Firefighter War Stories II

BOOKS BY LEW LEBLANC

War Stories:
    Some Memories from the Firehouse Years

Firefighter War Stories II:
    More Memories from the Firehouse Years

Firefighter War Stories III:
    Some Early Memories & The Firehouse Years

Firefighter War Stories II

More Memories from the Firehouse Years

Lew LeBlanc

Edited and Illustrated by Sue LeBlanc

ATP
2015

Copyright © 2015 Lew LeBlanc

Edited and illustrated by Sue LeBlanc

All rights reserved. This book or any portion thereof may not be reproduced or transmitted in any form or by any means, electrical or mechanical, including photocopying, recording, or by an information storage and retrieval system—except for the use of brief quotations in a book review or scholarly journal—without the express written permission of the publisher.

Although the author and publisher have made every effort to ensure the accuracy and completeness of information contained in this book, we assume no responsibility for errors, inaccuracies, omissions, or any inconsistency herein. All opinions expressed in this book are those of the author.

Andremily Tree Publishing, Natick, Massachusetts

FirefighterWarStories@verizon.net

Printed and bound in the United States of America.

First Printing, 2015

First edition, Georgia font, 12 pt.

ISBN 978-0-692-45570-8

Dedication

This work is dedicated to the men and women of the fire service everywhere, who do the job every day because they love it.

Contents

Acknowledgements vi
Introduction 1
The Stories:
    Experience Shows.. 7
    Never Again!.. 10
    Fire and Ice.. 11
    The Lady in White 13
    Hear That Whistle Blowing 15
    Those are the Rules 17
    Not Always as They Seem............................ 19
    English Cut 20
    To Get to the Other Side 21
    Snowman... 23
    The Pot Calls the Kettle Black 25
    Some Burn Permit Problems....................... 26
    Memorable People.. 29
    Something Nasty Coming 32
    The Right Call 34
    A Bad Apple.. 36
    Snowball.. 41
    Yes, There was Entertainment 43
    You Are What You Eat 45
    Wrong Hole 46
    Where Did He Go? 48
    Where are the Tools?................................... 50
    Victim Identified 52

What Stinks? 54
The Mural 55
Trouble with the Privates 56
UFO 60
We Didn't Forget... 62
Family Tragedy 65
Unique Position 67
Time, Manpower, and Disaster 70
Danger, Least Looked For 74
Where's the Fire? 76
Rebuilding the Call Department 78
Officer Down 81
Tag Up 83
A Firefighter's Funeral 86
The Roach Coach 89
Unwanted Responsibility 92
State Hospitals 93
Sometimes They Do Say Thanks 96
All Grown Up 98
Telltale Responding 101
Near Miss 103
Bicycles 105
Cream of the Crop 107
Fire Below 109
Hands Off 111
Chiefs Can't Dispatch 115
Mechanism of Injury 116
He Was Bad News 118
No Substitute 121
Special Request 123
Good Save 124
A Meeting Unexpected 126

I Feel Old	127
Food for Thought	128
A Privilege of Time	130
Making Us All Look Bad	132
Too Many to be Special	136
Shocked and Surprised	137
Any Time, Anywhere	139
Finding Your Way	141
Firsts	144
A Sight to See	147
A True Professional	149
Parent's Nightmare	151
That's the Way the Game is Played	153
Reminders	156
Old vs. New	160
Reputation	163
Nursing Home Troubles	166
Out of His Way	168
Steam Cleaned	170
Why?	172
A Generation of Weenies	175
Lemon House	176
More Inhumanity	179
Adapt and Overcome	181
Lucky Man	184
Here Comes the Sun	185
Death Ride	186
Adorable	188
All in the Family	189
All Mouth and No Guts	192
Around the World	194
Miracle Workers	196

15-2, 15-4, and 8 is a Dozen 197
Name Counts for Something 200
See How They Live................................... 201
Just Legs 204
Snots 207
CPR Instructor Class................................209
Modest and Afraid 211
What Else Could I Do?.............................. 214
Awestruck 216
Minor Injury 219
A Little Help... 221
Luck 223
Only a Candle..226
Man, What a Ride 227
Locations 229
Lessons in Scouting 232
Motivation 234
Equipment Delivery..................................236
Everyone Treated Equal 239
It Can Happen Anytime 242
Square Peg 244
Some Never Learn 247
The New Guy 249
Training Burn, July.................................. 251
Sorry, We Can Help 254
To the Rescue... 256
It Ain't Gone Yet 259
The Assistance We Provide....................... 261
The Principle of the Thing 264
The Unexplained.....................................265
The Way You Taught Me 267
Surprise! 269

Lesson Learned, Hopefully 271
Recognition 274
Not a Close Family 276
Hurried Up and Left 277
Evidence Tampering 279
Car Lock Outs 281
Santa Pants... 284
It's in the Blood 286
Lucky Shot... 288
Justice Delivered 290
Sad Coincidence 292
Memorable Moment................................... 293
Hole in the Ice 295
Just Not Right 297
Loved His Job.. 299
Abuse of Power 301
Gone with the Wind 303
Homecoming Surprise 305
First Big One... 307
Blood in the Water... 309
Boaters in Distress 311
Brain Cramp 313
Watch What You Say in the Firehouse........ 315
Constant Vigilance 316
CPR Save 319
DTs 321
Dog Struck 323
Meet My brother... 325
Damage Control 327
Confidence.. 330
Not Showing Off 333
Feels Like Home... 336

Cold Rain	338
Cursed	340
Beauty and the Beast	342
Bad Directions	344
A Reception to Remember	345
I Guess All Good Things Come to an End	347
Glossary	**350**

Acknowledgements

To all my former students, classmates, brothers and sisters in the fire service, friends all, who read and enjoyed many of my stories and encouraged me to put them together into a book, I give my sincerest thanks.

To Sue; my partner, assistant, editor, illustrator, critic, wife, and best friend; I can never thank you enough. Without your love, help, and encouragement this work would never have gotten done.

Introduction

Having worked in the fire service and fire training for more than 30 years, I guess it's no real surprise that in addition to living the life, I also like to read about it. In my personal library, I have stories of just about every disastrous fire and calamity that has ever happened in modern times. The collection is growing all the time. I also have books about careers, as well as the life and times in the fire service, written by those who lived and worked it.

One of the first books I got many years ago was Dennis Smith's <u>Report From Engine Co. 82</u>, a great work about firefighting in the South Bronx in the late 60s and early 70s. I am fortunate enough to have a copy of <u>Ready To Roll...Ready To Die</u> by Retired District Chief Paul F. Cook of the Boston fire department, autographed to me by the author.

Who can speak of books from the Boston fire department without bringing up the name of Leo D. Stapleton, retired chief and commissioner? I am very fortunate to also have an autographed copy of his first work, <u>Thirty Years on the Line</u>, covering happenings during his long career in the city of Boston. Mr. Stapleton has written many other works as well, and I have several of these in my collection.

I am a lover of nonfiction, so when I shop for reading material, I look carefully for what is available. Fictional stories about fires and the fire service abound. Maybe I'll read them after I finish all the nonfiction stories. Perhaps I'm just looking in the wrong places, but I have not run across stories from the smaller, suburban fire departments. A fire is the same no matter where it burns. Some are bigger—much bigger—but they are still fires.

The type of person who takes the job of firefighter is the same anywhere you go. Of course, you have some who just want it said that they are firefighters and love to wear the uniform. You get that element with any group. But the men and women who look for this job, this kind of life because they love it, are a unique breed. They live and work together. They socialize together. Everywhere they go they "talk shop." A firefighter from anywhere can walk into a firehouse anywhere else and be greeted as a brother or sister and feel like they're home. They are part of a culture that has to be lived to be truly understood. It's easy to tell fire stories to a group of firefighters. When firefighters tell stories with one another, they all speak the same language and use the same jargon.

Once I had retired, I found myself out in the world much more than I had been during my thirty-something years on the job. I had to learn to talk to non-fire people again. I got better at it. Like many people, I started using social media on my computer. I found very many old friends and classmates, many who were not involved in the fire service. I started to write some old memories for friends to read. I wrote these stories so the lay public could understand what was being said: changing jargon, simplifying, and explaining things in more detail.

I called them my "war stories." Well, I must have done something right because people loved to read them. Some told me that they looked forward to the next one. It was frequently suggested that I should collect these "war stories" together and publish them as a book. I was getting this positive feedback, not only from those in the fire service, like old fire buddies and former students that I had taught in recruit school, but also from many friends from the lay public—regular people!

I thought back over my long career and pulled together a variety of stories that stand out in my memory. In 2014, 126 of these short stories were compiled and published under the title, War Stories. Some are funny, some are sad, and some make you just stop and think.

Within days of the book going to print, I started thinking again. I kept remembering stories that I wished I had included. With over 30 years on the job, I had a lot of them. What else could I do but start writing them down? This project took about a year. The result is this sequel, Firefighter War Stories II, with 157 new stories.

In the interest of privacy, I removed and/or changed the names of people and places. Readers who might not be familiar with the jargon can look and refer to the glossary in the back. These stories are written for fun and are not meant to make anyone look or feel foolish. Although these events happened to me in a suburban town, they could have happened anywhere and to anybody.

Personally, I think that <u>Firefighter War Stories II</u> is even better than the first book. What do you think? Read it, and see if you agree.

The Stories

Experience Shows

They say, and I say it also, that there is no substitute for experience on our job. A good senior man who knows what he's doing is priceless. By the time I was promoted to captain, I had more than twenty-five years on the job, and had been involved in the training of new recruit firefighters for more than twenty years. One could say that I was pretty well experienced, even though I didn't come from a fire department that had a large number of fires when compared to some others.

On our department, a captain usually worked at headquarters and ran the shift. He drove car 2. The lieutenant would work at station 2. I took an overtime shift one night, filling in for a lieutenant, so I was at station 2. The duty captain was in charge at station 1. I was at a two-man house. My partner was someone that I had taught at the fire academy. As an officer, I didn't drive the engines, so my partner was behind the wheel. That also made him pump operator.

The night was quiet early, but after a few hours, we were dispatched to a house fire. It was just down the street from our firehouse, so we were first due with a response time of maybe a bit over a minute. When we pulled up in front of the house, there were neighbors standing around, looking at what was going on. I could see a glow through a window where I thought the kitchen was. I radioed back that we were standing by and there was fire showing in the kitchen. I probably should have investigated a bit more beforehand, because the shift commander just took me at my word, old salt that I was. He ordered the box struck and all off-duty firefighters recalled to duty. This is standard practice on our department for a working house fire. Trouble was that it was not quite what could be called a working house fire.

I got out and told the driver which hose I was going to use. I pulled it off, stretched it out, then called for water, just like we had taught my partner at the academy. He got water into the hose and I tested the nozzle to make sure it was going to flow correctly. I was preparing myself for the inferno to be found within. All this took about thirty seconds. I went to the door and opened it. When I looked in, I saw a small fire on an island counter top in the kitchen. One quick squirt put that out. With no more fire, I was feeling kind of stupid at not having held my report until *after* having a better look.

There was, however, plenty of smoke through the house. I radioed in that the fire was knocked down and we were checking for any fire extension. I said that we'd have a lot of smoke to clear. The captain and the second engine arrived. I was told to supervise the removal of smoke and to check the rest of the house, while the shift commander spoke to the homeowner.

We found out that there had been a small refrigerator up against the side of the island counter. There had been some sort of electrical problem with the fridge, and it sparked a fire, lighting some papers and magazines on the counter. It had the potential to become something serious, but we caught it early.

I got a lot of praise and pats on the back from the guys for a quick knockdown. Some people remarked about how experience shows and how the instructors really *do* know what they're doing. I never told anyone that I might have been a little too hasty when I reported it as, "fire showing." I also never told anyone that I could have put it out with a cup of water. I just took the praise and let it go. It's called self-preservation. I would have been eaten alive if I had ever confessed. Now, just so long as no one ever finds out about this…

Never Again!

This story came back to me from the distant past. We answered a call at a large residence in the north end of town one night. I don't remember what the call was for. It may have been for an odor of smoke. We responded with the captain in car 2, and I and a partner in the engine from headquarters. I remember that there were several older teenagers at the residence, and the parents were not home. The home had a huge, beautiful, stone fireplace with a huge, bluestone hearth out front. The family also had a great dane, who kept coming over to investigate us. He was no trouble and was quite friendly, but man, that was a lot of dog!

After checking things out and finding nothing wrong, we were standing in front of the bluestone hearth talking to a young lady who lived in the house, when the dog came over once again. Then, for some reason known only to the Great Spirit, the dog lifted his leg and peed on the hearth. That in itself seemed a bit unusual, considering how nice the house was kept. The poor dog let loose right onto an electrical outlet that was built into the stone hearth and facing up. There should have been some kind of cover on that outlet, I would have thought, but there wasn't, and the stream went right into the outlet. It responded with a crackle, and red and blue sparks shot up and hit the dog in the crotch. He yelped loudly and kept yelping as he ran off to somewhere else in that large house. We all stood there dumbfounded, residents and fire department personnel alike. Nobody could quite believe what we had just seen.

We wound up pulling the breaker on that outlet, and recommended that they call an electrician to check it out. There was no other problem, so we returned to quarters. The people living there were going to look after the dog. I don't believe he was much more than scared. However, I'll just bet he won't do *that* again!

Fire and Ice

In the town where I worked, there is a lot of water. There is a river, several large bodies of water, and many smaller ponds that are hidden in the wetlands around town. There was a time when there was a lot of skating on the large ponds, but not so much now. I couldn't really say why. Maybe people prefer the safety of skating rinks. Ice fishing is still going strong, though. I've seen many people ice fishing on ice so thin that I would never walk out on it. Maybe I'm just a coward.

There is one pond that has quite a history. The area has been built up all around it. It started out as summer cottages way, way back, and now there are some nice homes around the pond. Some years ago, it seemed to be a favorite pastime of certain groups to go out after dark and light fires on the ice. Then they would sit around the fire and talk, sing, drink, or whatever else they wanted to do. We don't really know who these people were. We always blamed the teens, but we never really knew for sure. People living around the pond would call and report a fire out on the ice. It wasn't going anywhere, but the law said that it wasn't supposed to be there so we would have to put it out. At first, we would walk out to the fire, but the folks out on the ice would see us park the engine and they'd run away. Then we would have to put the fire out. We tried water extinguishers and even dragging booster hose out to the fire. It all worked, but it was a pain in the neck.

One year, the fire department took delivery of a new engine. It was our first diesel automatic. It was loud, but it was easy to drive and the pump was a pleasure to operate. It also had a pre-piped gun on top of the engine. The gun was also portable with a removable stand, if you wanted to use it away from the engine. If not, then all you had to do was have a water supply, open a valve, and the gun would shoot from the top of the engine.

The next winter when the calls for fires out on the ice started coming in, one of our engine crews got innovative. They drove up a street that went right next to the pond. The fire was out a ways, but not too far from the street. They fired that gun onto the fire and everybody around it, using all 500 gallons in the tank. When they were all through, the engine crew simply hooked up to a hydrant right next to where the engine was parked, refilled the tank, and returned to quarters. I'd like to say that their technique put an end to it, but some people are slow to learn. After a few showers, the fires stopped. We never really knew who was lighting them, but I'll bet they took our department name in as much vain as they could think of.

The Lady in White

People call the fire department for many reasons: some are legitimate emergencies, some are perceived emergencies, and some are malicious. There are as many reasons as there are people. It can get interesting when we get calls from people whose mental status is questionable. We have several facilities in town for older people, from nursing homes to assisted living facilities to elderly housing projects. Towns with many residences for the elderly usually have a higher volume of ambulance calls because of the physical and medical problems common in these places. There are falls and requests for assistance that really are not emergencies. And as I said, there are some interesting calls, also.

One night while working at station 2, we were dispatched for an assistance alarm ringing in an apartment at the housing for the elderly, right down the street from us. With no phone call from the apartment in question and no knowledge of the nature of the emergency, the ambulance was also dispatched from station 1.

We arrived in about thirty seconds and entered the lobby. There we were met by a resident who told us which apartment the alarm was ringing in. All of these apartments are equipped with an assistance alarm on a wall switch in the bathroom, within easy reach of the toilet, should someone need assistance getting up. All they have to do is flip the switch up and the alarm rings. Flip it back down and it stops.

We went up to the door and rang the bell. We could hear the alarm clearly from out in the hall. I rang the bell again and the door slowly opened. There, in front of me, stood an elderly lady. She must have been in her 80s, very thin, and she was wearing a white lace teddy, complete with garters and stockings that just about hung off of her emaciated legs. She leaned up against the doorway with a coy smile on her face. Needless to say, I was feeling somewhat less than comfortable with this situation. It appeared that we'd been called for something other than an emergency. I asked her if there was any problem, and she said, "No," still smiling.

I said, "Excuse me," and slipped past her, into the bathroom, and switched off the alarm. She watched me, but did not leave the doorway.

As I had passed her on the way in, I had noticed something. I verified it on the way out. If her intent was to turn us on, she failed badly. But in all fairness, if she had been a shapely young lady in her 20s, she still would have failed. No one could get close to anyone that smelled that bad. I don't know when her last encounter with soap and water was, but she positively reeked of body odor.

We asked one last time if there was any problem. She said, "No," and never stopped smiling. I told her that I had reset the alarm, but I'm sure she knew that. We then said, "Goodnight," and left. We called on the radio and cancelled the ambulance.

Man, we couldn't get out of there fast enough. I was sure glad there was no emergency. It was getting hard to breathe in there. But then I thought, what the hell, it wasn't my night to work the ambulance, anyway.

Hear That Whistle Blowing

Back in the 80s, we went from a dispatch system inside the firehouse and staffed by firefighters, to a joint fire and police dispatch system staffed by civilians. These civilian dispatchers worked in the dispatch center in another part of the building. They worked an eight-hour shift, the same as our police: 7 a.m. to 3 p.m., 3 p.m. to 11 p.m., or 11 p.m. to 7 a.m. The dispatchers would be assigned one of these. There was no sleeping on the overnight shift.

At this time, the fire department still had a whistle on the roof of both firehouses. They were intended for calling off-duty firefighters back to the firehouse in case of fire. The whistle was not blown at night because the off-duty men had radio receivers at home to alert them. During the day, off-duty firefighters who were not home would be able to hear the whistle from anywhere in town and know that there was a fire and a recall was needed. The whistle was activated by a button on the firefighters' watch desk. There was also a button on the desk at the new dispatch center.

I was working one night at headquarters. I don't recall how the early part of the night went, but it was quiet around 10 p.m., so we started to get ready for bed. I went to bed and was in a rather deep sleep. We awoke suddenly to the sound of the whistle going off. It was set to blow a series of seven blasts, followed immediately by another seven blasts. A 7-7 is the signal for a general recall to duty. The whistle is loud under normal circumstances during the day, with all the other routine noise that happens around us. In the quiet of early morning, it is deafening.

The captain sat up, shook off the sleep, got up and quickly, but silently, got dressed. He was so pissed off that he was almost glowing red. He stormed out of the bunkroom and went to the dispatch center. I looked at the clock. It was four o'clock in the morning.

He came back a few minutes later, still angry, and told us what happened. We had a young lady working the dispatch center that night. She was friendly and we all liked her. There was also an auxiliary police officer there. The auxiliaries don't work regular shifts as a rule, but would often ride with a full time officer. I guess this auxiliary officer had either just finished his ride-along, or the full time officer he had been riding with was busy in the building. The auxiliary officer went into the dispatch area and was joking, or maybe flirting, with the dispatcher. Instead of sitting in a chair, he got up close to her to talk. At some point, he sat down onto the dispatch console—right onto the whistle button. They tried to silence the noise, but they didn't know how. Next thing they knew, the captain was in there. I guess he chewed them both out pretty good.

That never happened again. I'll bet that the chewing out the captain gave those two was nothing like the complaining from the public that the chief and the officers had to listen to, for blowing the whistle in the wee hours of the morning!

Those are the Rules

On our fire department, we have three specialists among the privates. The mechanic is responsible for vehicle maintenance; the electrician is responsible for the fire alarm system; and the inspector is responsible for marking and approving building plans and fire alarm systems, and ensuring compliance with the rules. All of these people work on a regular shift as firefighter/EMTs. They get a higher rate of pay for their extra duties.

I was on duty as the shift captain one day with the inspector. He said that he had to go out to inspect a construction site. Someone had tipped him off about the use of salamanders in a house under renovation.

Propane salamanders are a type of heating device with an open flame. They are illegal for use any place used for habitation. They are also illegal for use by a construction crew inside a building. With that kind of unit, in addition to the flame, there is the potential for the build up of carbon monoxide within a closed space. CO is colorless, odorless, flammable, explosive, and deadly if inhaled over time. Propane should never be stored indoors. Fire related laws, such as these, were put in place to protect the public. They are often the result of past tragedies, when people have gotten injured or killed doing something they shouldn't. Unfortunately, there are people who think the rules do not apply to them, and so they do what they want.

A short while later, the inspector came back with quite a story. He had gone to the house under renovation. He went in and found that not only was the builder using the propane salamanders, but he had twenty 100-pound propane cylinders stored in reserve, so they could keep the salamanders running. The inspector used his authority and shut down the job until those tanks and salamanders were removed from the premises.

The inspector was filling out his report back at headquarters, when the builder himself showed up a short while later and wanted to talk to the chief. When the chief came out of his office, the builder began ranting about the inspector and generally acting like a know-it-all and a tough guy. The chief turned and walked back into his office. When the builder tried to follow, the chief said, "Talk to my inspector," and shut the door.

Gotcha!!

Some people think they're exempt from the laws and immune from anything happening to them. It's true that almost everyone you can think of has a grill with a 20-pound tank of propane on their back porch, and a spare tank somewhere, hopefully stored outside, as required. But propane is used for a great many things, other than cooking your steak. It is transported in bulk, all around us, and is closely regulated. Still, sometimes accidents happen.

Propane gas is liquefied when under pressure and placed in a container. If the container is ruptured, the liquid will turn back into a gas as it escapes. As it does this, it expands to 270 times the space it had occupied in the container. It is heavier than air and will seek the lowest places, like basements or storm drains.

Propane is extremely flammable and can easily be ignited by something like, for instance, the flame on a salamander. If there had been a fire in that house, one tank rupturing would have caused all the others to rupture as well. With an expansion ratio of 270 to 1, I think most of the neighborhood would be gone. We would have one hell of a fire.

Not Always as They Seem

Working at the firehouse on the ambulance one day, we got a call to assist the police. They had gotten a call that a dead body had been found in a backyard and they wanted us to take a look and make sure the victim was indeed dead.

We got there and went into the back yard. The body of an older male was prone on a set of wooden, landscape tie steps with his head down. We went over and checked the body. There was a trickle of dried blood that had come from the side of his head facing the ground. The body was pale and hard: rigor mortis had set in. The police said that it looked like he had been coming down the steps, tripped and fell and struck his head. The man had been there a while, too long for us to do anything for him. Since he was expired, it was a police matter. We went back to quarters.

The police called the medical examiner. When he got there, he examined the body. Then they rolled the body over. That's when they found the gun. It seems that the man had stood on the steps and shot himself in the head with a handgun. When he fell, the gun dropped and he fell on top of it. Well, that changed the whole ball game for the police. Don't be fooled: Not everything is as it seems.

English Cut

We were dispatched one morning to a residence for the report of a man who had cut himself. Sometimes calls like this are pretty bad, but as often as not, they don't turn out to be anything serious. People really tend to overreact.

We arrived and were met at the door by a lady who led us into the kitchen. There was a man standing there with a wad of paper towels held to his hand. I asked him what happened, and he answered, in a very strong British accent, "Ah cut i' on a cat food tin. The blood was spurtin'."

I looked around and didn't see a drop of blood anywhere: not on the counter, not on the floor, not even on the paper towels he was using to cover the wound. Well, no matter. I got out some gauze and put on some gloves. Then I said, "Let's have a look."

He winced and removed the paper towels. There, running across his palm, was a red line, like something sharp had been dragged across his hand and had barely broken through the first layer of skin. There was no open wound and no blood at all. He wasn't even cut. I looked at my partner and he looked back. I think we both had to stifle our laughter.

The man asked us, "Are you gon' to stitch i' up roight 'ere?"

I said to him, "Well, we could, but you wouldn't want us to because we aren't qualified. I'm just going to bandage it up, and if you keep it clean and bandaged, it should be fine." He looked relieved and we left.

He cut it on a cat food tin and the blood was spurting. Maybe they judge things differently where he comes from. I'd hate to think that that would be considered a serious wound in England. I think it was more likely the man was a pansy.

To Get to the Other Side

I was working a day shift years ago and getting ready for shift change at 6 pm. Just shortly before the night shift came in, we got a call. It was a medical of some sort, requiring a transport to a local hospital. We never looked forward to these last-minute calls. It meant that we were not getting off duty on time, but at least there was some overtime pay for it.

We made our transport and were on our way back when the dispatcher radioed. We were sent to an MVA in a town next door to us. I knew that town pretty well, so I knew just how to get there.

When we arrived, we saw a young man lying on a low stone wall to our left. Just down the street a short distance was a car. It was a high-end, sporty convertible. As this was summer, the top was down. There appeared to be two people in the car. The firefighters from that town were on scene and directed us to the man on the stone wall. I remember being told that this man had been thrown from the car. Our patient was conscious and alert and was able to move his arms and legs. However, you never know what could be wrong, so to play it safe, we fully immobilized our patient, took him to the hospital, and returned to our quarters.

We found out later what had happened. There had been a young lady, probably in her late teens, driving the car. I suspect that it was her parents' car. She had a male friend in the front and another one in the back. She had been heading east and probably traveling faster than she should have been, when she made a turn off of the main road and onto a side street. The side street wasn't a real turn. It sort of bore off to the right, but did not require the driver to slow down much, and she didn't.

As she came onto the side street, there appeared in front of the car, a chicken. It was walking around in the middle of the street. Since the first house she had passed on the right was a small farm, that was probably where the chicken had come from. I guess she was startled and cut the wheel hard to the left to avoid the bird. She sideswiped the stone wall—hard—and the man in the back was thrown out and onto the wall.

The car continued on, crossed the street, and hit a tree head-on just a bit further down the road. I guess the driver was banged up a bit, but her front seat passenger could not feel anything from his neck down: never a good thing.

I never found out how any of them made out. The potential was high for at least some devastating injuries, all because someone was being careless and a chicken had wandered into the road. Sometimes truth is stranger than fiction. What were the chances that a chicken in the road would set off this chain of events? This still leaves us with one unanswered question: Why did the chicken cross the road?

Snowman

For a number of years, while working in support services at the academy, I was in charge of repair of the fire extinguishers used in our programs. I would repair and replace them, as needed. The program that used the most extinguishers was the gas firefighting school. They did spray some water around to control the vapor clouds, but firefighting and extinguishment was done with 30-pound, dry chemical extinguishers. These were filled with a dry powder, extinguishing agent and there was a small cartridge of liquefied CO_2 attached. To operate the equipment, a lever was pushed down, thereby puncturing the cartridge. The contents of the cartridge would fill the extinguisher, and the CO_2 would rush out of the extinguisher, taking the powder with it.

Often, the extinguishers would get jammed up with powder and need to be broken down and cleaned out. That's where I came in. There was a large storage building that was up at the gas school that had been converted into a shop for refilling the extinguishers. The filling station was at one end, opposite the end with the door, and a workbench was along one side. When I was working, I tried to get any extinguisher that had problems right away. There were a lot of them, but that school used a lot of them. So I tried my best to keep them all working.

One day, when I was working in the main building, I was called to the gas school for some clogged extinguishers. I headed up there right away. I got there and found a crew of three working at filling. Two of the men were outside putting the caps back on the filled extinguishers. The third man, a friend of mine, was in the room, filling. I walked in and saw some extinguishers on the bench, just inside the door. I squeezed the trigger on the first one I grabbed. It was clearly clogged. So, just like I always do, I put a wrench on the coupling that detaches the hose from the extinguisher, and turned it. It turned a few times. My aim was to take it off, unplug it, and clean out the nozzle.

As soon as the hose came free, «*WHOOSH!*» there was a loud noise, like rushing wind, and the whole room filled with powder. We couldn't see our hands in front of our faces and we couldn't breathe. The two men outside were looking as I fell out of the door, covered with the powder and coughing. We didn't see the last man, so I started to go back inside when out he came.

He was completely covered in that powder—and I mean *everywhere*. He opened his eyes and that's all you could see of his face. He had held his breath, so he wasn't coughing too badly. The look of him was funny. As soon as we made sure everyone was all right, we had a good laugh. I took a lot of heat for taking that hose off.

What had happened was that someone had pushed down the lever to activate the equipment, but it clogged and so it didn't fire. They put it in the filling room to be looked at. Trouble was, the extinguisher was still charged and under pressure. The clog was in the hose, so when I removed the hose, the clog was gone and everything blew out through the opening created by removing the hose. I just had taken for granted that the thing was unpressurized when I went to work on it. It could have been serious because it could have injured someone, but it didn't turn out that way.

We laughed about it and I got beaten up a bit, but I don't think I ever began work on another extinguisher without making sure it was not pressurized.

I still laugh when I think of the look of that man when he rolled out of there. Frosty the Snowman! But the lesson was learned.

The Pot Calls the Kettle Black

One of the deputy chiefs I worked with over the years was short and bald. He used to get a lot of harassment, but then, so did we all. It's just that if you had some special target for the guys to shoot at, they would! It helped if you had a good comeback and were willing to laugh at yourself. Almost nothing was sacred.

One day, back when I was losing my hair and it was starting to show, I was working on the deputy's group. For some reason that escapes me now, I was squatting or bending over. Anyway, my head was lower than the deputy, and *that* wasn't easy.

He looked down at me, and with an ear-to-ear grin, said, "Hey, you're getting a little thin on top."

I looked up at him and said, "Well, if you think that lets you off the hook, Curly, you're mistaken."

He was still thinking he had me, when he came back with, "Grass doesn't grow on a busy street."

To which I replied, "It doesn't grow on cement, either."

The conversation was over. Yet another lifelong friendship secured!

Some Burn Permit Problems

Our state permits the open burning of brush and garden debris from January 1 through May 15, inclusive. Some people burn when there is still snow on the ground, but most wait until weekend days when it's nice to go out and work in the yard. Citizens who want to get a burn permit have to come in to the public safety building and fill out an application. Then all they have to do when they want to burn is call and let the dispatch office know.

There are certain rules that have to be followed. The fire is supposed to be at least 75 feet away from any building and anything else that can burn, a hose has to be handy, and the fires kept small. Burning is permitted daily from 10 a.m. to 4 p.m., at the discretion of the fire officer in charge for the day. Nothing like logs, piles of leaves, household waste, or trash may be burned. Most people are pretty careful, but even when careful, things can happen. Most are good about following the rules, but there are those that think those rules were made just to inconvenience them.

When I was working one weekend morning, we were called to a residence for a fire that got away from the resident. We went to put it out. I was the duty captain in car 2 and I had the engine company from station 1 with me. I had the engine from station 2 covering headquarters. We were on our way back to quarters when we noticed a man burning brush in his yard. His fire was small, but he had six of them, and instead of having them in his yard, he had them in the woods near the edge of his property. The engine crew saw it, too, and stopped. The man looked up at us. I told the engine to keep going and I would speak to the homeowner. They continued on, and I stopped and got out of the car.

As I walked over, the man didn't even look up. He was an older man and he looked like he had no time for me. I told him that he'd have to move his fires out of the woods, and he had to cut them down to one fire. He acted like he didn't even hear me. Now I thought that things might get ugly. I was right.

He ignored me, until I spoke loudly and with an air of authority. Then he looked up and asked me what was wrong with the way he was doing things. I told him what was wrong. He walked away from me, picked up a rake, and began to rake more fuel into the nearest fire.

Well, that was about enough. Time to get serious. "Did you see that engine pass by a few minutes ago?" I asked him. "Well, you can either put the fires out or I'll call that engine back and *they* will put them out. But either way, the fires are going out."

As he looked at me, flames shot out of his eyes. Then he went and got his hose and put the fires out while I watched. Then I got back in the car and went back to quarters. My first stop was the dispatch office to inform them that if that man, or anyone from that address, calls to burn, they were to be informed that the permit had been pulled *on my authority*. All I had asked was for him to be reasonable and follow the rules. He couldn't even do that.

There was another call for a citizen burning brush that I remember going to that was stranger and dangerous. Years before, when I was a private working at station 1, we got a call for possible illegal burning. I seem to remember a permit for that address, but there was some question of just what was being burned. Two of us went with the engine and the captain went in car 2. We got to the residence and saw thick, dark smoke coming from the backyard. It was a big yard, so we had to pull the engine down a dirt driveway to get near where we saw the smoke.

The fire was in a pit and was quite large. We could quite plainly see the big logs that were burning in the pit. There wasn't much brush. It wasn't going to spread, so why bother with it, you ask? Because there were rules in place, we had to enforce the rules, and we had had a complaint. We were obligated to act. We pulled off hose and started to spray down the logs while stirring things up with a long pike pole. This pit was quite deep and was full of things that were not supposed to be burned.

The homeowner was a strange man. He said very little to us when we arrived. We said that we had to put it out and he said nothing. As we worked, he just continued to putter around the yard, not paying any attention to us. He got onto a small yard tractor and started to drive it around the yard. I don't think he was really doing anything, but driving around. Then he drove close to where we were working and deliberately swerved the tractor toward the captain. We all saw it and the captain got out of the way. The captain said that he was going to call the police.

We ran out of tank water and had to go out to the street to fill up the engine again at a nearby hydrant. We still had lots more work to do. While my partner and I were filling up, we saw the man drive his tractor across the access, blocking our way back in. We radioed to the captain to tell him what was going on. He called dispatch again requesting the police.

As we sat waiting, we saw a police car coming. It pulled up and out got probably one of the most useless police officers that I've ever known. This man was a sergeant and a big man, but he was just plain lazy. We could expect little help from this man. By rights, the homeowner should have been arrested for aiming at the captain with the tractor. Well, he wasn't. The police officer finally got the man to move the tractor, so we went back to work. I saw that police officer for a few more minutes, then I don't remember seeing him again.

We continued to work and the homeowner continued to putter. Now he was walking around with a big pair of loppers, the kind used for cutting larger shrubbery. Then he walked by the captain, opened the loppers, and made a lunge toward the captain's neck.

That was it. The captain called me over and asked me to get him an axe. I got the axe off the engine and the captain carried that axe with him until we left that yard. The police were gone. The man was still around, but not near us. We finished up and left. A report was made of the incidents up there and the captain had a talk with the police.

I never heard of anything ever happening to that man for his actions. About the only thing that the captain felt he could do, if the police wouldn't do anything, was to pull the burn permit for that property on *his* authority, for life—and he did.

Memorable People

Doing transport work in the private ambulance business, a great deal of our work involved taking people from one hospital to another hospital for special treatment, and back again. We would sometimes take people from their homes for treatment, and then back home again. These were scheduled in advance, so dispatch would often have the transporting ambulance stay in the area and do the return.

We would often see the same people many times. Many of these people were too sick to converse too much, but sometimes we'd get to know them a bit. The ones we got to know the most were the dialysis patients. They would often start out not too sick. They would be picked up at their homes and returned there. As time went on though, their problems would take their toll, and the patient would become sicker. They often moved to a hospital, and sometimes even a nursing home.

Some of the people I got to know still stand out in my mind. I remember one lady who wasn't strong enough to walk up the steps to her home. The fact that there were about two hundred steep, concrete steps probably would discourage anyone from wanting to try. Going and returning, two ambulances were always sent to this call. Each of the four crew members would take a handle of the stair chair and carry the lady up or down. When we'd bring her home and had to carry her up, even the strongest of us would be a bit winded. That was a hell of a climb. If memory serves, our company got that contract because a previous ambulance company crew had dropped her. I guess she wasn't hurt, but then it was her turn to drop *them*. I think she was satisfied with us.

There was another old woman who lived in a housing project in the city. This housing project had the reputation as a place where bad things happened to people. We would take this lady home to the project. She'd have us park in front of the building. We'd then take out her wheelchair and get her into it. Then she always sent us on our way. She used to say that she could make from there and that we shouldn't go in there. It was nice having someone concerned for our welfare.

The patient who stands out the most was an interesting lady that we used to take home to a kind of bad part of the city. She lived in a large, old, three-story home. The house was a relic from a time when this was a better, more-affluent part of the city. It had been a single-family house once, but had been converted to a three-family house. This lady could not walk far and was not good on stairs, so naturally she lived on the third floor. The company would often send a second ambulance for help in carrying the lady upstairs. She was short and she was huge. She was probably three fifty to four hundred pounds, even *after* she took off her prosthetic leg. Taking the leg off didn't really help. Neither did the second ambulance crew, really. There was a narrow, creaky staircase with two 30° bends in it. There simply wasn't enough room for the patient, the stair chair, and more than two other people. She would take off her leg and sit in the chair. Then we'd see who we had for help. The two biggest and strongest were always the ones who did the carrying. We'd strap her in the chair and up we'd go, all praying that the staircase held out for just one more trip. The other two crew members often walked behind the guy on the lower end of the chair for support, in case anyone slipped or the stairs broke or something. It never did, but we were sure worried.

After we nearly killed ourselves getting her up, she would give us a key and ask us to open the door. It was locked up with a hasp and a padlock. Unusual for a residence, but she explained that she needed to do that because her oldest son was a heroin addict. If he got in, he would steal everything she had. She told us once that if he were there, he would kill us for the money in our wallets. We worked in the ambulance business, so our wallets weren't exactly bulging anyway. It was disconcerting to think that we could be killed for that little money.

30

I do remember that she had another son who lived with her. He was already grown, over six feet tall. This son had Down syndrome and was mentally challenged, as well. I saw him often, but I don't recall where he was when she was out. I don't remember her locking him in the apartment. Perhaps he stayed at a neighbor's place. Anyway, he would walk around wearing nothing but a bed sheet. He never talked, but would get very close to you, and he loved to touch people. It was nothing really, but it kind of gave me an eerie feeling. We just wanted to get out of there as soon as we could, all the while looking out for her first son, the one who'd kill us for our money. She was a nice lady, but a trip there was quite an experience.

Something Nasty Coming

In the fire service, we see all kinds of things, good and bad. Most are in our own town, but sometimes we get to see someone else's messy calls. One night, while I was the attendant in our ambulance, we were on the way to a local hospital with a patient. I don't remember what was wrong with our patient, but I remember that it wasn't too serious. They really just needed transport to the hospital.

As we made our way to the hospital, we were listening to the fire department radio. The ambulance from another fire department was transporting to the same hospital. From what we gathered from their radio talk, they were transporting someone with a real emergency. There is a medium security prison in that town, and they were transporting a prisoner. They had paramedics working on board and had MAST trousers in place. We heard them start CPR several times, recover a pulse, only to lose it and have to do CPR again. It sounded like a real mess.

As luck would have it, we would arrive at the emergency room at about the same time. We got there about two minutes earlier than the other ambulance. We got our patient inside and got our stretcher made up, when in that other crew came with their patient. Coming from a prison, many things pass through the mind as to what may have happened. What actually did happen was about the last thing I would have expected.

The patient was a tall, well-built man. He was unconscious and there was blood everywhere. We stayed, in case our brothers needed help. I looked over. The patient had a piece of wooden board, about six or seven inches long, that had passed through the skull and stuck in his head. There was gray matter showing around the wound. It's never a good thing when parts of the brain can be seen.

It seems that this man had been working in the prison wood shop. He had walked in front of a big planer as someone had sent a board into it. The machine fired the board out and right into the man's head. The firefighters on scene cut the board to a manageable length, secured it in place, and transported the patient to the hospital.

As I remember, the patient did not survive. With gray matter visible, that's not surprising. The damage was severe. There have been many calls through the years that have been bad and messy and tragic, but I'm glad that it wasn't me who had to deal with that call.

The Right Call

The very nature of a police officer's job puts him out on the road. He can often arrive sooner than the fire department apparatus to a call for a fire. Most of the time it really isn't a problem, and often they are a great help, but sometimes there is a cop who creates more problems than he solves. He is the type of person who arrives before the firefighters and proceeds to report on something he knows nothing about and starts "fighting the fire" by breaking out windows. This person usually parks his cruiser right in front of the fire building and gets in the way of the arriving fire apparatus.

In talking to many brother and sister firefighters from many places, it seems that every town and city has at least one of these types of police officers. We had one such man, too. He would respond to fire calls and make reports over the radio that were not accurate. We'd find his car parked in front of the house and he'd be walking around the house, breaking windows. Once he threw a hibachi through a plate glass sliding door at a house fire before the firefighters got there. Feeding air to the fire like that only helps it grow bigger. It's a wonder that he didn't burn the place down. He made our work harder. He'd also get angry when we refused to move the apparatus so he could get his cruiser out.

Working at station 2 one Saturday morning in the summer, not too far into the shift, we got a call for smoke in a house. We got dressed and left with our engine. We were first due with about a one-minute response time. Guess who beat us to the call? That's right: our police officer friend. The first thing he did was to report, in a loud, excited voice, *"Smoke showing!"*

We were almost there, and as I looked up the street, I could see no smoke at all. We passed the fire chief's home. He was getting into his car to respond to the fire. When we pulled up in front of the house, things seemed to be normal. There was no smoke. I looked to the rear of the house at the peak of the roof and saw what might pass as smoke. I called in and reported we had a very slight smoke condition at the peak.

You might think, "Smoke is smoke, so what's the difference?" There is a great deal of difference, economically speaking. If we have a light haze of smoke just hanging there, it could be, and usually is, something very small that can be handled by the engine crew or duty shift. If we have thicker dark smoke pushing up from a structure, that is, moving under pressure, it usually is a working fire. That would require more help. A report given over the radio, like the one this police officer gave, would make the dispatcher think that we had a major fire. If we put out the recall tone and get all firefighters back to duty, everyone who shows up on the recall is guaranteed a minimum of 4 hours overtime pay. This can get expensive for something minor. On my report, the responding captain delayed the recall. We investigated things.

Well, we found no problem in the house, though we could smell a burning kind of odor. I opened the trap door to the attic and saw a slight haze inside. We got a short ladder and up I went. There was no floor, so I had to balance on the rafters. I eventually found about a handful of rock wool insulation that was smoldering. There had been a thunderstorm the night before and it was thought that the house received a minor lightning strike. There was no damage, really just some of the insulation was smoldering. It surely would have developed into a big problem, but we had caught it early.

As I was making my way over the rafters back to the trapdoor, my knee slipped and went between the rafters. A large piece of the plaster ceiling almost hit the chief and the captain as they walked through. What could I say, but "Awww, shit!" They didn't laugh. The chief told the captain that I had made the correct call on our arrival, but as things turned out, I did more damage than the lightning strike.

A Bad Apple

At the firefighting academy, I worked with people from all over the state, as well as an occasional person from a neighboring state. The common denominator was that they were all firefighters who loved the job, and even if one was a person that I didn't really hit it off with, there was always that common ground we had to share. That's not to say that we didn't have any weak links or bad apples through the years. We certainly did. We had people who just wanted to come and play, but not really work. They never lasted long, and even with that group, most of them weren't bad guys, even though they were lazy.

There was one person though, that stands out in my mind. I only knew him for a couple of days, but they were the longest couple of days that I can remember. I was working in support services then, building and lighting the fires for live fire training. Back then, we didn't have the facility that we have now. We did these training burns in several locations, depending on what kind of burn we were doing (i.e. structure fires, car fires, flammable liquids).

We used to do structural burns in the burn building at a county training area a couple of hours away. The recruit firefighter class used this training facility for their bigger live burns. Each half of the class would have two days. While we were training in this location, the students had to arrange for lodging for themselves. The academy put the staff up in a hotel for the time we were there. At the end of a day of burns, two or three support staff would take a truck full of the empty, used air bottles to a firehouse about a half hour away and refill them. This wasn't anybody's idea of a fun job. It was long and tedious, but it had to be done, so we made the most of it. The staff then would get together and go to dinner. Sometimes a few of us would go out for a drink afterward, but we had to take it easy as we had a day of hard work coming up the next day.

I had been assigned to work three of the four days for one recruit class. As our new facility was nearing completion, this was going to be the very last days of recruit burns ever at that place. When I got there on the third day, I knew almost everybody. There was one that I didn't know. He was a new guy in support. He had been assigned days two, three, and four. We introduced ourselves and seemed to hit it off. He seemed like a pretty good guy. Boy, was I in for lesson!

We worked together all morning. We had a good time and got along fine. Lunchtime came and I was going to drive down the street for a burger. My new friend wanted to come with me. After he had eaten and paid for his lunch, he told me that he didn't have any more money. I didn't have much extra, but I loaned him a ten so he could eat dinner. That's all I had to spare.

At the end of the day, three of us took the truck full of air bottles and went to fill them. My new friend was not with us. His name was soon taken in vain by my two partners. One of them was already on his third trip to fill tanks. He told me that my new friend hadn't even gone once. Seems that the new guy made himself scarce when it was time to go fill the bottles and somehow avoided doing a job that nobody enjoyed.

When the work was done, one of my partners was not assigned to work the next day, so he headed home. He was through with those burns. The other guy and I took the truck back, dropped it off at the training ground, and drove our cars to the hotel. It turned out that I was assigned to room with the new guy. He was down in the lobby waiting with the other staff, after avoiding what should have been his job.

I took a quick shower and changed clothes. The staff would usually travel together or meet at one particular restaurant and eat dinner together. My new friend and I got into a car with another guy and went to a restaurant for dinner.

For some strange reason, we usually wound up all getting the same thing, and this night was no exception. When we were done, everybody chipped in the same amount of money. That gave the waitress a good tip and paid for our meals. That guy never said anything to anybody, just ordered his meal. There was no way he could pay for it with the ten that I had loaned him. Anybody would have helped him out, if he had asked, but he said nothing. At the end, when everybody threw in twenty dollars, he threw in the ten, said nothing, and left the restaurant. The waitress had to pay for the rest of his meal, I guess. He found somebody that was going out for a drink, and asked if I wanted to go. I went along, but said that we couldn't stay late. I don't know where he expected to get any money to pay for his drinks, but that wasn't my problem.

Over the next hour or so, we socialized with a few people. I was sitting with two women and talking, when a waitress came up to me and asked for money. It seemed that my buddy was running a bar tab. I said that she'd have to take it up with him. My beer was paid for.

For a while longer, he was dancing and having a great time. He always had a drink in his hand. I thought maybe he'd hit someone up for some money. I got up to use the men's room. When I came back, the two women I was talking to were standing up and getting ready to leave. It seems that when I was away, the guy had come over and invited the women to our hotel room for some fun. I guess he had gotten quite descriptive about the kind of "fun" he meant. They told me that they thought my friend was a pig, and then they left. I didn't want to pick anyone up. I had a hard day ahead, and besides, I had a steady girlfriend and wasn't into fooling around. I must admit that I was a bit angry at what he had done.

Shortly after that, the guy came and got me. He said we had to leave. We walked out with the guy who was our ride. The new guy kept hurrying us along like he didn't want to be seen. On the way back to the hotel, he told us that he had skipped out on his bar tab. What a jerk. He could have gotten all of us in trouble.

Back in the hotel room, my roomie had the TV on. I was tired and not too pleased with him at that time, so I lay down and fell asleep. In the morning, I got up and got ready for work. I was ready to leave the room as he was just getting up. I told him I'd see him at work.

At the desk while checking out, they told me that I owed them some money. When I asked what for, they told me it was for the movie. I told them that I knew nothing about any movie. Apparently, they had some kind of setup where you could get some dirty movie on the TV in your room. If you turned it to that movie and left it on for a certain amount of time, it would be charged to the room. I guess my roommate watched it while I was sleeping. I told them at the desk that they would have to talk to him, and he would be down soon.

Then I left and went across the street for breakfast. There were several of us staff members there, all in various stages of breakfast. Suddenly, in walked the new guy. I have no idea of how he talked his way out of paying for that movie. Maybe he said that he didn't have any money, but I don't think he was an honest enough man to do that. He ate breakfast and pulled the same thing he had done at dinner. This time, he just threw in nothing and said nothing to anyone. I don't know who else might have noticed, but I was looking for it.

At work that morning, I wasn't in a very good mood. I could have gotten arrested, thanks to this guy. After realizing what a scumbag he was, I wasn't talking too much. This day was to be the very last recruit burn day there. The boss decided he wanted to have a barbeque lunch cooked on a grill that was there. They collected money from the guys and sent someone to the store to shop. Of course, our buddy had no money to give.

I was still not in a good mood when the boss came up and told me that I had to come out and help him cook. I tried to reason with him but he wouldn't have any of it. He said that I had to cook. That did it. In a rage, I walked out of the burn building and found the incident commander. I told him that I had been ordered to cook. I said that I didn't believe that that was in my job description, and if they told me that I had to cook, I was going to drop my gear, get in my car, drive up to the academy where I could talk to the support coordinator and find out for sure. I guess I was telling him that if I was ordered to cook, I was leaving. I don't usually get like that, and the IC was kind of laughing when he said not to worry, that I wouldn't have to cook.

We did all the burns the first half of the day and ate a late lunch. We were all cleaned up and sitting down for burgers and hot dogs, when who do you think I saw stuffing his mouth with food? That's right: our favorite deadbeat. I was just pissed off. I ate and left for home.

I made a call to the boss of support services and told him all about that jerk. I wasn't the only one who thought this guy was a scumbag. In the next few days, the boss received a few more reports. The deadbeat was never scheduled for those burns again, and it wasn't too long before he disappeared completely from the schedule.

Those guys never last long, but he was there just long enough for me to learn a lesson. I never did see that ten bucks I lent him. That's no surprise. He'd better save his money. I did hear that a couple of years later he lost his job with his fire department. Looks like he has fans everywhere.

Snowball

It's just amazing how much we depend on electricity. How for want of it, even just a little, disaster can strike. There was a house in town that was for sale. It had been on the market for a while, and as I remember, the owner had done a lot of work inside. The place was still for sale in midwinter when the owner showed up to check on things. If I remember right, he had someone interested and wanted to show it. He came to make sure everything was well. He noticed icicles all around the front door. He opened the door and saw ice everywhere. The presence of that much ice inside the house was evidence of a major water problem. He called the fire department, as everyone does for a water problem.

I arrived on an engine and the captain showed up a few seconds later. We went inside and couldn't believe what we were seeing. As we walked through, we could hear water running somewhere upstairs. It was running down the walls and through the ceiling in torrents. The weather was below freezing and had been for days. As the water flowed down, it froze. The inside walls had huge icicles on them, and there was ice on the floors and ceilings. It was a mess.

We went upstairs and followed the sound of running water. We were able to trace it to a broken pipe inside the wall in an upstairs bathroom. The water was free flowing. We didn't waste time looking for a local shutoff valve for this pipe. We went to the basement to shut off the water to the whole house at the meter.

The meter was in the partially finished basement. We came into the basement down the stairs into the unfinished part, the old part of the basement. The finished part was a playroom. It had a door leading to the outside from there, but that door was encased in ice; thick, thick ice; from top to bottom. No one was going to open it.

In the basement, we found between four and five feet of standing water, with more flowing in every second. I've never seen it that deep in a basement. Furniture and appliances were floating around. Looking around, we were able to determine where the meter should be. I stepped off the stairs and onto an appliance. I think it was a washer or dryer. Sitting on that appliance, with the aid of a pike, I poled my way across the basement to where I thought the meter should be. I looked down, and sure enough, there it was: near the floor under several feet of water. I managed to get my coat and my shirt off and stretched out so I could reach down. I had my arm, shoulder, and part of my neck in that freezing water, and needless to say, my t-shirt was soaked, too. I shut down the meter. Then I poled my way back to the stairs and got dressed again.

Before we left, we spoke with the owner. He hadn't been there to check on the house for about two weeks. We figured out that the battery in the thermostat had died sometime about a week before. The empty house quickly got colder in that weather. As things froze, a pipe burst inside the upstairs bathroom wall. This started everything. I would say that pretty much the whole interior of the house was destroyed. I guess the owner had to put off showing the place for a while, at least until he could rebuild.

It's amazing how something as small as a triple-A battery could cause such a disaster. For want of the little bit of electric power in that small battery, the problem snowballed and the home was ruined.

Yes, There was Entertainment

Back in the olden days, working at station 2 was sometimes kind of dull. It was just a two-man house, so if you weren't really friendly with your partner, conversation could dry up kind of fast. Back then, for some reason, the department didn't really condone taking the engine out to ride around and check out the district.

That kind of thinking turned into a big problem when taxes were going up and the town was looking to make cuts. With the firehouse doors shut and the engine parked inside, people just *knew* that we were in there sleeping. We wound up having to justify our manpower levels.

Things are different now. The fire companies are always out in the community, doing inspections, checking new construction, or maybe just looking around and seeing what might be new in the district. The people see us out. We're visible and they know that we're doing something.

In those old days, if things were quiet, it could get downright boring. We did, however, have some "entertainment." The intersection near the front of the firehouse had no traffic lights. There were stop signs, however, at the two streets that crossed the main street. The main street was just a clear shot across the intersection.

Well, there were always people running the stop signs. Many would forget that there was a stop sign there, and some would swear that the stop sign was for the traffic on Main Street. There were many minor crashes, not too often was there a serious one.

There was also a popular restaurant at that intersection, and their parking was in the rear of the building. Back then, it was a haven for the senior citizens at lunchtime. Every day, you would see a great many of them out for a nice lunch with friends. They would often have a few drinks with their lunch, and maybe some before, and often some after lunch, too. Then they would get in their cars and drive home. Drinking and driving never makes a good scene, but factor in some people who, just maybe, weren't too sharp driving in the first place, and you could have a problem.

I remember being on duty one spring day just after the lunch hour. The captain was at station 2. He, my partner, and I were talking inside the firehouse, when we heard a loud crash. I ran outside and saw a car stopped in the intersection.

I don't remember too much about the car in the intersection though, because I was looking at all the smoke that I saw coming from the other car. It was head-on into the building housing a liquor store.

There was a lot of noise coming from that vehicle also. My partner drove the engine out into the intersection. I grabbed the medical bag, and ran to the car which had crashed into the liquor store. When I got there, I saw an elderly man in the driver's seat. He was alone in the car. It seems that he had had a few too many drinks at lunch. He got into his car and drove out, and ran the stop sign.

There was a car traveling on the main street. The elderly man had cut the wheel to avoid a collision with the other vehicle. He didn't hit the car, but he wasn't so lucky with the building. He hit dead center. That was the crash we heard.

The old man wasn't hurt, but decided that he needed to get away from there—fast. He was sitting in the car (fully conscious, though inebriated) with the gas pedal to the floor. The wheels were spinning fast on the sidewalk, burning the tires, thus the smoke. It never occurred to the man that the car wasn't going anywhere.

I reached in, put the car in park, and shut off the ignition. We checked the man out. I don't remember him being injured at all, so our part was done. It then became a matter for the police to handle.

I've seen many things happen at that intersection, but that's the only time I saw someone try to drive straight through a building. Yes, we did have some entertainment there!

You Are What You Eat

If stories of the fire service are going to be told, you have to take the good with the bad, the funny with the sad, the gross with the...not gross. This story falls into the second to last group.

There was a man that I worked with some years ago, who would eat just about anything. Anything, that is, as long as you put hot sauce on it. I swear, if you gave him a bowl of Napalm, he'd put the hots on it. You also really didn't want to be at the table with him eating. He had little by way of table manners, and you could usually tell what he had eaten for lunch by looking at the crumbs and stains on his shirt. Knowing the kinds of things that he shoveled into his mouth, one can only imagine what came out. If I ate what he did, I'd have no stomach left. One thing that you never wanted to do was to follow him into the bathroom, or use it for some time after he was through.

One afternoon, I was sitting in our day room reading, when I heard a noise. I looked up and in came this man, heading for the bathroom at the far end of the room, and he was moving fast. He pushed the steel door to the bathroom open. As it closed, I could hear the door to the toilet stall slam and almost immediately I heard the passing of gas, a lot of it, loudly. I looked back down at my book, thankful that I didn't need to use the bathroom for a while.

Suddenly, through the wall and a closed steel door, came an odor that was probably the raunchiest thing I have ever smelled. I had to get up and go out onto the apparatus floor so I could breath. Don't know what he ate, but it must have been good. Yeah, right!
Oh man, if we are what we eat, I couldn't tell you what this guy was.

Wrong Hole

Ventilation is a common practice—a staple in firefighting—in one form or another. We have different ways to ventilate. The way we do it depends on where the fire is located, the type of building, the weather conditions, and some other factors. A common way to vent is to cut a hole in the roof above the fire. We have a variety of tools for this purpose, from power saws to the old standby: the axe.

Fire is always looking for a way up. Heat, smoke, hot gasses, and flames tend to rise. This is basic fire behavior. Cutting a hole in the roof will allow the heat and smoke to rise and escape the building, and it draws the flames with it. This makes the seat of the fire easier to find and extinguish, not to mention providing a clearer atmosphere for search and rescue work.

Care must be taken when deciding on a good location for the vent hole. If you cut in the wrong place, it is possible to draw the fire across unburned portions of the building, causing even more damage. We say in training, "If you're going to cut a hole, make it a big one." Knowing the reason for the vent hole should make it clear as to why we don't place a hose line into the vent and spray water: it effectively blocks the hole and the escape of the heat and smoke. This is taught to the new recruits at the beginning of drill school.

In our town some years ago, there was a fire in a medium-sized supermarket one day. The fire got large and quickly went through several alarms, bringing in help from other towns. Among the many people there, was a man who used to show up at local fires and videotape the action. Afterwards, he would give us a copy of the tape to keep in the firehouse. At this fire, he captured on tape men climbing up ladders to gain entry to the second floor through two, double-hung windows at one end of the building.

He then panned to the action on the roof at the other end. There was a crew from another town, busily cutting a large hole in the roof. For one reason or another, the chief from that town was there, and on the roof with his men. This was somewhat unusual. The hole was cut and heavy smoke was pouring out. Then this chief picked up a charged hose line, and with an open nozzle, stuffed the line into the vent hole. This chief had come from one of the small cities in the eastern part of the state. He had been an engine company captain, and most certainly should known better, even if this wasn't *Firefighting 101*.

Next, the film panned back to the other end and showed the results of that chief's handiwork on the roof. Heavy black smoke was being pushed out of the windows at this end of the building. The men working inside also poured out of the windows, onto the ladders to escape. Well, the building was heavily damaged, but was rebuilt as a different business. By some miracle, no one was hurt. We also now have the evidence of what happens when you put a water stream into the vent, thanks to an unthinking chief and a fire buff with a video camera.

Where Did He Go?

We have a pond in town that has a long, interesting history. The area around the pond is built up with many newer homes overlooking it. There used to be many small, older cottage type homes all around the pond, the remains of a time when this area was considered the "country." The property around the pond was loaded with these little cottages that people could come out to the country and rent. Over the years, a few were added on to and turned into year-round homes, but most were torn down. Most, if not all of these, are gone now.

When I was growing up, there were still some cottages left. I had a summer friend from the city whose family owned one. I found another one years after, when I was in my first winter on the fire department. I don't remember exactly how the call came in, but we did receive a call at night from a person saying that he could see fire across the pond. We didn't know exactly where the call came from. The caller had hung up before we could get that information.

So we sent engines to both sides of the pond to look. I was coming from headquarters with another man, while the station 2 engine got to the pond first. That south side engine reported their location and said that they could see a building on fire across the pond from where they were. We arrived in the area and quickly found the fire. It was in a small home on property abutting the pond. As the other engine was making its way around to give us a water supply, my partner told me to take an attack line to the house. He set up the pump and prepared to give me the water in the tank as I took the nozzle and an armload of pre-connected attack line. I stepped over a low wall in the direction of the house. It was mid winter and we had had a lot of snow. When I stepped over that wall, I quickly sank almost up to my neck in deep snow.

I hadn't realized it, but that house was set probably eight feet below the level of the road. The wall was there and there were steps, but they were covered with snow.

As I fought to move in the deep snow, my partner came around the engine, but didn't see me in the dark. He called out and started looking around. He saw the hose where it fed off of the engine and saw where it disappeared over the other side of the wall. He looked over and chuckled a little when he asked me if I needed help. By this time, I was moving forwards through the snow, pulling the hose to the house.

When I got to the house, I realized the place was boarded up. One piece of plywood had been torn off a window overlooking the pond. That's where vandals had gotten in and that's where the fire was coming from.

I remember trying to knock down the fire from there, since my partner hadn't joined me yet with entry tools. I wasn't having much success. Then other engines and more men arrived. They managed to find the steps that I hadn't even looked for, and they came down with tools to open the place up. They pried off the plywood covering other windows. We were able to enter with our hose and properly attack the fire and put it out.

I remember while we were checking for fire extension, there was an older call man on a ladder with a pick head axe. I don't know what he was chopping, but on his back swing, I narrowly missed getting the pick from his axe through my helmet. A lesson was learned about paying attention to those around me. Another lesson was learned by me, too. I learned to pay attention to where I was going, to look for an easier, more practical way down, instead of taking things in one stride. My partner got a good laugh though, seeing me in snow up to my neck.

There was quite a bit of damage done from the fire, as well as from the people who had broken in. The cottage was knocked down and something bigger and modern built on the property. All that waterfront property around that pond is worth a lot of money now. There are some beautiful homes built along the shore. But if you look closely, you can still see in some of them the image of the cottages that they once were.

Where are the Tools?

We have all kinds of tools to effect rescue these days. If we don't have what we need, we generally know where we can get it. Ahh, but things weren't always so organized.

I remember working a night at station 1 years ago when there was a rollover motor vehicle accident in the next town over. The driver was still in the car. When the car rolled over, the roof was partially pushed down, trapping the victim's head between the seat back and the car roof. The patient was conscious, but unable to move. With their head being trapped and the extreme danger of neck injury, a lot of care and planning had to go into any type of rescue attempt. It seems that the hydraulic rescue tools that we all had were not going to be of use in this rescue. So, a lot of time was spent trying to think of what to do.

The best idea anyone came up with was to use special airbags which were designed to lift heavy objects. Trouble was that not too many departments had them at that time. So the search went on for air bags. I don't really know how long all this took, but it seemed to take forever. While the search was going in, we sat beside the fire radio and listened.

Finally, a set of airbags was located in a fire department a couple of towns away. That department was contacted and assistance was requested. They responded to the accident with their airbags and people trained in their use. Shortly, the bags were in place and inflated. When the car was lifted gently, the pressure was taken off of the roof. This freed the patient's head. It was a young lady. She was told to stay still, but I guess that time spent trapped was too much. She scrambled out of the car, with no obvious injuries at all. She was taken to a local hospital for examination, but was uninjured and very lucky.

Those airbags saved the day. I don't know how we would have been able to have the same outcome without them. In our business, we try to be smart and learn from past experiences, but it was a long time before there were more airbags around. Now, it seems like every fire department has them, and has trained their people in their use. We also have more knowledge of what tools are available from other towns, if needed. This eliminates the need for time consuming searches. Things are a bit different now in these modern times, thanks to lessons learned in the olden days.

Victim Identified

Many years ago while I was on duty as part of the ambulance crew at station 1, we got the tone from dispatch telling us that we had a medical call. What came over the speaker next had us kind of horrified. The dispatcher said that they had just gotten a call from a man who went walking in the sandpit near the high school and had come upon a body. The caller had told the dispatcher that the man had blown his head off. After hearing that, I was dreading what we would find when we got there.

The sand pit is up a short dirt road behind the high school. The high school lays about halfway between our two firehouses, so the apparatus from each station will arrive at about the same time. We got there in the ambulance as the engine from station 2 pulled up. I went up the dirt road toward the sandpit with a man from the engine. The police were already there, a short way up, as was the man who placed the call. He was in tears. We looked just beyond them toward a group of logs standing together, and sure enough, there was the victim.

Without going into all the gory details, it looked like the man had walked up the dirt road with a shotgun. He probably sat down on a log, put the barrel of the gun in his mouth, and pulled the trigger. Basically, there was nothing left above the lower jaw making it impossible to tell who he was. Anyway, as this man was obviously deceased, this was a police matter.

I walked back down towards the school parking lot to the ambulance to get a sheet to place over the body. Something caught my attention and I looked up. This was a weekday afternoon so school was in session. A teacher was running across the parking lot in our direction, closely followed by about half a dozen students. Everybody wanted to know what happened. Being a police matter, I'm not able to tell anyone anything, and I told them so. The teacher started to move past me to go up and see for himself. What lay up there was a sight that nobody needed to see. I asked him several times to "Please get back," and "Don't go up there," but he still tried. Some people just won't give up. I finally called over a police officer, and he made the teacher and students get away. Since our further assistance wasn't needed, we returned to our quarters, full of thought about what we had just seen.

The story isn't over yet. In an effort to try to identify the victim, the police started to check cars in the parking lot, near where the dirt road goes up to the sand pit. Most belonged to someone at the high school next door. Then, they hit on one. It didn't belong to anyone at the school or anyone else that should have been there at that time. It turned out that it belonged to the father of one of our own firefighters. That firefighter wasn't working that day, and had been away for the day. It seems that the father had been very sick and got tired of being sick and in pain. He decided to put it to an end.

How do you deal with that? We see so much in the course of our work that we forget sometimes that we have families, too, and sometimes things happen to them. Still, we feel a special closeness to things like this because it's one of our own that's involved. Imagine how it would have been if the victim's son had been working and had to respond to that call. That happens too often that one of us goes to a call and finds a family member dead or injured. There's not much we can do, except provide support to our fellow firefighter in any way we can. When a person joins the fire department, he joins a brother/sisterhood, a huge family, that will provide the support for the family to pull through. We take care of our own.

What Stinks?

One day, when I came on duty as the shift captain, I went to put my gear in car 2. When I opened the door, a smell nearly knocked over. I couldn't identify the smell, but it was rancid. I put my gear in, and cursing the off-going captain, I opened all the car's windows and doors to air it out. The off-going captain had already left before I discovered the smell, so I hadn't asked him what the stink was. I looked in the car and couldn't find anything wrong. Everything looked like it should, clean and orderly. I mentioned it to my crew and they all went down and checked things out, too. They couldn't find anything out of place either. I had to work all that shift, twenty-four hours, in that stink. I kept the windows open. I don't recall what the weather was, but it didn't matter. The smell was positively gross.

At the end of the shift the next morning, I told the person relieving me about the smell. He said he'd try to find what it was. Then I left.

The next morning, when I came back, I put my gear into the car again. The smell was gone. The off-going officer told me what had happened. Two days before, he had been working. He hadn't brought any lunch, and as the crew wasn't cooking lunch that day, he had gone in car 2 to a local take-out place. He had ordered a fried fish meal. When he was on his way back, he had to stop fast for something. The container with his meal in it slid onto the floor and got fish juice all over the floor and seat. He got back to quarters, got a towel, and wiped up the mess.

He got it all cleaned up, but he hadn't used soap to really clean it. By the time I came on duty two days later, it was disgusting. Once he remembered what had happened, he had his crew use soap and really clean it all up. The smell was gone.

It's interesting that the guy never thought that the fish that he spilled would start to stink and cause a problem later. I mean, old fish stinks. I guess some people don't worry about things unless they are bothered by it.

The Mural

One day many years ago, I went to a home in town in car 2 with the captain. The reason we went there escapes me, but since we brought no engine or special tools, it couldn't have been too serious.

When we arrived, we got out of the car and walked up to the front door. It was a split-level house. There was a large window to the left of the door that went the full height of the door. As we waited for someone to answer the door, we looked around from where we stood. That window allowed us to see inside to the entryway. We looked in, rubbed our eyes, and looked again.

Inside, right in front of us on the wall to the left of the door, was a mural, from floor to ceiling, about eight feet high, featuring a beautiful blond woman, fully nude. It was really a very nice piece of artwork. We did try not to stare too much, and after another minute or so, the door was answered. Can you guess who answered the door? That's right: the model for the mural.

As I said, it was a very good piece of artwork. It looked just like her, except that now she had clothes on and wasn't eight feet tall. The captain was glowing, he was so red. We didn't have to try too hard to figure out what she might have looked like without clothes. The artist took the guesswork out of that. We did, however, have to work hard *not* to stare, at either her or the mural, and not to seem too uncomfortable. I still don't remember why we were there, but we finished up our business quickly and left speechless. I don't suppose that she was the shy type, but I'll bet she had a pretty good laugh after we left.

Trouble with the Privates

Off and on, I spent a good many years in the private ambulance service. I worked a lot of hours, but I never worked there full time. As a full time firefighter/EMT, I was familiar with ambulance work from an emergency standpoint. The work in the privates was mostly routine transport work. This involved transporting patients for things like dialysis, radiation, or chemotherapy. Often we'd transport non-ambulatory people home from hospitals and things like that. I got my chops busted a lot at the firehouse for doing that type of work, but truth be told, even without any emergency work, there was plenty to be learned.

There were three big things that I learned working in the privates. First, I learned my way around as I went to distant medical facilities. My knowledge of the roads in cities and towns was greatly expanded.

Second, I learned to communicate with people. We dealt with all kinds of people. Some did not speak English, but we still had to communicate with them. Sometimes I got a chance to use my limited Spanish skills. There were people who were scared, tired, or disgusted. We had patients who just wanted to die, and others who were just happy to be going home. We were the ones taking them for the ride, and we had to learn to communicate with them all if we were to keep them comfortable and reassure them.

Last, but probably most important, was that I learned to move patients without hurting them or myself. I've seen those who didn't learn how to do this. They ended up damaging their backs, knees, shoulders, and other things. Some of these injuries were career ending. Either way, you had to take that injured part with you when you left in thirty years or six months.

It wasn't bad work, and I was getting paid to learn. There were a large number from the fire service that worked in that field. But as they say, all good things must come to an end, and it did. The economy was hurting, and with taxes going up, the towns were looking for ways to cut costs.

A firefighter from a neighboring town caused some friction between the town's fire department and the privates. This man also worked for the ambulance company that I worked for, but he worked in the sales office. I think his allegiance changed depending on who he was working for on a given day. It seemed he forgot where his primary job was. Either way, something possessed him to approach another local town to offer to help them cut costs by providing emergency coverage for the town from the private service at a reduced cost. The town in question ran two emergency ambulances. Firefighters staffed them twenty-four hours a day. To convert to a private service would mean sixteen of that man's union brothers would lose their jobs. It wouldn't be just positions lost: it meant layoffs.

The union went nuts, from the locals to the state level, and rightfully so. Those of us who were union firefighters and also worked for that private company were forced to stop working there, pending some sort of settlement. There was some sort of agreement after a short while and we all went back to work, but the bad taste never left the mouths of the union. Shortly after, I left to work at another part-time job, and didn't return to the private company until seven years later. Those bad relations between the private ambulance companies and the fire union were still there.

Around this time, that town that ran the two ambulances did indeed vote to go with the private company for emergency ambulance service. Instead of layoffs now, the town just eliminated sixteen unfilled positions. The union went crazy again, but this time there was nothing they could do about it. There was no official job action by the union, but we were constantly getting badgered by our union presidents to leave that company. I was going through a tough time in my life then, and money was tight. I wasn't making tons of money at that job, but it was something I knew how to do, so I really had to stay. That salesman had left the fire department a few years before, but stayed with the ambulance company.

There was constant feuding between that ambulance company and the union locals, but no union was more bitter than the one that the salesman had once belonged to. They had a president that was opposed to any firefighter working in the privates and would get in your face and yell and argue with anyone who disagreed. He didn't want to hear what anyone had to say. He thought he was right and that was that. I needed the money, so I had to stay.

One morning, on a day when I was working for the ambulance company, I put on my uniform and headed off to work. I stopped at an ATM. While I was in there, that union president walked in. He recognized me and started speaking loudly and criticizing me for wearing that uniform. He got kind of abusive, and wouldn't let up. He didn't want to listen to me. Finally, I got loud, too. I told him that I had earned my EMT certification myself, and the fire department hadn't paid me a dime to get it. So he didn't have any right to tell me what I could do with it. He yelled that I was costing firefighters their jobs by working there. I challenged him to name me *one* firefighter who had lost his job because I did transport work for that company. I said that if he could name one, just one, I'd leave right then.

He couldn't.

I then said that he should remember that it was a loose cannon from *his* department who caused all this trouble in the first place, and that he should clean up his own house before getting in my face. Then I turned and left.

I was wound up like a spring back then, and I might have taken a swing at him if I had stayed. Of course, then I would have lost my job. My relationship with that man continued on like that for years afterward.

One day some time later, I was in one of those private ambulances when someone walked up and reported a bad accident up the street. I started over there. I called my dispatcher and told him what I was doing, and requested that he notify the fire department. Since it was in their town, it was their call, but we were there to help if needed.

I arrived and found a bad two-car crash. There were eight people with various injuries, all of them potentially very serious. Then up came a ladder truck from the local fire department. Who do you think the lieutenant was? That's right: my friend from the ATM. I tried to tell him what he had for patients, but he didn't listen. He gave orders to his company and yelled at me not to take anybody to the hospital. His company had their hands full with three badly injured people in the first car. He told us to take care of the patients in the other car, but *not* to take anybody. He began to call area fire departments for help. No skin off my nose. He wanted to play games with people's lives. It was his call. He was in charge, but it made no sense to me. The other people were examined by us, but transported by other assisting fire ambulances.

That's the kind of thing that went on back then. As long as we had someone like him stirring up the shit, things stayed bad. Funny how when that man retired, things calmed down quite a bit. There doesn't seem to be that same level of animosity between the privates and the fire union these days. The privates have gone into emergency work in other towns and taken a bigger bite of the pie, with no problems. Maybe everyone took a step back and looked at the big picture. Health care is expensive. Playing games and starting fights won't solve the problems.

UFO

An EMT certification is not something you earn and just keep for life. We have to accumulate hours of review and education toward recertification every two years. In Massachusetts, I had to accumulate twenty-eight hours in order to recertify. I also kept my national certification, which required forty-eight hours of training to recertify. When I became an EMT, there was no Massachusetts registry for EMTs yet. Massachusetts honored the national standard. This is what I earned and what I kept through my career. The national certification wasn't required for my job, but since I did so much training, I had very little trouble getting the hours I needed, so I just kept it.

Over the years, the classes offered towards getting your EMT recertification hours tended to be the same ones, over and over. It got old, so I started to look for other, less common things to do. One opportunity that I found was a ride-along with a non-transport ALS team based at a local hospital. We got to ride with the paramedics and observe for half of their eight-hour shift. I signed up and reported on my assigned day. At first, it was mostly just the usual things that I saw every time I went to work, such as a cardiac arrest.

Then we got an unusual call. We had to report to a small airport and were told to stand by. This airport was divided into a civilian part and a military part. We reported to the military part. There was an armed guard on the gate who got us an escort out to where we were to stand by. We were told that there was an aircraft coming in and its landing gear would not lower. Coming in to land without wheels sounded serious to me, so I felt a nervous excitement as we waited.

After a short time that seemed like forever, we could see the plane as it approached. It was a small, two-seater, delta wing jet. It was coal black, with no markings on it whatsoever. We watched as it came in and touched down. It slid along the runway, with sparks flying, and came to a stop. When there was no explosion or fire, the authorities couldn't hustle us out of there fast enough. They gave us a fast escort off of the base. I guess there was something they didn't want us to see. Maybe it had something to do with that black, unmarked aircraft that came in. Must have been a secret. (Don't tell anybody.)

We Didn't Forget...

Routines are often nice. Schedules can make life run smoothly. When we do the same thing many times, we develop habits, but sometimes with these habits comes complacency. In our job, that's never a good thing. Instead of thinking ahead or planning what to do with a situation, we just do what we have always done. There are lessons to be learned from complacency. Sometimes we get lucky, and other times the learning process can be devastating.

We have a three-story elderly housing project on the south side of town, just up the street from station 2. It was converted from an old school building. We get the usual kinds of calls from there: the medical emergencies, falls, "smells and bells," and the list goes on. Except for some medical emergencies, nothing is too serious. Burned food on the stove is a common one. The smoke detectors are in the halls, and when the residents burn food, they nearly always open the apartment door to let the smoke out. This trips the smoke detector, which in turn, trips the alarm system. Then the box is received at the firehouse and we are dispatched to respond to the housing unit.

One night while I was working at station 2, not too late in the evening, we got the box for the housing for the elderly. My partner responded in engine 2, with about a thirty second response time. Car 2 and the ladder were coming from headquarters, about three miles away. We pulled up, and seeing no signs of trouble from the outside, reported to dispatch, "Nothing showing."

We went to the box and opened it to determine whether the box had been tripped from inside or pulled from the box itself, outside the building. It had been tripped from the inside. The panel showed that the alarm had come from the third floor. All this was routine. We had done the same thing a hundred times. I remember thinking, "Burned toast again," as we got our keys, gained entry, and started up the stairs to the third floor. Usually we are greeted by a resident outside their apartment, smiling and full of apologies. As we walked up, at about the second floor, we met people coming down. They reported that there was a fire and they were telling us where the fire was.

Guess what we didn't bring? We didn't forget. In our complacency, thinking this was another "burned food" call, we didn't bring the high-rise pack or any forcible entry tools. The high-rise pack consists of two fifty-foot rolls of 1¾" hose, joined together with a nozzle on one end. The other end is accessible to attach to the standpipe connection in the stairwell. Then we could open the valve and advance with the nozzle with a charged hose to fight the fire. Well, we hadn't brought it from the engine. I went back down to get the high rise pack, an axe, and the Halligan tool, while my partner kept going on to the third floor to check things out.

When I got to the third floor with our equipment, I opened the hallway door and looked. The hall was filled with smoke. The apartment with the problem was across the hall from the door where I was. My partner was there, talking on the radio, and reporting what was going on.

This incident had the potential for disaster. We were fortunate that it hadn't gotten that far. The lady who lived in the apartment was not a very neat, clean person. She had her household trash in paper bags, piled one on top of the other against a wall, just inside her door. There were many bags in the pile. She was also a smoker. All around the apartment there were ashtrays, literally overflowing with ashes and cigarette butts. What she had done was to empty one of the ashtrays into one of the bags in the trash pile. There was a butt in it that was not extinguished completely. After a while, the trash in the bag began to smolder and fill the apartment with smoke. The resident opened the door to clear the smoke, which tripped the alarm. My partner was able to extinguish the small fire with water from the tap inside the apartment.

The unsafe way this person lived was a hazard to herself and everyone else. It was reported to the housing authority and would be dealt with by them. Everybody got lucky that night. My partner and I got very lucky. What would we have done if we opened the door and found the hall filled with fire and people needing evacuation? I'm grateful we didn't have to find out. Lesson learned. We never left those tools behind again. We can't afford complacency and those typically human mistakes. Too many lives depend on us. If someone had died because of our mistake...I don't like to think about that. That's a piece of baggage I don't need to carry around for life.

Family Tragedy

Years back, in about the late 70s, we ran a Basic Life Support ambulance. Paramedics, with all of their advanced live saving equipment, were rare in the state, and nonexistent in our area. We worked with our hands and some basic equipment, that's all. If someone had a cardiac arrest, all we had was CPR and oxygen. Still, we managed to save a few. Most, however, didn't make it.

One night shift, we got a call for an unresponsive man in a section of town that is not on any main roads. It is very difficult to make any time getting there. The roads are windy and narrow, and the neighborhood is a confusing mess of little streets. It's bad in the daytime and can be very confusing at night. If you were smart, you would drive around in that area whenever you got the chance, just to stay familiar with the roads.

We got to the residence all right. It was the home of a large family. The children of that family ranged in age from much older than me to much younger. They also had a son and daughter who were my age and were in my class in high school. I spent some time with the son because he had some of the same friends as I did so I knew him reasonably well. The father of the family was found in full cardiac arrest. CPR was started. He was transferred to the ambulance and they started to the hospital.

At some point, someone in the family called this man's son to let him know about his father. He lived in a nearby town. He immediately left in his car for the hospital. He was someone who had been driving from the time he was old enough, and maybe before that. He was known to drive fast, but was thought of as a pretty good driver.

I never did find out exactly what happened, but on the way to the hospital, the son got in a car crash. I guess it was a bad one. It happened in another town, so we were not involved. He was taken to a hospital, where he was pronounced dead.

At another area hospital, his father arrived. He was in full arrest with CPR in progress. Unfortunately, the CPR was not successful and the father was pronounced dead, too. It was a double tragedy. Two loved ones lost in the same night.

Unique Position

It's interesting, sometimes, to look at maps of our local towns. I look and often wonder how the borders got so crooked and messed up. We had places in our town that we were responsible for, yet we had to go into another town to get there.

It can be interesting if a building lies right on the town line. We once had building in such a place. It was well known as a kind of a tough bar back in the day. The old timers can tell stories about things that happened in there. The building sat right on the town line. The way I heard it, part of the building was in our town, and part was over the line into the neighboring town. One town did not allow any bars and the other town did. So, even though this whole place was known as a bar, the actual bar was in the part of the building that was in the town where bars were permitted. The rest of the place was taken up with tables and chairs where people could sit and drink, all perfectly legal in the other town.

The bar was in operation for many, many years before the owners decided to sell. I think that the bar had a bad enough reputation to put a bad taste in the mouths of those living in the area. Plus, new neighborhoods had sprung up in areas where there was once woods or sand pits. These people just didn't want another bar to open on that site.

A few years later, a restaurant opened in the building. The restaurant also contained a bar, but its location was, once again, carefully chosen so that the bar was on the correct side of the town line, in the town where it was allowed to exist. It was a very popular restaurant for quite a few years.

One night, when I was on duty at station 1, there was a fire at that restaurant. It happened late, well after bed and closing time. Because of its unique position straddling the town lines, there was a rather unique response for any box alarm struck, or received, from that building. The alarm system for that building was tied into the fire alarm system for the other town. We monitored the radio channels for our neighboring towns, so if an alarm was transmitted for that building, it would be received by our dispatcher, who was supposed to retransmit the alarm through our alarm system. The result would bring two full first alarm responses to that building. That's a lot of men and apparatus to respond to a building that wasn't very big in the first place. I don't even recall if somewhere in the plans it said which officer from which town would be in charge.

Though our dispatch center was elsewhere in the building, we always had scanners and radios, over which we could hear what the other towns were doing. It made it hard to sleep for your first couple of years, but after a while, you got used to it. It was a strange phenomenon that we could be in a deep sleep and yet wake up relatively alert if something came over the radio that we needed to hear. That was a good thing, because on the night of the fire in that restaurant, our dispatcher (a civilian) screwed up. When the alarm system tripped the box, it rang in the next town over, like it was supposed to. But our dispatcher just thought it was a box for that other town coming in over their tapper, so he did nothing. That strange phenomenon kicked in and our captain woke up to their radio traffic.

The captain got us up. He could have called up dispatch to tell them to start the assigned apparatus, like they should have done in the first place, but instead, our captain made the decision about what to send. He instructed dispatch to send him in car 2, the engine from station 2, and to call in men to cover station 2.

The dispatcher clearly didn't know what he was doing, as he had trouble with the procedure for calling in men to cover a station. I remember having to tell him how to do it. I think I had some colorful remarks to him about learning his job.

I also had a new guy in the station with me that night. He was all kinds of angry that the dispatcher had fouled up and that the captain had changed our response, thereby depriving him of the chance to go to the fire. It got to be a pain in the ass listening to him after a while and I had to tell him to shut up...several times.

I wasn't at the fire, but from what I heard, it was just another building fire, nothing special. There was quite a lot of damage and the restaurant closed up. It sat in its own ashes for a few years before a builder bought the property. Now two big houses stand on the property and both are in our town. Nothing but the back yards are in the next town over, so the town line has become insignificant. I guess that we are the only ones slated to respond to fires in those houses. The other town will respond on mutual aid, but the fire would be ours to start.

That dispatcher never did learn his job. He applied for, and got, a job with the police department. He is good with the books, so he advanced quickly to a commanding rank. Hope he's better at that than he was at dispatching.

The new guy that was with me that night has left the fire service. He quit our fire department to take a job at another. He quit that one, too, but thought better of it about a year later, and asked for his job back. The chief of that department did give him his job again, only to have him quit again a while later. Today he is not in the fire service anymore...and life goes on.

Time, Manpower, and Disaster

I have often told my students over the years that the public, for the most part, doesn't understand what we do for a living. They don't understand our job, and generally speaking, they don't care, as long as *we* know our job and do it well. I usually followed this by saying that while they may not understand the job, just wait and see how quickly they pick up on it if we even *look* like we don't know what we're doing. They always understand that—or they think they do.

One of the many things the public doesn't understand is that this job is manpower intensive. We need people. Unfortunately, people are expensive, so we never have as many as we feel we need. This being the case, we set up procedures that work well with what we have, and also try to have a "Plan B" in case "Plan A" falls through. There have been times when we were not able to adapt to conditions fast enough and tragedy resulted. Sometimes misunderstanding and arrogance resulting from this tragedy can compound the problem.

This happened in a town close to where I worked. I was not involved in any way. The story I'm going to tell was told to me several times over the years. While maybe some details might be wrong, the story, as I'll tell it, is true.

Often, people are their own worst enemy. A common saying in this business is something like: If people ever stop doing stupid things, we'll all be out of work.

One winter day some years back, a young woman took her dog out for a walk around a frozen pond. The dog was running loose and ran out onto the ice. The ice wasn't strong enough and the dog fell through. As is so often the case, the young woman ran out onto the ice to save her dog. If the ice was not strong enough to hold the dog, it was certainly not strong enough to hold her, and she fell in, too. She was seen holding onto the edge of the hole where she had fallen in. The water was deep and she needed rescue.

I'm not aware of anyone else going out on the ice to rescue her, thank heaven. Cell phones were not yet a common thing in people's pockets, and 9-1-1 hadn't come into our area at that time. Someone saw her and ran through the woods to where they knew there was a telephone at the town library. It took time for them to get there through the woods. The call was made to the fire department and it was reported as "a person through the ice near the library."

The town where all this happened is a small, quaint little town. It's mostly residential and many residents are quite wealthy. There is one firehouse, and at that time, there were only two firefighters on duty at any given time.

The firefighters brought all the ice rescue equipment and responded to the caller at the library. When they arrived, they were told that the emergency was not there, but on the other side of the pond. It was a short distance through the thick woods, but a much longer distance by road. The two firefighters knew they would not be able to get their equipment through the woods, and so they drove their vehicle around the pond to the location where the young woman had fallen in.

By the time the firefighters got there, the young woman had disappeared under the ice. The firefighters tried everything they could, but they were not able to find her. Some time later, I believe, divers were able to recover the body. This was a tragedy for all: the young woman's family and the firefighters alike. There is no feeling like working your heart out to save someone, and being unable to.

The story doesn't end here. I'm sure there was an investigation. The woman did not die due to any negligence on the part of the fire department. It was a tragic accident. However, the young woman's family didn't see it that way. They held the firefighters at fault. One can understand the family's feelings after such a loss. They went on a campaign to endorse training in ice rescue, totally discrediting the fire department. They weren't interested in hearing any reasons or circumstances affecting this rescue.

The family members spoke at various functions and sponsored an ice rescue symposium each year. They spoke of the fire department's lack of training and lack of knowledge of their job. This went on for some years. It created some very bad feelings on the part of the public toward the firefighters.

From a firefighter's perspective, we know how things worked and why it ended up like it did. There were several factors that worked against the firefighters that day:

- There were no other known telephones, so the caller had to run through the woods to the library to make the call. This took a lot of time.

- The caller failed to give the true location of the emergency. The firefighters had little choice but to respond to where the caller was.

- When the two firefighters on duty learned the actual location of the accident, there was no one else to call and send. Larger departments could call and have another company respond. They did not have that kind of luxury here.

- The responding company had brought all of the fire department's ice rescue equipment. Since they could not get it through the woods, they had no choice but to take the longer way by road.

- They used their training to try and find the young woman in order to save her life, but they just couldn't find her.

The combined effect of all of these factors resulted in the tragic outcome. There was contempt and anger from the firefighters for years, as they watched their names and reputations dragged through the mud. They did the best they possibly could with the resources available to them, yet there seemed to be no recognition of the limitations forced upon them. They still talk of this incident in hushed voices.

Was this whole accident preventable? I think most certainly. The firefighters train and are familiar with what they do for a living. I guess no one can blame a person for wanting to save the dog. Maybe it would have been better to call and report a dog through the ice instead of running out, as so many people do. After all, we do dog rescues, too.

Danger, Least Looked For

All emergency vehicles, under all the fancy paint and lettering, are nothing more than regular vehicles. They are usually more powerful and rugged, but mechanically they have the same things that all vehicles have, which means that they can malfunction. They are often better maintained, due to the nature of their use, but they can malfunction.

The same goes for all the extra stuff that goes on them. Electronics can malfunction, too. If you believe in Murphy's Law, then you have to believe that they will malfunction at the most inconvenient times and places. Ambulances and police cars are usually equipped with electronic sirens. The one I'm familiar with is the "federal." That's the one you hear that will sometimes be a whining noise or a yelping, or even that Star Trek phaser type noise, all sounded at the whim of the operator. Fire vehicles have that type of siren, also. Many times however, they are also equipped with the Q-siren. That's the one where someone steps on a button and it produces a loud whining sound that gets louder and more intense the longer you keep the button pushed. With this siren, you can really move traffic. Few people who are not stone deaf can say that they didn't hear it. Trouble is that this type of electronics can malfunction.

On a quiet night at station 1, it was the wee hours of the morning and the crew was asleep when they were awakened by the noise of the Q-siren on the engine parked in one of the bays in the rear of the firehouse. They came out of the bunkroom and onto the apparatus floor, and as the noise grew louder and more intense, they had to try to determine where the noise was coming from. The whole building was vibrating. They finally realized what was going on. They tried to stop the noise using the button, but to no avail. Finally, with their ears having reached the threshold of pain, they managed to disconnect the battery and silence the noise.

I think they decided it was an electrical short that did it. What a time to have that happen, when everything was quiet and the crew was sleeping peacefully. Then, the worst possible siren was the one that sounded and grew louder with the seconds. It's enough to make your ears bleed!

A few years later, I was asked to move another engine out of the firehouse. I forget the reason why. I got in and turned the key. Almost right away, there was an explosion. My heart was pounding fast, I ducked and shut my eyes, quite sure that I was about to breathe my last breath, and I think I might have messed my pants. Then everything was quiet. I didn't know if the engine would run or not, and I didn't care. At least I wasn't dead. I just wanted to get away from there—fast.

The mechanic was there and he looked and found that one of the batteries located behind and below the cab had exploded for some reason that I can't remember. That sure cleared out my arteries and I finally stopped shaking.

The job of firefighter does have its inherent danger—it's true. But we don't expect to find it in the firehouse!

Where's the Fire?

There are many factors that will affect a house fire and its outcome. This includes things like weather, traffic problems, accessibility, and water problems, just to name a few. Another thing that isn't as much a factor now as it was years ago is locating the fire. Back in the days before home fire alarms and companies that provide 24-hour security against break-in or fire, people had to pull a fire alarm box and wait for the firefighters to come, then direct them to the fire. People might call and report the fire in the next house, and so on. If there was no one around to see and report the fire, it would often lead to problems.

Many years ago, just before I got on the fire department as a call firefighter, there was a fire reported in the early morning. I don't remember what time the calls started to come in, but it was daylight and a time when people would be up and about and perhaps already gone to work. Phone calls started coming in from people who could see thick smoke rising in the distance, but could not be sure where the fire was. The town next door was getting calls also, and they were out searching for the fire, just as we were doing in my town. Calls were coming in from a wide area, all reporting the smoke rising from a certain direction. The fire department was going crazy trying to find that fire. They started to drive up and down all the streets in an area, gradually narrowing the area down.

When the fire was finally found, it was on a dead-end street that was off of yet another back road, in an area where the roads all wind and twist and are narrow. There were about six large, high-end houses on the street, and no one was home in any of them. The houses on the street were spread out, and the one with the fire was near the dead-end. By the time the location of the fire was found, the house was still standing, but burning badly. I was told that one firefighter entered and a bathtub fell through the ceiling from the second floor and almost hit him. When the battle was over, there was nothing left standing but the front wall of the house. It was a total loss.

That house was rebuilt years ago, and it's bigger and better than it was before. Now there are alarm companies that monitor homes. They call in any report of fire to the fire department. Home alarms will sound and people nearby hear them from all around, but not back then, when no one was home on the whole street to report the fire.

Rebuilding the Call Department

Our fire department, like many others, was once an all call department: part-timers who came in when there was a fire. As the town changed, there came a need for full time, professional firefighters. It started off small, with a few full time firefighters and a very large number of call men. I started with the fire department when I was appointed to the call department, one of eight who were hired that year. The following year, a group of six was appointed.

At first, they kept a lot of call men on the department. With fire prevention working, fires were down. As taxes started to go up, the town started to whittle down the number of call men. Those call men did not work shifts in the firehouse. They were only called in for help in fighting fires and for station coverage, if an engine went out of town or the ambulance transported to a hospital.

Over the years, the call department was reduced to ten people. It was still ten extra sets of hands for work, and perhaps more importantly, it was a pool from which to draw our next full time people. When a job opened up, we would give a competitive exam open to all, but the call people had the best chance of getting a job because of their experience and training. It also helped that we knew them and knew what to expect from them. They still had to pass the test and do well in the rest of the testing process. It seemed to work well as everyone appointed full time for many years came from the ranks of the call firefighters.

Years later, we had a chief who didn't pay much attention to that call department. For a while, he appointed people who lived a long distance away, making it impractical to expect them to come back to the firehouse when we needed help. When I became the training officer, many of the call people had left and I wound up with a call force of just three people. With only three men, if just one of them couldn't make a drill, there were a great many things that I couldn't drill on. This was a nearly impossible situation. It was no way to teach these people how to work as firefighters.

Finally, one day I asked my captain to come with me as a witness while I talked with the chief. I told the chief that I didn't want to train the call department anymore. I said it was a joke. He didn't staff it and he didn't equip it. The money would be better spent in the training budget for the full-timers.

He looked at me and said, "You're right."

I almost fell over. I wasn't expecting him to agree with me. He handed me a stack of applications for call firefighters and told me to pick six. I went through the stack and picked six that looked good to me. They were interviewed and hired. With nine call people, now the training could begin. Shortly afterward, we picked up another call firefighter, bringing our number up to the max. It took some time, but after a while, I was able to get the chief to buy them new turnout gear. We started some more advanced training, like driving, pump operation, and ladder work. We drilled them with the department boats and water rescue equipment.

The call firefighters had a probationary period of one year. By the end of that year, they were expected to know all the equipment and the streets, and have their EMT certification.

At one point, I asked the chief for an assistant, and not just anybody. I asked for a particular man. This guy liked to drill and could teach. He was a man who was good at his job. We got the OK for him to join me, and so the "training division," such as it was, was born.

The position of call coordinator had existed in the past. We brought it back and gave it to a very senior call man. He was the head call firefighter and answered to my assistant, who answered to me. Now the call department had a chain of command.

As time went on, we got other officers to help out with drills. Not everyone likes to work from square one with a brand new person. I never minded though. We'd start at the beginning with the very basics. I would get on the floor and show them how to do things.

When my call coordinator left, the next senior person who showed an ability to do the job was promoted. This is by far a shortened version of the story, but suffice it to say that we wound up with some very enthusiastic people as part of a well-run training division, and we produced very good call firefighters.

I saw many of these people join the ranks of the full time firefighters on our department. One of them later told me that he learned his job well because, as far as the basics went, I got down on the floor and *showed* them how to do things.

We had put together a pretty good training division and produced a good call department, thanks to my willing assistant, some very good call coordinators, and a group of people willing to work and learn.

Officer Down

Among the many debates that rears its ugly head from time to time is that old argument of "flagman vs. police officer." Often, at road construction sites, there needs to be someone to watch and direct traffic. I don't know what the law is. Not all cities and towns do it the same, but my town uses police officers for these details. There is usually something going on in town that requires a detail.

There are periodic attempts to save a lot of money by being able to use a civilian flagman, instead of hiring an expensive police officer at his detail rate of pay. I suppose each side has a rather good argument and I do have my opinions, like everybody else. However, my opinion isn't important for this story, and no one cares what it is anyway.

We had a police channel on our radio in the firehouse. We listened all the time, since the police sometimes get calls that also require fire department response. Plus, with the police being already on the road, they might come upon the scene of an emergency and could then call us to respond.

One summer day when I was on duty at station 1, there was roadwork going on in the neighborhood not far from the building that we shared with the police. It was a residential area with not an awful lot of traffic during the weekdays. But then again, it was a kind of wooded area, with windy roads and blind turns, so I guess they could justify a detail.

It got to be late morning when suddenly, over the police radio, we heard the frantic call for an *"Officer down!"* and calling for help. The call had come from the officer working the detail in that neighborhood not too far from us. There was no other information given. Several officers who were in the station went running out, got into their cruisers, and headed off in a hurry.

We kept listening, waiting for the fire department to be called for the ambulance or some other kind of assistance. No call came in for us. After a short while, there was a voice that came over the police radio. I don't remember exactly what was said, but it indicated that there was no problem.

We found out later what had happened. The officer working the detail was someone who was about as popular as tooth decay with his fellow officers and the firefighters, and even a large number of the citizens, at least all the ones I've ever spoken to. He was a rather small man with a huge ego. He was arrogant with an incredibly high opinion of himself. He always liked to show off what he had. Everything was kept spotless so as to be ready to impress someone, should the need arise suddenly.

It seems that there was little for him to do on this detail since there was hardly any traffic. He decided to polish his motorcycle. I don't remember what kind or size his bike was, but it was nice looking (he always saw to that) and it was a big one. I guess maybe he got it because it made him look bigger when he was on it. Who can say?

But anyway, as he was polishing it, he squatted down beside it. He bumped something and the bike fell down on top of him. He wasn't hurt, but he couldn't get the bike off of himself. It must have torn his heart out to have to make the call that he did. He wasn't the sort of guy who took criticism or ridicule well. But he had no choice and made his frantic call.

I was told by other officers who were there, that as soon as they found that he wasn't injured, they were laughing so hard that they almost couldn't lift the bike off him. They did get it off of him and he was all right, and the day went on.

The story was told often over the years, but that officer always left the room when someone brought it up. I guess it bruised his ego kind of badly. Maybe if they had had a flagman there, he could have lifted the bike off of him and saved him from having to make that call.

Tag Up

I remember the "bad old days" when we had no accountability system within our department. Accountability systems were a bit rare back then. There was no organized way to know who was there. Companies would show up and often get mixed up with other companies. People would lose track of others in their company. Sometimes guys would get lost or in trouble, and no one even missed them until it was too late.

I was at the funeral of a man from a neighboring town years ago, who wasn't missed until his company was packing up to return to quarters. No one had seen him for a while, so a search was launched. His body was found on the second floor, not far from a window. He had run out of air and died up there. This, while not necessarily common, happened far too often.

Gradually, a system of accountability was developed. Each man was given a tag with his name, number, or something else that would identify that it was his. When that company arrived on the scene of an emergency, before they went into action, each man would give his tag to a designated staff person on the scene. That way, someone would know who was in the building and where they were most likely to be.

Along with the tags came better training. Firefighters were instructed to stay with their companies, and each company officer was responsible for his crew. The crew answered to the company officer, the company officer answered to the sector or operations officer, and so on. As companies got their orders from command, it would be recorded where that company was sent to work. The theory is that everybody is accounted for and their location is known. If someone were to go missing, you'd know where they should have been working and where to go looking for them.

The problem was to get the guys to use the system. Of course, there are the people who hate anything new, but most of the people could see the value in the system. They just had to break old habits and remember to use their tag.

This system was added to the recruit program at the fire academy. Each recruit is given a tag with his recruit number on it. They clip it to their coats and carry this tag everywhere they go. When they arrive at a workstation, there is a place for them to "Tag up," meaning to place their tag in the proper place with the others. Like all lessons, sometimes it slips someone's mind and they have to be spoken to.

I remember that I had a kind of routine when we were at a workstation and I saw a tag still hanging on someone's coat, instead of where it should have been, with everybody else's.

I would ask one of the recruits, "What was the last order given?"

If they had been listening, the answer would be, "Tag up, Sir."

I would then say, "That's correct. So why am I still seeing accountability tags hanging on coats?"

Everyone would check, even if they remembered having already tagging up, and the guilty party, or parties, would go and hang their tags up where they belonged.

I wouldn't be done yet. When the guilty returned, I had a speech for them. I would ask if they knew what those tags were for. Then I'd tell them, "If you don't tag up in the real world, the commander would have no way of knowing that you were even in the building, so if something happened, no one would be sent in to find you. And," I said further, "if you call for help, help might be sent to the wrong location, putting even more lives at risk."

Finally, to try to hammer in the point, I would say, "It's not just about you. I, as the incident commander, don't want to have to talk to your wives, husbands, families, *mothers*, and tell them that you're dead because I didn't send anyone in to look for you *because I didn't know you were in there!* I don't need that kind of baggage." My voice would rise considerably as I got to the "mother" part. "These little 50¢ tags could make the difference between you going home at the end of the shift or someone finding your body after the fire was out."

Then I would offer a deal. I told the recruits that today would be free: no repercussions. Tomorrow, there would be subjective reports written if someone forgot to tag up. They always took the deal.

That is a lot of attention given to something seemingly so small, but it is a very important, lifesaving tool for the firefighters to use. Many of my fellow instructors would laugh at me when I went off on my tirade, but I didn't get too many repeat offenders.

A Firefighter's Funeral

The funeral of a firefighter killed in the line of duty is usually a sight to behold. Bagpipes sound and drums beat, as long lines of uniformed men and women from all over the state, country, and sometimes the world, come to pay final homage to a fallen brother or sister. Firefighters not killed in the line of duty are sometimes given the same type of sendoff, but a line of duty death is always something special.

There was a funeral that I attended some years ago, which was that same kind of special, though this man was not killed in the line of duty. This story goes a long way to show how callous and ignorant some people can be, and how seriously we, as brother and sister firefighters, take these occasions. There was a fire captain from another town who was very well known. He was very big in our union. I never met this man, but I'm told that he was the kind of man you couldn't help but like. He always had the well-being of his brother and sister firefighters first in his mind. I'm told that this man was so well known and well liked, that he could call the governor of the state on the phone and actually get through!

One day, the man was off duty and riding with his wife and another couple in his car. The two men were in the front seat talking, and the women in the back. They were driving along when they were suddenly hit, head-on, by another car driven by a drunk driver. If I remember right, the two women escaped injury. I'm not sure what happened to the other man in the front seat, but our friend, the captain, was killed.

His funeral was of the type one would come to expect for a firefighter who had died in the line of duty. There were firefighters from all over the state, and I'm not sure from where else. There was a very heavy union presence, because of his position in the union. The funeral was attended by the governor of the state, as well as other dignitaries. There were far too many of us to all fit into the church for the service. The members of his fire department got in, and the rest of us waited in long lines on both sides of the road in front. The road was closed to traffic.

As we stood in our two walls of blue, waiting for the service to be over, a car came up a side street behind me and a bit to my right. I was close enough to hear what was being said. The driver wanted us to break ranks so he could continue across the street and onto another side street. He didn't ask, or even request. He ordered us out of his way. He was told, very matter of factly, that we were *not* going to break ranks for him. The man started to get nasty and a bit abusive, and he exchanged words with a few of the guys. I guess he could have pushed the issue by driving forward, but he was smart enough not to. Instead, he just sat in his car and cursed us.

He finally told us that he was a doctor and his office was down the street. He said that he had to get back to the office. Nobody believed this story. It came far too late into the incident, after the situation had already gotten very heated. If he really were a doctor, I think he would have found another way around, instead of just sitting there in the car. Then, in an attempt to boost his own feelings of self-importance, he said, "I hope that there is no one dying."

From somewhere in the ranks, a smartass was heard to reply, "Don't worry. If there is, they'll call the fire department."

That shut him up for a little while. A little later, while he was mouthing off again, a motorcycle cop stopped and had a short talk with him. This quieted him down through the rest of the services.

When the services were over, the doors to the church opened and we were called to attention. Out of the doors came the members of his fire department, his friends, and family, as well as the governor of the state. They got into their cars and limos and drove to the cemetery, passing between two rows of uniformed firefighters, saluting as the hearse drove by. The man in the car was still sitting there.

After everyone had passed, we broke ranks and started to head for the gathering that always takes place after these things. Except, not everyone headed to their cars. There was a large number of people who headed over to the jerk's car. When last I looked, I couldn't even see the car for all the blue uniforms surrounding it. I don't know if there was any physical altercation, although the man really should have been slapped in the head. I never found out just what was said, but they no doubt spoke to him about respect.

The Roach Coach

People doing stupid things is what keeps us, in the emergency services, working. Oh sure, there are accidents and acts of God. These can't be helped, but by far the most calls we deal with involve someone doing something stupid. Sometimes these calls are sad, especially if someone is hurt or killed. But there are times when something happens that just hits you right, and you have to laugh at how foolish or just plain dumb someone can be.

Every once in a while when things were slow, we would leave the grounds of the fire academy for lunch. The students had to remain on campus, but we, as staff members, could leave, as long as we got back on time. We heard that a new place had opened up a few miles from us, and so we decided to check it out. The place was one of those vans with the window in the side where someone takes your order. The food is cooked inside. We call these things "roach coaches." Sometimes the food is pretty good, other times it's the pits. Either way, you're not getting any gourmet cuisine. It's just that the food at some is edible, and others will make you sick.

This one looked pretty good. It was nice and clean, and the people inside were friendly. There was a large awning out front to shade you as you ordered. There were several of those PVC plastic picnic table and chair sets there, too. These things are really not good quality, and you have to be careful. They're not made for heavyweights.

Well, three of us went there one day and placed our orders. After exchanging some pleasantries with the owner, we went to one of those tables to wait. I'm a big guy, but I took a chance and sat down. The chair seemed like it was going to hold me all right. I was sitting facing the front of the coach. There was another set of table and chairs in my view. One of my friends was also sitting. He had his back to the coach and was facing me. The third guy in our group was standing right next to me, looking in the same direction as I was.

As we waited and talked, another man walked up to the window to order. This man was huge. He was short and very fat. But for his head, he was the shape of a very large ball: he was that round. He placed his order and wandered over to the table and chairs. I was thinking to myself, "No. He can't be going to sit on that!" But I was wrong. The man pulled up a chair and sat down. It's not like the chair was broken or anything we could have warned him about. What would we say to him? "You can't sit there because you're too fat." I don't really think anything we could have said would have been well received. Anyway, as I watched, I had the feeling that this had disaster written all over it. I'm over two hundred pounds, and

this guy had to have at least a hundred and fifty pounds on me, probably more.

Sure enough, it happened. There was a loud snap, like a rifle shot, as the chair disintegrated underneath this massive man. The next thing we knew, he was on his back, kicking his legs and flailing his arms in the air. There was no doubt that he had not broken his neck and was not paralyzed.

In the milliseconds after the chair had blown apart, I looked at what had happened with a shocked expression on my face. My friend sitting across from me knew something was wrong by the look on my face. Then he looked into the face of the friend standing beside me. Something told him not to turn around. I slowly looked up. My friend had tears in his eyes from trying to hold back laughter. He couldn't help it. What that guy did was just so stupid. As soon as our eyes met, we both lost it. We had to quickly get up and run around the corner so no would see us roaring with laughter. A lady working in the coach came out the back and told us how evil we were, but she was laughing hysterically, too. Well, the guy got up on his own. He wasn't hurt.

Our insides ached all the way back to work, and for many years after, each time this story was told. There are some who might think we were cruel to laugh at the man. Rest assured, his girth had nothing to do with why we laughed. We laughed because a man who should have known better did something he shouldn't have done and made a fool of himself in public. This was mild compared to some of the things we see people do. But like I said, sometimes something just hits you right and you gotta laugh.

Unwanted Responsibility

There was an interesting call we had years ago, before any paramedics came to our area. Every town's fire department ran their own BLS ambulances. I was working at headquarters one afternoon, when my partner and I were dispatched to a neighboring town for the report of an unresponsive male. That often means the person is in cardiac arrest and we will likely have to do CPR. We figured that both of that town's ambulances must be tied up. We left in our ambulance and made good time with our response.

What we found was not what we expected. There were no firefighter/EMTs from that town at the scene. There was only a police cruiser, parked out front. Two police officers were walking toward us. One officer came up to us and said that they thought that the guy inside was gone, but he needed to have someone verify it. Legally speaking, we were no more able to declare a person dead than the police officer was. Of course, if certain conditions existed that pointed toward certain death, there would be nothing we could do, so we wouldn't work the patient. It would then become a police matter.

Well, we went into the house and into the room where the patient was. He was stiff, hard, and pale. It was pretty clear that this man had been gone for some time. We told this to the police officers. They said, "Thanks," and we left to go back to quarters.

This was a strange call. The police could have just as easily done what we did and come to the same conclusion. These were not new, young officers, who maybe weren't sure of themselves. These were a couple of old salts who knew, or should have known, what they were doing. I think that we had two guys who just didn't want the responsibility. If that's not it, then I have no explanation.

State Hospitals

I worked for years in the private ambulance industry. Though there was some emergency work, I mostly did routine transport work. I got my emergency work at the firehouse, so this was, in a way, kind of a break from that, and a chance to see some other things.

One place I remember having to go often were the state hospitals. They were all places for the insane or mentally challenged. I don't know how many state hospitals there were, but they were spread all over the state and there were a lot of them.

Funny thing about them was that they all looked the same: several dismal-looking, dark-red brick buildings spread over sprawling lawns of perfectly manicured grass with neatly trimmed shrubbery. The buildings were depressing. They all looked old, and I guess they were. There were bars over the windows.

Before we could enter, we had to remove everything that we had on us that was sharp and leave it locked in the ambulance. That meant pencils, pens, badges, name pins, other uniform pins, combs, and of course, the buck knives that we all carried on our belts back then. The company issued us a tie to wear. It was a clip-on. If you wore the other type, you'd better take it off. We were going into a hospital where there were insane and otherwise mentally unstable people, and if one were to grab you by the tie and it didn't unclip, well I guess you were going to be in trouble. We'd have to ring a bell to get inside and they would either buzz us in or someone would come down and take us up. The corridors were all dimly lit. The places were not dirty. They were just old and rundown.

We would come up to a ward and get buzzed in, and that's where the fun started. As soon as we would enter, people would crowd around us. You see, the patients were not locked in their rooms. Perhaps that might be true for some patients at some facilities, but at most state hospitals, they just locked the door to the ward and the patients could walk around where they wanted.

We would be kind of a distraction for them. There were some who had severe mental challenges. They would follow us around and touch us. Sometimes they would get really close and look at us, or perhaps make noise at us. It was a very eerie experience.

At the nurses' station, we'd have to borrow a pen to do paperwork. The patients would all be looking at us and coming in, until the nurses made them leave. You had to run the gauntlet going in and going out.

One day, I looked around for someone to let me out. I was kind of new at this at the time. I looked around and I realized that I didn't see any staff around. I started to get nervous. My partner found someone to let us out. I asked my partner where the staff members had been. He explained that you really couldn't tell the difference between the staff and the patients, unless you saw a big ring of keys. Those were carried by staff, and it was the only thing that set them apart from their patients. That was a scary thought. What if one of the patients got ahold of a key ring? Imagine the chaos that could have ensued.

We did an awful lot of work in and out of those places. Back in the olden days, people would put their mentally challenged children into a state hospital. Back then, anyone who had any mental issues was called "retarded," and many spent their entire lives in those institutions. It was thought that they were incapable of being productive members of society, and so they were shut away. Heartbreaking, if you thought about it.

The general opinions of the medical community and treatment methods have changed greatly over the years, and most of those places have shut down now. You can still find them, if you know where to look. The lawns are still cut and the bushes trimmed. The buildings are empty, for the most part. Now they just stand as monuments of another era, when we would take those who couldn't help themselves and shut them away, away from our sight for life.

Sometimes They Do Say Thanks

The ambulance is about the busiest single piece of equipment the fire department has. Many of the calls are real emergencies. Some are emergencies only in the mind of the person who calls. I guess that would be a matter of perception. I suppose if you think you're having an emergency, you can make a good argument for calling the ambulance. We also have those who call the ambulance for other reasons, and almost never have an emergency.

Among our many "frequent flyers," there was one lady who would call often. Then the calls would stop for a short time, before picking up again. Then we might be going to that residence as often as several times a week.

It was always the same person: a rather young lady. She was heavy and not very clean. She was always drunk, and generally not pleasant to have to deal with. She also was loud and a bit abusive to us. We heard that she was married and her husband was much older than her. We were never sure if that was true or not. For all the times we went there, we never saw anybody but the lady.

Every time we went in, we would find her lying on the same sofa. She always had some reason for calling. Sometimes she had taken too many meds, and sometimes she just didn't "feel right." She told us many different things, but she was always very drunk, so we always took her to a local hospital. Then the calls stopped. We didn't hear from her for quite a while.

One day, I was on the ambulance when we got the call for that address. We got there, along with a paramedic team from a local hospital. The lady told us she was bleeding. An exam by the paramedics revealed that she was indeed passing blood vaginally, a lot of blood. We quickly got her on the stretcher and into the ambulance. The bleeding came in waves, and each time, she would just gasp.

The medics got two large IV lines started. She was losing so much fluid that while the medic was getting the next bag ready, I would squeeze the fluid from the first bag, to get it into her as fast as I could. We did this all the way to the hospital. I don't know how many bags we went through on that five or six minute ride, but there were many. We left her in the care of the hospital, got our ambulance cleaned up, and returned to the firehouse.

We didn't see that lady again for a couple of years. Then one day when I was working, a man and woman walked in. The woman smiled and was nice looking. She walked in straight and proud. The man was quiet and a lot older than her. She came up and introduced herself. It was the same lady that we had taken so often, but now she was clean and sober. She told us that she had quit drinking. She wanted to thank us for all our help and to say she was sorry for all the hard times she had given us. Then she introduced us to her husband. I guess he really *did* exist.

Don't know what got into her to turn her life around, but turn it she did. She was nice and friendly and attractive after all. I haven't seen her for many years now. I still drive by that address often. I look over and remember all the times that I went there and remember how she changed. We don't often know what ever becomes of our patients. However, once in a while, they come back to say, "Thanks." I'm glad that this one did.

All Grown Up

When I was still kind of new to the job, I was assigned to a two-man station with an older guy that no one wanted to work with. The man was loud and in your face, and he was always trying to stir up trouble. Me, being a new guy, kind of just kept quiet and let him walk all over me. I had grown up in a house where Dad ruled the roost, and we had all better shut up and listen and do as we were told. With this in my background, I just sat there and took everything that this guy dished out. It made me miserable for the whole two and a half years that I worked with him. Then I quietly went to the chief and requested to be transferred away from that man. The chief knew very well about the problems that everyone had with this guy. He got me away from him quickly.

As the years went by, I worked with the man very little. In fact, I would turn down overtime to avoid working with him. He used to talk about me behind my back and tell stories about me, but what the hell. He did that to everyone else, too. This guy was a non-EMT assigned to station 2. Our shifts were back-to-back, but since I worked at headquarters and he was at station 2, I rarely ever saw him.

One night shift in the fall, a man from my group assigned to station 2 was out, for whatever reason, and it was my turn to go over and work his slot at that station. I got to work and went in the kitchen to cook something to eat. The kitchen was a mess. I started moving some things around to make room. The glass coffee pot was sitting there and I went to move it. I grasped the handle and picked it up and the thing came apart in my hands. I'll swear on a stack of bibles that I did nothing else to it. Well, since it was broken, I threw it away.

The night went pretty well, as I remember, until around midnight. We got a call for a brush fire in a nearby aqueduct, a place where we usually had our worst brush fires. It's not that those fires were really worse than other brush fires. They were no bigger. It's just that we always seemed to get them at night.

We got there, put water on the fire, and it darkened down. This made it hard for us to see and to wet down the places where it was still burning. We were there for the rest of the night. It was hard, dirty work.

We came back to station 2 after sunrise. We were tired, dirty, stinking, and wet. We got our engine back in service then went and sat down and waited for the day shift so we could go home. The day shift arrived, one of them being that same guy who had made me miserable for so long. He went into the kitchen right away and saw the coffee pot. He yelled out, "Who broke the coffee pot?!"

I tried to explain what had happened, but he wasn't listening. He blamed me for breaking it. He complained loudly that now he couldn't make his coffee. Then he proceeded to tell me that I had to buy a new one. He told me where I had to buy it and how much I had to spend. All the while, he was yelling over my attempts to explain. If I had broken it, I most certainly would have replaced it. I might have anyway, but not after the way I was being treated. I finally yelled back at him, "Buy your own coffee pot!" I think I told him to kiss something, too, but I don't remember.

Then I started to walk to the door. I couldn't wait to get home and clean up so I could rest. I had just made the door when his voice boomed out again. "I'll have my coffee, but you won't have any!"

I snapped. I stopped and did an about-face that any military man would have been proud of. I marched right up to the guy and got right in his face. I stuck my finger in his face, too. I spent the next five or six minutes loudly telling him what I thought of him, and warning him that he'd better stay the hell away from me.

The guy was quiet all through my tirade. I think that was the last thing he expected from me. What do you know—he found out that his ex-partner had grown up and now it was *his* turn to shut up and listen. When I was done, I turned and left.

He spent the next few years not talking to me. On those occasions when we would work together, after he did his required housework, he would then take a lawn chair out to the apparatus floor and spend the day out there. It was sure OK with me.

Two and a half years after that incident came a time when we had to speak. He acted and talked like there was nothing wrong. The only thing that was missing was the abuse.

Though he is long since retired, I still have little use for that man, and the sooner he leaves this earth, the better off we'll all be. But he never tried to push me around again. Hell, if I knew it would be that easy, I'd have told him off years ago. On second thought, I probably wouldn't have. I needed to grow up first.

Telltale Responding

Years back, when my oldest daughter was still in elementary school, I was at the school one afternoon to register her for Girl Scouts. I was walking up the front driveway of the school when I heard a siren in the distance. It was a Q-siren and it was wound up and screaming, without letting up.

I hear sirens and watch emergency vehicles responding to calls all the time. I can usually tell by the way the siren is used what type of vehicle; ambulance, fire, or police; is using the siren, as well as the seriousness of the call. Though fire apparatus is often equipped with the federal three-way sirens, we always like to use the Q. It really moves traffic and leaves no doubt that fire apparatus is coming through.

Police often use the siren very sparingly, unless they are going to a potentially bad call, then the hi-lo siren comes on. The same is basically true for ambulances, unless it is a fire ambulance driven by a firefighter. Then, that hi-lo comes on, alternating with the wail, and stays on until the traffic is cleared.

Driving is also an indicator of how serious the call is that they are going to. It's not just about speed, but also the way the driver moves through traffic. I once watched as a police cruiser passed me like we weren't moving at all. He was heading to a fire call. I don't know why he thought he had to get there first, but he did a very dangerous thing trying to beat us there. He was putting himself and others unnecessarily at risk.

I once drove the fire ambulance into Boston in weekday morning traffic, going to Children's Hospital with a small boy who was seizing. This patient had a life-threatening seizure disorder. We went there often and always took him to Children's Hospital. We never took him to a local hospital. Traffic going east, to the city, is brutal in the morning.

I drove the ambulance straddling the line separating the lanes and left the siren on as I made my way toward the city. I couldn't always go fast, but I did drive aggressively for the whole trip. The traffic parted before us. There was no doubt in anyone's mind that I needed to get through.

My wife and I have visited Manhattan a number of times. With the amount of vehicle and pedestrian traffic in New York, cars and people get green lights at the same time. Pedestrians always have the right of way, but you'd be a fool if you took that for granted and crossed a street without paying attention.

One evening we were crossing 6th Avenue, which has a traffic flow from south to north. We could see a vehicle with emergency lights coming in our direction down the side street. We started across the avenue and were about half way across when a ladder truck, lights and siren operating, came into the intersection. I was watching closely and saw the driver's arm come out the window signaling for a left turn, against the traffic flow. My wife just stood there in the intersection. She hadn't seen the arm come out the window. I moved quickly and pulled her out of the way as the truck turned against traffic. It went down one block before turning onto another street and going with the traffic flow. I never saw anything like that. Think they were going to something that sounded important? I would say so.

That siren I was hearing when at the school belonged to an engine from the south side of our town. They were responding to a report of an 18-month-old that had been found floating in a backyard swimming pool. I found out later that she was the grandchild of one of our own firefighters. The child, sadly, didn't survive. I didn't get all the details until a day later, but there was no doubt in my mind that they were going to something bad.

Apparatus trying to make time, aggressive driving or not, and use of the siren are a dead giveaway to the seriousness of a call. I can usually tell.

Near Miss

One day when I was duty captain, we were running a drill on drafting at a small pond on the north end of town. For those who don't know, drafting is the act of picking up water with a pump from a static source; like a pond, lake, or even a swimming pool; adding pressure and then sending it out through hoses to fight the fire. Often at brush fires, it is required to draft in order to get a water supply. That's the simple explanation.

We had the whole shift there with the two engines and another vehicle, which was designated as an engine. In reality, this "engine" was a pickup truck with a pump and water tank mounted on a skid in the back. It was used for brush, and because of its size and four-wheel drive, it could go places that the other engines could not. Well anyway, the drill progressed. At some point, one of the men, a good friend of mine, got up onto the tailgate of the brush engine. He squatted down and bent forward to pick something up. This made his shirt come untucked, revealing a plumber's crack like you read about. It was at that point that I heard the "Voices." They started out slowly and quietly, then got louder. Before I could help myself, I picked up a spanner wrench, held it up over his backside, and let it go. Bull's eye! Got it, dead center.

Then, from the corner of my eye, I could detect movement. The "Voices" were quiet now. Funny how they quiet down in times of danger. I was left all on my own. I stepped back a full step and turned my head—just in time to see an enormous fist fly by my head. I could feel the breeze as it passed.

My buddy had felt the spanner drop, and without another thought (except getting that maggot that did that to him), he swung his fist back. He nearly got me, too. We all enjoyed a good laugh, at his expense, and I thanked my lucky stars for that near miss. Hell, he could have broken my face!

Bicycles

As far back as I remember, I had a bicycle. When I was a kid, most households where I grew up had only one car, and Dad took it to work. If we kids wanted to get anywhere without walking, we took our bikes. I'm sure we can all remember skinned knees and elbows from falling off our bikes.

Over the years, things have changed and we don't see as many kids riding anymore. Bikes themselves have changed, too. They're not those rugged things we could ride down stairs and off small cliffs anymore. Bikes now are high-tech, expensive, and they go very fast. We also have many more serious bike riders than there used to be. I suppose it's always been true that there was potential for serious injuries in any bike crash, but we see much more of that now.

I remember the first serious bike crash that I saw. It was a couple of years before I started on the fire department. I was working for a DPW. I watched a man on a bicycle, clearly on his way to work. He was holding a briefcase and was dressed for office work. He pulled out of a side street without looking, and right into the path of a young lady, also on a bike. She was dressed for biking and rode a nice street bike. She looked to be on a ride for exercise or training or something. She crashed into the man and they both went down. He was all right, as I remember.

A doctor driving by stopped to help, and someone produced a big first aid kit. As I helped that doctor bandage up the gaping wound to that young lady's head, she kept saying, over and over, "He was on the wrong side of the road!" She was right: he *was*. That wasn't thought about much, back in the day, but it's important now.

I've seen people hit small stones or sand and go down. Thank God they were wearing a helmet. On the way to the hospital, they would keep saying the same things over and over to me, the result of the concussion they suffered. Without that helmet, they probably would have died.

We're told often that bikes need to follow the same rules as autos, but we still have people on the wrong side of the road, running stop signs and red lights without looking, or riding two or three abreast. I've seen broken limbs and split heads. I've seen people that have left all the skin from one side of their body on the road, as they slid to a stop on their side.

I'm still a rider, but I try to stay where there isn't any traffic. I go out of my way to avoid major intersections and high traffic areas. Yes, I have certain rights and right-of-way, sometimes— on paper. There's no guarantee that someone in a car will yield the right-of-way to me.

Everyone tends to do what they want and then points the finger at the other person when something happens. I can't fault just the cars or just the bikes because they're both guilty of not following the rules. We all need to be more careful, observant, and tolerant. Just having the right-of-way won't keep anyone safe. In the end, when someone is lying in the street, dead or seriously injured, does it really matter who was in the right?

Cream of the Crop

It has been said that the firehouse is not for the thin-skinned. The same can be said for the state firefighting academy. The academy is staffed with active firefighters or retirees from various fire departments across the state. These men and women come to teach the art and science of firefighting. No one does it for the money. We don't get paid that well. Some who come from far away don't make much money at the end of the day when the cost of fuel and meals are factored in, but they come back because they love it. The staff at the academy is the cream of the crop, and that also means that we have professionals in the art of harassment and ballbusting. I heard one fellow instructor say that no one from his department could survive one lunchtime in that room with the guys at the academy. I'm proud to say that I've survived many.

Among the many things that have been done to be inhuman to one another, there are two that stand out in my mind. One guy, in an attempt at payback for some slight, put an egg into the pocket of a man's turnout coat. The idea was, the guy would put on the coat and a while later the egg would break. He'd then stick his hand into the pocket and find broken egg. Great idea, except that he put it in the wrong guy's pocket, and the gear wasn't worn for a while.

The next time the owner of that coat came in and put his gear on, the egg broke, but he didn't notice it right away. Out in the drill yard, the man put his hand in the pocket and felt the slime. He took his hand out and brought it up to his face to see what it was. Then he smelled it.

During the time while the egg was in the pocket, it had plenty of time to spoil. As soon as he got one whiff of the rotten egg, he immediately projectile vomited. What an attractive thing to happen in front of the students!

The ensuing investigation uncovered the whole story. There were no real repercussions. People were just asked not to do things like that again. None of us is fool enough to think it won't happen again. It will, just as soon as possible, after things cool off.

The other thing was interesting, and perhaps a bit dramatic, and it was funny, too. We had a guy who liked to joke around a lot. He was always pulling a joke on somebody. He was good at it, and he could take it when people played jokes on him, too. One morning, he started off the day by pulling some kind of prank on another guy. Shortly, his victim found the jokester's car keys lying on the table in the instructors' room. He took those keys, put them in a coffee cup, and filled the cup with water. Then he put the cup in the freezer. There it sat all day. The keys were in a block of ice, frozen solid in the cup. I didn't hang around to see what happened when the guy came looking for his keys. It was time to go home. Still, it was a pretty good joke. Simple, but effective.

Fire Below

I go to Manhattan often to visit my wife's family. Her parents, especially her father, seem very interested in the craft of firefighting and the science behind it. When we sit in their apartment on the 7th floor looking out over a busy avenue, there are always sirens to be heard going by. One particular day, my wife said to me that they had stopped in front of our building. I came to look out the windows. There was no doubt by the activity that was going on, that there was a fire somewhere below us on a lower floor of the building. There were two ladder companies with their aerial ladders raised, an engine hooking up to a hydrant on the corner, and firefighters entering the building.

I looked out and watched. My father-in-law was amazed as I gave a running commentary on what was going on and why. I also told him what they were about to do, before they had even started. The operator of the engine on the hydrant, besides the LDH to feed his pump, had a piece of 3" hose connected. My father-in-law asked what the smaller hose was for. I think I said the LDH should get him all the water he needed, but he used the length of 3" hose to get all the water possible out of that hydrant. He asked how I knew it was 3". I told him that I worked in the business and I know my tools. He had trouble believing that I could tell what size hose they were using from up where we were.

We went out for food before the firefighters were done. As we started walking down the sidewalk, my father-in-law left us for a moment. He went over to talk to the pump operator at the hydrant. He came back and we continued on our way, without a word said about what he had said to the firefighter.

When we returned a while later, the fire department was gone. We went into the building and back up to the apartment. Shortly, my father-in-law left and went down to the apartment that had had the fire. The firefighters had apparently had to force entry through the steel door. When my father-in-law came back, he told us what he had seen. He was appalled at the damage that had been done to the door, and couldn't imagine what could have done that. I went back down with him to look. The door had indeed been forced. It bore the unmistakable tracks and marks of the mighty Halligan tool. I told him that and described the tool and how it is used.

Back at the apartment, I asked my father-in-law, "When you talked to that firefighter before, were you asking him about the size of the hose?"

He said, "Yes."

I asked, "Was I right [about it being 3"]?"

Once again, he said, "Yes."

He looked at me in amazement. What can I say? I know my business.

Hands Off

I worked with an older guy at station 2 from time to time. Actually, it was six months at a time, plus some times when it was my turn to fill in for someone who was supposed to be his partner, if they were out that shift. He was not an EMT so he could not work on the ambulance in station 1, so was assigned to station 2 permanently. We had no officers assigned to station 2 at that time. The remaining members of the crew were all EMTs and rotated through station 2 for six months at a time. With only two people working at station 2, if someone was out, a man from station 1 would have to come across town and fill in for him. We couldn't have just one guy by himself working there.

Working with this guy was a real trip. He wasn't a bad guy, once you got to know him and got to know what he expected from you. This was in the "bad old days" when some of the older guys didn't think about what they were doing. Sometimes they would have a few beers, sometimes more than a few, and sometimes far more than they should have had, and still come to work.

One night shift, I came to work a bit early and relieved one guy on the day shift. At 6 p.m., the other day shift guy left. I was alone in the station. That should never have happened. I called headquarters and the captain answered the phone. I asked who was supposed to be there with me that night and told him that I was alone. He said that my usual partner was supposed to be there. Right then, I saw a flash that was my partner's truck, roar through the intersection out front and pull around to the back of the firehouse. I told the captain, "Never mind. He's here," and hung up the phone. It rang again a second later. It was the captain. He told me to be sure to log my partner in at 6:15. I said, "OK," and hung up.

My partner came in and listened while I told him what the captain had said. Then he exploded. He called me names and said that I had "screwed him," and that I was supposed to call his house if he wasn't in on time. This kind of thing wasn't really unusual for him, so I just let him run on. He ended up not speaking to me for a couple of weeks. No loss on my part.

Sometimes he would come in and it was very obvious that he had had a few too many beers in him. He'd come in talking a hundred miles an hour, with a cigarette in his mouth. Yes, smoking was allowed in the firehouse back then. He would put the cig down and forget about it, and then light another one. Sometimes he would have two or three of them burning in ashtrays around the room. When he came in like that, the man's partner would spend that night shift hoping and praying that they didn't get anything serious. I was lucky enough not to have anything too serious happen when he was in that condition working with me.

One time I had a headache at work, so I asked this guy if he had any aspirins.

He said, "Yes. Go into my locker, on the top shelf, and look in the bowl."

I did as he said, and when I looked into the bowl, I couldn't believe what I saw. There was a potpourri of pills, unwrapped, and mixed together in the bowl. There were all different colors, shapes, and sizes. I had to look hard to find two that even *looked* the same. I decided that I'd rather live with the headache.

The funniest thing about this guy was his food. He always kept canned goods in his locker, but he would also bring in a ton of food from home. He'd bring in half a smoked ham that his family didn't finish. There were huge bowls of meatballs, packages of cold cuts, and pickles. He loved those really long, fat ones. He used to cut them in half and suck out the inside. Then he would put the pickle skin in the ashtrays. He would sit and smoke all night with the ashtray on the floor next to his chair. He'd flick the ashes and they'd fall on the floor, around the ashtray. When the cig was done, he would blot it out in the ashtray, right on top of the pickle skin. The smell from that is something that has to be experienced to be believed.

All of this food was his, and heaven help you if you touched any of it. Make no mistake: he knew exactly what was there. At that time, we worked 10s and 14s. That would be two 10-hour-long day shifts, followed by two 14-hour-long night shifts. Then we were off for four days before the cycle would repeat. Our time on duty was spread over four days, and he would monopolize the refrigerator for all that time.

Most people will have a small snack while watching TV. Not him. His snack would be a double fried egg, tomato, and mayo sandwich. Sometimes he'd have two. He'd get up during a commercial and start cooking. Then he'd come out of the kitchen with his sandwich and take a bite. Wait...this gets better.

He had none of his natural teeth. He had had an upper plate and a lower at one time. Somewhere along the way, he'd lost the lower. It made no difference anyway. He would take out his upper plate and put it in his pocket. When he went to bite his sandwich, he was all gums. His gums would just squish the bread. The contents of the sandwich would squirt out of the back and onto the floor. Sometimes he'd wait to bite until he sat down again, and he'd have the sandwich on his lap. It was disgusting, but I had to laugh. He just never learned.

Once I saw him come back from his locker with a box of generic brand mac and cheese mix. He opened the box and saw many little flies in with the noodles, and they were all dead. "Wheat bugs," he called them. No problem for him. He just strained out the dead bugs and cooked the pasta. While it was cooking, we had a run. He just left it on the stove. When we got back, the pasta had absorbed almost all the water in the pot and was all bloated. I have never seen an elbow macaroni that big in my life, or one that soft. They even *looked* mushy. It didn't bother him, though. He ate it.

He used to stay up very late at night. I'd go to bed long before him. In the morning, I'd get up about 6 a.m. and go into the kitchen to make coffee. The kitchen would be positively heinous. All the cupboards would be open, every useable dish in the place would be dirty and left out all over the counters, and the sink would be full. The air would be scented with the fragrance of burnt pickle skin. I would make coffee, bring it into the office, and drink it. If the engine needed washing, I'd wash it. I'd do all this alone. If I woke my partner up, soon it would become my job and he'd expect me to wake him all the time. So I let him sleep. When the day shift came in, I'd leave. He'd get up and have to clean up the station. He asked me once why I didn't wake him. I told him that I wasn't his mother. Maybe he should have set the alarm clock next to his bed.

One night, he insisted that he was going to watch the Miss America pageant. I don't care for those things, so I went to bed at my usual time. As I lay awake reading, and for a while as I was trying to get to sleep, I heard him talking loudly to the contestants on television. How loudly, you ask? The bunkroom was on the opposite side of the station, across the apparatus floor, and I slept in the rear room, furthest from where he sat. I heard him as clearly as if he were sitting right next to me. I have to think he would have gotten slapped if he talked to those girls in person like he did when they were on TV.

Usually, at the end of our four-day stretch, he would get a paper bag and collect all of his leftover food to take home. Once though, he forgot a container of meatballs. They must have stayed there in the fridge for a month. One day, he was looking for something to eat and found them. He recognized them as his. When he opened the container, there was a thick skin of grease on top. He got a spoon, broke through the skin, and scooped out the meatballs. He heated them up and ate them, with no ill effects, I might add.

This guy was something, and on top of all this, he wasn't much of a firefighter and not an EMT. As I said before, he was fine as soon as you learned what was expected of you. What was expected was you do all the housework, keep your mouth closed, and *hands off* of everything that was his, especially the TV, and above all, his food.

Chiefs Can't Dispatch

Many years ago, when the fire department used to run their own dispatch desk, there was a call for a fire in a house. It was not too long before the day shift would be coming on duty. I was scheduled to come on duty that day, so instead of throwing on some clothes and responding to the firehouse, I got myself ready for my shift. I shaved and put on my uniform and left for station 1, ready for work.

When I arrived, it was mayhem. Because it had been so close to shift change, and with anticipating the day shift coming in, the chief ordered the man on the dispatch desk onto the engine responding to the fire.

I guess the chief and his deputy thought they could take care of things until someone came in. They were mistaken. Things were a disaster. They had been scribbling down bits of information they needed on little pieces of paper. Now they were scattered all over the desk. The chief was seated at the desk and the deputy was standing behind him.

There was indeed a house fire. It had started when an elderly lady in a long nightgown had gone to the stove to make herself a cup of tea. She turned on the flame on the gas stove, and then reached over the stove, setting her gown on fire. The fire spread to the kitchen. I don't remember how the call came in. The fire was quickly knocked down, and the woman was badly burned.

When I walked into station 1, the chief looked up and told me to take over. He and the deputy couldn't get out of the dispatch office fast enough. I don't remember how long it took me to sort through all the pieces of paper and notes to finally make sense of things. Sadly, the woman injured in the fire did not survive her injuries.

I never minded doing the dispatch work, just as long as I didn't have to take over and straighten out that God-awful mess after the chief officers had gotten things started!

Mechanism of Injury

The term "mechanism of injury" should be familiar to everybody in the emergency medical services. It should most certainly be known to those who answer emergency calls. We can treat those injuries that are obvious, but injuries that we don't know about, those injuries that we can't see, can be deadly. We try to take in the whole scene as we arrive, to try to determine exactly what happened through what we are told, what we can see, and what we learn from investigating the scene.

Often, I have found victims walking around and telling me that they are all right when the mechanism of injury will tell me that more potential injuries may exist. That information can give us a little more leverage when trying to talk a victim into taking an ambulance ride to a hospital to be examined for injuries.

Early one evening years back, I was on duty at station 1 when we got a call for a motor vehicle accident on the south end of town. The dispatcher sent a paramedic team, the ambulance, and the engine from station 2. The engine was first due. It signed off at the scene. After a few minutes, they reported that they were unsure of any transport. The paramedics had not arrived yet and we continued with our ambulance.

When we pulled up in the ambulance, I saw a car with front-end damage. I don't remember what it had hit, but there was an elderly lady seated on the ground a short distance from the car. She had been the driver. As I remember, the engine crew had taken her out of the car and sat her down where I saw her. The EMT with the engine crew told me there would be no transport. He was getting release papers for the lady to sign.

I decided to take a walk around the car. I walked over and looked in. The first thing I saw was a bent steering wheel. It was bent inward towards the dashboard at the bottom, so the lady probably had hit it with her abdomen. Steering wheels don't bend too easy. They have to be hit pretty hard to bend like that. With that in mind, the mechanism of injury indicated possible internal injuries.

I walked back to the EMT who had told me there would be no transport and asked him if he had looked in the car. He answered, "No." I told him that the steering wheel was bent and she really should go to the hospital. He glared at me as I started to examine the patient. Almost right away, I found a kind of protrusion in her upper right abdomen. It was rigid. Just then, the medics showed up. They looked at the car as they walked up to the patient. I filled them in about the steering wheel and what I found during my exam.

They looked and did their own assessment. They agreed that she really *did* need to go to the hospital. They wanted her to go into a trauma center in Boston. They volunteered, and it was agreed, that they, the ALS team, would do the transport. We explained what was going on to the patient and she was agreeable. We put her on a stretcher, loaded her into the medic's ambulance, and they left.

I later heard that this lady had spent several days in surgical intensive care at the hospital in Boston. I never found out the full extent of her injuries. If someone hadn't looked in that car and realized what may have happened to her, that lady might have been sent home. Who knows what would have happened then. I'm sure it wouldn't have been good.

Some people in EMS, far too many, forget the basics of trauma care and the survey of victims of trauma. We always have to remember the basics that we learned in school, as well as the education that is picked up through experience. Then we have to use all of that knowledge to conduct ourselves with a good professional attitude and thoroughness. Someone's life, sure as hell, depends upon it.

He Was Bad News

I guess every town has its share of kids that grow up to be real trouble. Ours was no exception. We had some colorful characters hanging around back in the 70s. I'm not talking about those who had a run-in with the cops for drinking or smoking a little dope. I'm talking about the kind that grows up to be really bad news.

We might have had a lot, but a certain few come to mind. They didn't bother the fire department much, but they were always trouble to be around, and it wouldn't have taken much provocation for them to become a problem for us in the firehouse. I remember one guy who used to hang out around town. He was younger than me, so I didn't really know him until he got into his early teens. Around then, I was in my late teens. A friend of mine was walking down the street with his girlfriend when he chanced to pass this kid and his friend. They made some remark about my buddy's girlfriend. I guess he should have kept walking, but that's not an easy thing for a young man of that age to do. He stopped and had words with the two other guys. Things got ugly very quickly. My friend had had a mouth full of metal braces the whole time I had known him. He had just had them removed prior to this confrontation. Well, that kid hit my friend with a bottle and broke his teeth. That incident was a long time ago, so I don't remember what ever became of it. However, I think it spoke volumes about the kind of person this guy was growing up to be. Things only got worse from there.

The guy became a real bad ass, the kind you were always better off avoiding. He was a drinker and a druggie. Though I couldn't say for sure what drugs he was taking, I've heard stories that he tried just about everything.

I did hear a story once about how he offered to help out a few of his friends. He said he could "take care of" their boss who they didn't like. It involved doing some bad things to the boss's family. That was a story I heard and I can't confirm that. But it kind of fits right in with what I knew about him.

One night years back, this guy was supposedly on heroin when he had a fight with his girlfriend. He left for work on the graveyard shift, got on his motorcycle, and took off. He never made it. I was on duty at station 1 when we got a call after midnight for a motorcycle accident. I think that someone was driving by and saw the bike all smashed up near the street. It happened in an area near where a river passes through town. The road is almost at the same level as the river, and there is marsh and weeds all over. We got into the area. We had no trouble finding the bike, it was just off the road, but we couldn't find the rider. We looked all around without any luck. Then we expanded the search area, and sure enough, we found him. He was quite a ways into the marsh and weeds. He's lucky we found him. He was pretty well smashed up and unconscious. We used full spinal immobilization and transported him to the hospital. He did survive, but with his back broken he was paralyzed from the waist down.

That didn't slow him down any, though. He was still trouble wherever he went. I was on a call a few years after his accident. We responded to a local bar for a man down in the parking lot. We arrived to find that same guy lying in the lot next to his wheelchair, all bruised and skinned up. I guess he must have been having some trouble inside, and one of his "friends" gave him a push down the stairs. He wasn't hurt too badly, and was soon home again.

One time, years ago, we had a murder in town. Two young guys heard that an old lady had some money. They broke into her home and tortured her for hours before finding that she didn't really have any money. Then the two young guys stabbed her to death. As I remember, they weren't too smart about it and they stayed local. I had the job one day of operating the boat for the state police as they dragged the bottom of a local pond looking for the murder weapon.

They didn't find it. I know that they liked our friend in the wheelchair for "complicity after the fact." They thought that he might have let those two guys hide in his house for a few days. They did catch those killers, but I guess they couldn't prove anything about our buddy in the wheelchair.

Shortly after that, I heard that he moved to Florida. A while after that, I heard that he died. I never did hear what he died from. I'll bet I could put together a list of possibilities, but I won't. I doubt that anybody really cares. He's gone, and that's enough for many.

No Substitute

During my off time from the fire department, I spent many years working in the private ambulance business. I worked for several companies over the years, but I started with, and worked the longest for, one local company. I met many people there. Some I have no use for, even still. Some just came and went. Others I have known and respected all these years. Some of these wound up as brothers and sisters in the fire service, some are still involved in ambulance work, while others have gone on to other things. There were some great EMTs and medics working there. Although I personally did mostly routine transport work, you never really knew when something would go wrong and you had to use your knowledge and experience.

I was posted one morning on a main street at the town line. My partner was a new guy. He was very young and about as exciting as a root canal. I had my doubts about him. Well, we probably wouldn't need to really do anything extraordinary anyway.

Suddenly, someone came up to our ambulance and reported a bad car accident up the road. Everybody always reports an accident as "bad," but we had to check it out. I headed in that direction, while reporting on the radio where I was going and requested that they notify the fire department in that town. It was really their accident to deal with. Then I heard another company ambulance come on the air. They had been stationed on the same road, only further down. That ambulance had two experienced men on it, as I remember, but one guy was as old as me, with as many years of experience as I had. Considering who I had for a partner, I was glad I was going to have experienced help coming also.

The accident was a head-on, right on the town line. One car had three men in it. All were unconscious and bleeding heavily. That first car was enough to keep that town's firefighters busy. They told us to take care of the patients in the other car. In there, we found two large women and three young children. None were wearing seat belts. All were injured in various degrees and in full panic mode. The fire department called for other fire ambulances. We had, at the time, somewhat strained relations with the local fire department, and they wouldn't let us transport anyone. Meanwhile, we were able to assess and stabilize our patients and get them ready for transport.

My partner proved that he was as useless as I had thought when he couldn't take a set of vitals before an IV line was started. As he packed up the cuff and stethoscope, I asked what he got for vitals.

He looked at me and said, "I couldn't get any."

I looked back and said harshly, "You *have* to get them. Do it again."

He did. I guess he finally got something they could use. The three of us with the most experience managed to get things under control and in some order until even more help arrived.

I never saw that new guy again. He's probably making big money doing something that the world could easily live without. No matter. I liked what I did and found that I was pretty good at it, at least after a few years. There's no substitute for experience!

Special Request

Working at the private ambulance company one day, I do remember being paid a subtle compliment. In the morning before we went out on the road, I was approached by a member of the family that owned the company. He told me that I and my partner were going to be taking one specific call at some point in the day. All morning long, we were kept in the local area, driving around and waiting. It wasn't until mid-afternoon that the patient was ready to be transported.

It seems that one of the family was being transferred from a local hospital to a Boston hospital for emergency heart surgery. The patient was very unstable. The man who was telling me this was the son of the patient. He said that he had put in a special request to have me be the one to transport his Dad. Wow, what a compliment!

The call came in and everything went off without a hitch. The patient's son said that he knew it would, and he didn't want anyone else to do this call. He could have had anybody in the entire company take that call, but he asked for me. I guess I must have had a pretty good reputation.

Good Save

A choking person can be a very dramatic thing to see. If something cannot be done quickly, the victim could die. It's incredible to think about it. A group of people are sitting together, sharing conversation and a meal. They're laughing and enjoying themselves. Suddenly, one of them is stricken, and with no help available quickly, someone's life is cut short.

One night when I was the duty captain, we were dispatched to a local restaurant for the report of a person choking. I responded in car 2, and so I arrived about a minute ahead of the ambulance. It was very crowded and I had to request the police to clear traffic that was blocking the way for the ambulance. The ambulance was right behind me. The ambulance arrived and we entered. We had to fight our way through a crowd of people standing around. We had to get loud to get the people to move and to get someone to tell us where the patient was.

It turned out that the patient was a middle age female who was having dinner with a group. She had swallowed something wrong and was having difficulty breathing. She got up and ran to the ladies room. We found her there, still conscious, with all the signs of a nearly obstructed airway. The EMTs went to work doing the Heimlich maneuver, while I went to call for an ALS team to meet the ambulance en route to the hospital. We were not going to delay transport to wait for them.

It is incredible how people can act when there is an emergency. Everybody wants to see what's going on, and they crowd around and get in the way. This place was very busy and many people wanted to see. The EMTs did abdominal thrusts with no success, until the patient lost consciousness. I'm thankful that we had the police officer there that we did. He was a man who knew his job and had no hesitation to move the people out of our way. The engine from station 2 had arrived and brought the stretcher inside. The unconscious lady was secured to the stretcher quickly, hustled through the crowd out to the ambulance as quickly as possible, and put inside. There was no paramedic team available to meet them en route, so I had an EMT from the engine join the ambulance crew to help, and they left for the nearest hospital.

When the ambulance returned to quarters, the crew told me that they had kept up abdominal thrusts in the ambulance. Then at one point, a large piece of meat dislodged itself and came up and out. They cleared the mouth and checked for breathing and pulse. The patient had both. She had begun to breathe again on her own. If I remember right, she was still unconscious when they left her at the hospital, which is to be expected, but she recovered. I seem to remember a call or letter from the lady, something low-key thanking us for saving her life. We don't get much of that.

That night, I typed a letter to the chief explaining in detail, what had happened and what I had been told. I recommended a letter of commendation for all of the people on that call who worked on the patient. The chief did indeed write letters of commendation for each of them. It was well deserved. They did a fine job and made a good save.

A Meeting Unexpected

I was brought up in a certain religion. I did what I was supposed to do and went to church. When I grew up, I stopped going to church. I still have my beliefs, but I no longer practice that religion, or any other for that matter. I also try to respect the feeling of others, as I feel that someone's religious choice is their own personal matter.

There is part of a big lake that is in our town. The lake also extends to several surrounding towns. In that lake, people water ski, fish, swim, and pleasure boat. There is also a nice woods surrounding the lake for walking through.

One day, there was another thing going on in the lake that I had never known to take place there before. It seems that there was some kind of minister that was baptizing people in the lake. This was taking place in a neighboring town, and we were listening on the district fire radio system.

Having grown up around the lake, I had explored and swam all over. All of us locals are familiar with conditions in the different areas. Where these baptisms were taking place, the water is shallow for about twenty feet out. Then, the bottom drops suddenly and it gets deep. Well, I guess no one involved in this baptism ceremony knew about this.

The minister was a bit off shore. I don't know how many people had already gone, but when the minister laid this one person down backward in the water, it seems that he lost his grip. All of a sudden, the person was gone. That poor person had sunk like a stone and had not come up.

The call went out for help. This was not our call and our assistance was not requested, but I listened to things play out on the fire radio. Fire, police, boats, and divers came as quickly as they could. As I remember, the person did not survive. The body was recovered shortly. I remember thinking that I hoped the ceremony had been completed before the victim had sunk. They had an unexpected meeting with the Almighty.

I Feel Old

One day while working at the fire academy, I had been assigned to do a lecture. The topic of the lecture was "Communication." At the time, all lecturers used overhead projectors with some other props and techniques thrown in. Now all the lectures are on PowerPoint. More to learn, but once you've got it figured out, it's a better way of doing things.

Anyway, one of the things I had to do for part of the lesson was play a little game. You know that game "Telephone"? You whisper something into the ear of one person, then they do the same, and when it goes all around the group, you see if the message has changed. Well, a recruit was to read from a prewritten scenario involving a traffic accident between a ladder truck and a car. Then the recruit was supposed to report what she had read to the next person, and so on. This was to show how much care has to be taken when exchanging information to make sure the right message is delivered.

I handed the paper to a young female recruit in the front row. She stood and silently read the paper. She had a funny look on her face. Finally, she said, "Ahhh, Sir. I think there is a typo here."

I came over to look and she pointed to the word "Corvair." She then asked me if it should say "Corvette."

I answered, "No. Corvair." She still had that funny look on her face.

I asked her if she had ever heard of a Corvair, and she answered, "No."

I looked up and asked the class if anyone knew what a Corvair was. Not one person raised their hand. Out of 44 students, no one had ever heard of any such thing. It was time to put plan B into action...as soon as I thought of it. Boy, did I feel old!

Food for Thought

When I first started work at the fire department, there were two nursing homes and two elderly and handicapped housing facilities in town. Over the years, the number of facilities of this type has gone up. We went to those places a lot for box alarms, which almost always proved to be false or minor problems, easily handled. We went there for medicals and assistance calls very often, more often than anything else.

Did anyone ever think about what we would do if we had an actual fire in one of those places? I don't think anyone on my fire department ever did. We operate with a minimum of manpower, as do most departments. Out in the smaller towns in the suburbs, the number of people working on a fire department can be very small, with sometimes only one or two people on duty at a time. The nursing facilities tend to have the highest number of staff during the day, but only a bare minimum at night.

Early one morning, somewhere between 5 and 6 a.m., we got a call from one of our nursing homes for a fire in the building. This was before the start of their business day, so the small night staff was on duty.

The first engine that was due to arrive was engine 2 from station 2, and it had two men on it. I was coming with the ladder company with three additional men from headquarters. All the way coming across town, I was thinking about what the hell we were going to do if the building really was on fire. It wasn't a large nursing home, but that didn't make any difference.

Most of those people would be in bed. Some were confined to bed. Many who could walk used walkers or just moved very slow. Add this to the confusion of an emergency that strikes at night, when people are least aware and half-asleep, and only a minimum number of staff available to help. Plus, there is no real plan in place for such an emergency. I was thinking about all this while answering the alarm. I wasn't an officer then, so I didn't have to anticipate what orders I might give, I only had to think about just how we would get those people out.

Before we arrived, we received word that it was a mistaken alarm. As I recall, someone smelled smoke in the attic, panicked, and reported a fire in the building. I breathed a sigh of relief. But still I wonder: what would we do if we had a real fire? There still wasn't any plan in place.

A Privilege of Time

When a person is new to the fire service and to a firehouse or company in particular, there are expectations to be learned and lived up to. They are eventually passed on to the next group of newbies, once the current group has some seniority. When you first start on the job, you have to shut up, make coffee, learn your job, respect your seniors, and learn to live with the ballbusting that goes on, much of which is directed at you, the new guy. We've all been there and it's a rite of passage into the fire department family.

When I started, there was a man from down south on my group. I don't know how long he had been up north, but he'd been with our fire department for thirteen years. He still had that southern accent, as well as the speech, attitudes, and prejudices that one might expect from someone who had grown up in the south during that era. He was very loud and not shy about busting the chops of the new guys. This was the mid 70s, and as television went, there was no cable or any pay TV in our area at all. It was also the age of the mini-series. There were several that aired in my first couple of years on the job. One of these was "Roots," and was based on the book of the same name by Alex Haley. It told the story of a man who was captured in Africa and brought to America to be sold into slavery.

Back when I had hair, it was very curly. I never shed a tear when it fell out. I never could do anything with it anyway. Plus, it made me the object of jokes. At the firehouse, that southern co-worker began to call me "Toby," the same name as the main character in the Roots mini-series. Well, the name caught on, and soon I was known as Toby in the firehouse. Time went on, and new guys came on the job. None of them knew where the name had come from, but they knew that people called me Toby.

There was one new guy that came on some years after me. I had known him prior to his appointment, and I think he knew where the name had come from. He was still a newbie when one day he came up to me in the firehouse and said, "Hi-ya, Tobe."

I looked at him and said, "You haven't been here long enough to call me that."

He just kind of looked at me. I don't remember if he said anything or not. I think he was kind of insulted. I had only said that just to bust his chops, and also because I knew it bothered him. Well, the name Toby gave way to other nicknames in the years after our southern brother retired.

Funny though, that younger guy never forgot that day when he was still a probie. He used to bring it up once in a while. On the job, he demanded respect from all rookies that came after him. One of his great beliefs was that newbies needed a certain amount of time on the job before it was acceptable for them to show familiarity by using nicknames. Many a new guy heard that from him.

Years later, when this guy had earned some seniority, I told him that I had only said that because I knew it bothered him. He insisted that it hadn't bothered him though, but the proof is in how he deals with others under him in seniority. I think it bothered him plenty!

Making Us All Look Bad

On my days off, I worked for many years in the private ambulance business. The company had contracts to provide emergency service to several cities and towns, but I did mostly routine transport work. There was one city where the company did the emergency work that contained a hospital, many nursing homes, and a host of other medical facilities. We had an ambulance for BLS service, as well as a paramedic ambulance, dedicated for service to that city. There were also many other ambulances in the city at any given time. If the dedicated ambulances were tied up at a call, others would be called to answer any additional emergencies. Some of the people I worked with got really excited at the idea of emergency work. They wanted very badly to be assigned to one of the emergency ambulances. I didn't get too excited. I got my fill of emergency work with the fire department ambulance. The transport calls with the BLS ambulance were pretty laid back and I didn't mind doing them.

However, one Friday I was in that city when I and my partner were assigned to an emergency call. The call was for a 30-something year old female in cardiac arrest. I was driving and my partner knew that city pretty well, so off we went with him directing me. We had been told over the radio that we were going to have an ALS ambulance responding with us. Sure enough, as we crossed over a highway, our assigned ALS vehicle came off of the ramp in front of us. About that time, I looked in my mirror and noticed another ambulance behind me, with lights and siren going. I couldn't read the vehicle number. I got on the radio and asked dispatch which vehicle was supposed to be our ALS unit. I reported that I had one in front of me that I could identify, and an unidentified unit behind me. I asked if the dedicated units were responding also. I was told no; the dedicated vehicles were tied up at a motor vehicle accident. Then the dispatcher asked who was behind me. I said I didn't know.

When we were arriving at the call, the first thing I saw was the BLS vehicle assigned to the city parked outside the house.

The crew was inside. Our ALS unit (that had been in front of me) arrived and went inside. Then the unit behind me passed. I saw that it was indeed, the dedicated ALS unit. They pulled over and went in also. I thought something wasn't right. With all those medics inside doing patient care, it would be our job to move the patient onto the stretcher, out of the house, and to the ambulance.

I pulled our vehicle over, and as we got out, the BLS crew from the dedicated ambulance came out of the house. They very quickly opened the door of the parked ALS truck. Inside, I saw a large woman, fully immobilized, on a long backboard. She had been left alone in that ambulance. It was just for a few minutes, but that should *never* have been done. The BLS crew took the woman on the backboard out and moved her to their own ambulance. As they opened the door of their ambulance, I saw that they, too, had a fully immobilized woman, on a backboard, unattended in their vehicle. They put the second patient inside their ambulance and left for the hospital.

Now things were becoming clear: those dedicated crews fancied themselves heroes. When they heard the call over the radio, they were so eager to get some emergency work that they jumped on the call, in spite of having responsibility for two accident victims.

I went in the house with my partner. It was a split-level with a landing inside the front door. As we entered, I could hear laughter and joking from upstairs. I looked up and saw four paramedics working on a woman who was unconscious on the floor. I looked down to the lower level and saw the woman's family and a police officer. They were all well within earshot, and were looking up at me, as they, too, heard the joking around and insensitive chatter from upstairs. The medics were doing what needed to be done, medically speaking, but the job doesn't end there. Professional behavior is required, too. It was not being practiced here.

When the medics were ready, they called for us. We put the patient on the stretcher and carried her outside, where we placed her inside an ALS vehicle. All four medics got into that one ambulance and left for the hospital. My partner drove the remaining ALS vehicle to the hospital and I drove ours. We didn't have any patient.

When we got there, one of the medics, a man I didn't know, told me that the patient didn't make it. I said, "I know." He gave me a kind of arrogant look and asked how I knew. I told him that I had worked many calls like this, and I knew. This wasn't new to me. He nodded and walked away.

There is a room at the hospital for the ambulance crews to do their paperwork in. The phone in that room rang. It was the dispatcher, asking for me. He asked what had gone on. I explained to him everything that I saw that had happened. He told me that the higher-ups were asking questions and things were getting serious. Well, I worked the rest of my shift with nothing else said.

The next day, I was on duty at the firehouse when the phone rang. It was that dispatcher again asking for me. He told me that things were getting ugly. The company wanted an incident report from me on Monday. I really didn't want to get involved in this, but I had been told to write a report. I spent the weekend trying to write something as general and impersonal as possible, trying not to cast blame. It wasn't easy to do. As I was finishing it, I thought, "Hey, I wouldn't tolerate crap like that in the fire ambulance." If it had happened with the fire department ambulance, I would have written a report in an instant. These guys were all guilty, in my eyes, of jumping a call and shirking responsibility for the patients they already had. That "Hero Syndrome" is not acceptable.

As a professional, I knew how I needed to end my report:

> "I HAVE HAD MANY YEARS IN THE EMS FIELD AND HAVE WORKED MANY OF THESE TYPES OF CALLS. IN MY OPINION, THE ATMOSPHERE CREATED BY THOSE INVOLVED IN PATIENT CARE WAS MUCH TOO LIGHT AND CASUAL, CONSIDERING THE CLOSE PROXIMITY OF FRIENDS AND FAMILY. ALSO, IN MY OPINION, THE ABANDONMENT OF ANY PATIENT IN AN AMBULANCE IS IMPROPER. THE ABANDONMENT OF THESE TWO

LADIES WHILE FULLY IMMOBILIZED WAS UNFORGIVABLE."

Then I signed and dated the report and handed it in.

The two crews who had jumped the call were severely reprimanded. One supervisor was demoted. Those involved were allowed to read my report. When they had finished, they started to tell stories and lies to get themselves off the hook, or at least get me up there on the hook with them. They were told by the powers that be that it looked as though *my* crew was the only one who had done what they were supposed to. If it had been up to me, four or five people would have lost their jobs that day—but it wasn't up to me.

The people involved stayed employed, however they started to engage in a campaign of harassment against my partner. Funny, though, not one of them had the guts to say anything to me. Oh, they'd become quiet when I walked into the room. They wouldn't talk to me at all. I never considered *that* to be much of a loss.

As the years went by, I had left the ambulance business and was instructing at the state fire academy. I saw a few of those people come through as recruits. They recognized me and avoided me, when possible. I'm glad they had finally developed some brains. Maybe they also developed a sense of responsibility and a proper ethic that they could carry into the fire service. I hope so. That *I'm-a-Hero-and-Nobody-Can-Do-the-Call-Like-Me* crap has no place in the emergency services. It just makes us all look bad. Just do your job. It's not that hard.

Too Many to be Special

There are all sorts of medals, pins, certificates, plaques and such, that can be awarded probably almost anywhere, including in the fire service. They can range from a medal of valor, for saving a life while your life is at grave risk, all the way down to some certificate of recognition for giving your time to help out with something. The point is that they are awarded for having done something special. If everyone had them, they wouldn't be really worth much to anybody.

Early one morning years back, just before shift change, the ambulance was dispatched to a home for a lady in labor. I didn't go, as it was my turn to stay back to cover the station. The ambulance, the engine from station 2, and the captain in car 2 responded. I think an ALS team was also dispatched to the scene. They did indeed find a woman in labor. It was just a short time later that the baby was born, delivered by the EMTs on my group.

The next week, everyone was still feeling good about this when we came on duty for our next shift. In the fire service, there is an award called a "stork pin." This is just what the name implies: a small pin of a stork with a sling in its beak, carrying a baby inside. This is supposed to be awarded to those members who have assisted in the birth of a baby in the course of their duty. I guess the chief didn't see it that way, or didn't see it at all. Or maybe he didn't really think. He had gotten ahold of some stork pins and started handing them out to everybody. When he handed me one, I told him that I hadn't been there on that call.

He said, "That's OK. Take it."

I did, and that pin is in the jewelry box on my dresser at home. It's still in its original plastic bag. I didn't know what else to do with it, so I put it there and there it will stay. I didn't earn it.

When you start passing these out like candy, that makes them meaningless. The boss just didn't understand that, or maybe he just didn't care.

Shocked and Surprised

At the firefighting academy, the student recruits are given a number based roughly on the first letter of their name and the alphabet. We refer to them by this number. They also refer to themselves that way. Recruits must address instructors as "Sir," "Ma'am," "Mr.," or "Ms." So-and-So.

Shortly before a new recruit class was scheduled to start, I got a call from a good friend who was a lieutenant on an engine company in a town nearby. His department had just hired several new firefighters and they were going to be in the next recruit class. My friend told me that he had one of these new guys on his company. He told me that he had taken this new guy aside and told him that he was going to meet one particular instructor up there, and he told him my name. He told the recruit that the only way he could get any respect from me was to come up to me on his first day and say, "I already know everything there is to know and there isn't a goddamn thing you can teach me!"

This kid smelled a set-up right away. He told the lieutenant that he wasn't going to do that, and they all had a good laugh. He, of course, didn't know that I knew the lieutenant.

Well, the new class started, and of course the kid didn't say anything to me. So one day about a week into the recruit program, I looked up his number. His name began with an "A," and he happened to be #1. I had had some interaction with the class, and spotting him with a small group engaged in some small task, I called him over.

He came up to me and said, "Yes, Sir?"

I looked at him and very sternly said, "Number 1, I understand that you already know everything there is to know and there isn't a goddamn thing I can teach you. *Is that correct?*"

That poor kid. His eyes opened wide, his jaw dropped, and no sound came out. He looked horrified. Finally, he sputtered out, "I never said that, Sir. I really didn't...I wouldn't..."

The poor kid looked so terrified that I started to laugh. He looked somewhat relieved. He was properly relieved when I told him about the set-up. I told him he should have seen the look on his face.

He got a good laugh out of it, too. Just another incident on just another day in the life of a new probationary firefighter—especially as a recruit!

Any Time, Anywhere

Firefighters face many dangers, even death, in the course of their work. But let's face it, bad things happen to good people every day in the course of living. Being a firefighter just increases someone's chance of injury or death. It may come at the hands of a drunk driver in an auto accident. We've seen that. It may come as a work-related accident, as pretty much all of us have a side job. It may come from an accident in or around the home.

Several years ago, after I had retired, I was home one afternoon reading in the living room. I live in a neighboring town from where I worked. My wife was outside working on some project, when she opened the door and told me that something was going on at a house close by and down the street. There was a firefighter who owned and lived in that house with his wife, son, and baby daughter. The man was on my fire department and I worked with him often. I got up, went outside, and looked, just in time to watch an engine company pull up in front of the house. The crew got out and ran across the yard to a car parked in the driveway. The police were already there. There was a sense of urgency in their movements: something bad was happening.

I came back inside and made a call to our fire department to tell them to turn up the radio and listen in because something bad was happening at the home of one of our own.

I put on my shoes and walked across the street. When I got there, the ambulance had arrived. They were setting up equipment to raise the car in the driveway. I watched as they raised the car, and sure enough, there was my brother firefighter lying on the ground under the car.

He had been working under the car when it somehow came down from the ramps that held it up. My friend was trapped completely underneath the car. We don't know how long he was under there. Some time later, the mailman came to deliver the mail. He walked across the driveway, put the mail in the box, and returned to his truck. He didn't drive off right away, because something just didn't seem right to him.

He smelled something like blood, he thought. Blood does have a very distinct smell and is remembered by all those who have ever been where large amounts of it have been spilled. The mailman went back and looked under the car. That's when he spotted the man under it. He then made a 911 call.

My friend had been caught in such a way that he couldn't breathe. When he was taken from the scene and placed in the ambulance, I'm told that he had no pulse. The pulse was restored by the ambulance crew, and so he was technically alive when they got him to the hospital. It was determined that too much damage had been done to his brain from lack of oxygen. The decision was made to remove him from life support. He passed away shortly after.

The brotherhood/sisterhood, came alive and did everything they could to help his wife and children. They still stand by in case she needs anything. The firefighter was buried with full departmental honors, with hundreds of firefighters in full dress uniform in attendance, myself among them.

To think that after all this man had seen and done, he met his end at home.

Any time...anywhere.

Finding Your Way

When we train new recruit firefighters how to search, they're taught to make entry and follow and maintain contact with a wall. Left or right makes no difference, but stay on the wall. The wall is a reference point. You count how many doors or windows you've passed, as well as feel, with gloved hands, any other feature of the room within reach of the wall. This can give you an idea of where you are in relation to where you entered. Staying on the wall helps when having to exit, especially if you have to get out in a hurry.

I've often told recruits that we work in the dark. They have to get used to finding their way without their eyesight. Part of their training includes learning to use a thermal imager, which allows some surprisingly good vision in the dark. I'll tell them, "You have to stay on the wall unless you have the imager. Then it's all right to leave the wall. Correct?"

A great many say, "Yes." Some will say, "No," and then I ask why. Some will get it right, but the answer is that the imager is run by a battery. I am a firm believer of Murphy's Law. As soon as you leave the wall, the battery could die or something else could go wrong, leaving you in complete darkness with no reference point with which to find your way.

Recruits are also taught that any time they move through heat or darkness, they must be on all fours, crawling and feeling all around with their hands. The general rule is: If you can't see your feet, you should not be on them. Walking on knees is unacceptable also, as you tend to be unstable, especially in the dark.

They are taught from the beginning that they should always carry a forcible entry tool with them, like an axe or a Halligan. As they are crawling, they should be probing with the tool. I've told them to feel, but not to go around smashing things and pulling things down on top of themselves. One never knows what people have stored in their homes and on their property. Basements, sheds, garages, and pool houses could contain almost anything.

I once went into a home for a medical call. The home was owned by a chemist who lived alone. Except for the kitchen and bathroom, every room in the house had floor-to-ceiling, handmade shelves. They were loaded with books, large and small, and glass containers, some filled with liquids. I didn't know what was in them, and I sure wouldn't want to knock any of these things on top of myself, especially in the dark when I wouldn't see them coming.

If you pull a lot of things down and move things around too much, it can cause problems if you have to get out quickly. When you enter and make your way in, you make a mental map of where things are. It can be confusing if things don't feel the same as how you remembered. That can slow you down.

Many people think they know the basic layout of certain types of houses. That is just fine, until you come upon some change the homeowner made himself, like the chemist with his shelves.

I like to tell the story of an early morning fire years ago in a town near mine. A firefighter was searching in the dark. He was crawling along and feeling his way around. He went to place one of his hands on the floor, but the floor wasn't there. Instead, his hand went down—into the indoor swimming pool! No one even knew it was there. Can you imagine crawling around in a house in the dark, in the wee hours of the morning, and suddenly finding yourself in the water? Things could go bad, very quickly. That firefighter was doing things right, so all he did was feel the water, but he didn't fall in.

Making that mental image of the building you're crawling around in; finding and counting windows and doors; trying to identify what room you are in by the things you find, like furniture, toys, tools, cooking utensils, or a host of other things; makes search a very dangerous thing to do and requires a lot of concentration and training. It requires mental discipline to keep you doing things correctly, as well as discipline in air consumption, to get the most time possible out of an air bottle. Search is used to search, locate, and rescue victims who may be trapped in a fire situation, making it, at once, one of the most dangerous and one of the most important things to learn as we make our way through drill school and the rest of our careers. The learning never stops.

Firsts

Sometime back in the 80s, HIV and AIDS came out of the woodwork to haunt us. I know that there was much talk and studies on it as we watched it become an epidemic. I really don't remember much of that. It seems like it wasn't there one day, and the next day it was. We got some early information about it and got some special suits that we were supposed to wear if we encountered a patient with AIDS. Universal precautions were a new concept then. I remember an officer getting mad and yelling at us when we used latex gloves. "Those things are expensive," he would say. I guess we were supposed to just look at them. As we all know, if you don't use something, it stays new, fresh, and clean forever! We never really worried about hepatitis or any of that other bad stuff you can catch from blood. We were just cautiously anxious about AIDS. I don't really remember any special training to deal with it. But I suppose that with the little anyone knew about it then, what training *could* be put together? No one really knew where it came from, but there was a lot of gay bashing and casting the blame on homosexuals and I seem to remember a particular immigrant group. (It might have been Haitians.)

We coasted along for quite a while, until one night when I was on duty at station 1 with the ambulance. We got a call for an unconscious male. The call was on the south side, so the engine from station 2 was there before us. The engine crew was inside when we pulled up. My partner knew a bit about the patient, having grown up in the same general area. Before I got out of the vehicle, he said to me, "Lew, this guy might be a good candidate for gloves." He meant that I probably should wear them, so I put them on.

We went inside and saw a male patient, apparently unresponsive, and an EMT from the engine crew was trying to clear the patient's airway. He had his fingers in the patient's mouth without any gloves on. The family of the patient was there, but everyone was very tight-lipped about what might be wrong with him. Finally, the captain took the patient's father into the other room to talk. It was here that the father confessed that his son did indeed have AIDS. I guess he was afraid that if we knew that, we would just abandon the patient and leave. I have heard that things like that had happened elsewhere, such was the hysteria over this new disease. Well, we certainly weren't going to just leave. We had a job to do.

In retrospect, it all seems so silly now, but we went out to the ambulance and got our special suits to put on. They were disposable and so the department had them sealed in a package to keep them clean. We never even drilled with this equipment. I looked around for a suit that would fit me, but there wasn't one. I got the next size down, since that had the best chance of being useable. I put it on and zipped it up, but when I moved, the suit tore right up the back from top to bottom. It stayed in place, so I left it on, but I must have looked ridiculous. We had these suits, gloves, and masks on as we moved the patient into the ambulance and transported him to the hospital.

It is there that my memory fades. I don't remember what his problems were or how he made out. But this was such a production, born of fear. I have treated and transported AIDS patients many times since then without all the extra steps. With research came knowledge, and with that, the blind fear gave way to understanding and procedures that make sense.

My luck with "Firsts" didn't end there, either. Back in those early days, I was at an MVA with an unconscious patient. When he regained consciousness, he spit out the blood that had pooled in his mouth and throat that I hadn't had a chance to suction out yet. I got sprayed in the face and eyes with his blood. This was a large, unprotected exposure. So, per protocol, I went with the ambulance to a local hospital to report the exposure and get treatment. Turns out that I was the first one at that hospital ever to come in and report this kind of thing. Lucky Me! The fact is that they didn't know what to do for me. There was no procedure in place then. They took my temperature and my vital signs, which I guess were within an acceptable range. They gave me the name of someone to go and talk to the next day. I really got nothing out of that, either, except that it was set up for me to go back to the hospital every three months for the next year for a blood draw. They tested it and I guess they found nothing wrong.

After a year, I was cleared. What a year it was, too. I had to be careful what I did, and had to take all kinds of precautions, and I chewed my fingernails down to nothing.

There was an unprotected exposure and the hospitals didn't know what to do about it. So you go for tests and have to walk on eggshells for a year to be cleared. That was not good for the nerves.

A Sight to See

Many years ago, when I lived in a different house, I had a long driveway. It was probably four times longer than the one I have now, and I had no snow blower. That was the house I had grown up in, and I had shoveled that driveway every winter all my life. Dad would get home around 5 p.m. and he had better not have any trouble getting in the driveway. As a youngster, I'd get it shoveled and then go out with the shovel over my shoulder and walk the neighborhood offering to do some shoveling for people to make some money.

Later, after I had grown and become a member of the fire department, I bought that house from my father and lived there with my family. I was still a young buck and didn't mind shoveling the snow off the driveway. I was used to it. The kids were too small and the wife didn't shovel, so if it snowed when I was at work, I just had to make the best of it when I got home. If I was off duty, I used to like to go out at night, later in the night. I really enjoyed working in the quiet, with all the new fallen snow. Call me crazy, but I enjoyed that.

One night, after a big snowstorm, I was out doing my thing with the shovel. It had snowed heavily and they were still working to get the streets clean. As I worked, I could hear a siren off in the distance. It was constant, yet far away. I thought it was something happening in a surrounding town, as sound really travels on a night like that. As I continued to work, I noticed that the siren noise was getting closer. I started paying more attention to it as I kept working. Shortly, the siren was very close and I noticed another noise mixed in with it. I really couldn't put it together, until suddenly a snowmobile came roaring out of a side street and onto my street. The snowmobile had no trouble moving very fast on the snow covered streets. When that snowmobile had burst out of that side street, it was closely followed by a police cruiser. The cruiser had no traction at all. It was sliding all over the road as it tried to keep up with the snowmobile, siren blaring.

As the snowmobile passed me, I noticed the driver was laughing as he sped away, up the street and out of my sight. The police, vainly trying to keep up, slid sideways onto my street, straightened out, and kept after the snowmobile. I looked at the cursing face inside the car, and when I saw who it was, I wasn't really surprised. This would be just the man I would have picked to do something so stupid as to drive like that in an attempt to stop a snowmobile on a snow-covered street. The snowmobile was out of sight, but the police officer gunned his cruiser, fishtailed all over the road, and continued his pursuit.

Eventually, even the noise faded away. Even after all these years, that has got to remain the stupidest thing I've ever seen a public safety official do, and I've seen a lot. Oh, and I now have a snow blower and a much shorter driveway. No more shoveling for me.

A True Professional

One of my favorite jobs, while working at the fire academy, was the building and lighting of fires on the burn days when training new recruits. I did that when I worked support services. When I became an instructor, I would lead a crew in to fight the fire, and eventually when I was the incident commander, I was in charge of the training for those burn days. That was all great, but it didn't give me the same thrill as building and lighting. We liked to see how difficult we could make things for the line crews coming in to put the fires out.

Looking at it from another angle, it was also good training for the support staff. We could build fires any way we wanted, and as big as we wanted, and then sit back and watch. We got to study fire behavior, a very important thing to know in this business. We watched as crews entered and went up or down stairs. We watched them move hose. We saw what worked and what didn't, and we listened to the instructors as they spoke to the students. We learned, had fun, and got paid for it, too.

I always liked to work in the basement. Basement fires are very difficult to fight. People keep just about everything you can imagine in their basements. You have to go down through the flames, smoke, and heat that are coming up at you. We tried to make the training fires in the basement as difficult as possible. There was one fire I liked to build in a particular room in the basement. The stairs coming down were enclosed with a door at both ends. That is, it had walls on both sides and a ceiling above. I would build it so I could dump all the smoke and heat right up the stairway. I used to make that stairway a miserable place to be. The attack crew couldn't do anything about it until they got to the bottom, left the stairway, and turned right. Then the fire would be in front of them and they could put it out.

I remember one day, just after a crew had made its way down and put that fire out, the line officer came up to me and said, "That was the stairway from hell. Did you do that?"

I proudly answered, "I did."

This instructor was a man who knew what he was doing and never hesitated to do what needed to be done.

There was another instructor, a younger guy, that worked with us for a while. He was a pretty good guy and fit right in with the instructor staff. He came from a place where they have fires, a lot of fires. He knew his way around a fire ground.

On the fire ground at the academy, the guys were always setting each other up. On a day when I was lighting basement fires, this young instructor was bringing various groups of recruits down to the basement on a line. In between scenarios, another instructor came to me and told me that that young instructor had said that we were lighting "pussy fires." I smiled. The gauntlet had been dropped. I asked them to let me know the next time that man was leading a crew to the basement where I was.

Sure enough, before long I got the word that he was coming down in the next fire. I built a monster of a fire. I extended the fuel for the fire all the way up the staircase. When it came time to light it, I opened the back door to the outside. This would allow the breeze that day to push every ounce of heat up that staircase. It was fine work, if I do say so myself! I lit it right on cue and the fire took off. It did everything I intended for it to do. Everything; flames, smoke, and heat; went right up those stairs in great quantity. That crew fought their way slowly down, made the turn, and put the fire out. They worked hard.

When it was over, I went looking for that instructor. When I found him, he looked tired and beat. He was sweating all over. I think even his eyeballs were sweating. Laughing, I asked him how he liked *that* one.

He answered right away, "pussy fires!"

You might think that his answer popped my bubble, but no. I could see it in his eyes he thought that was a good fire. He'd be damned if he was going to admit that to *me*. He was a true professional.

Parent's Nightmare

It has to be the worst nightmare imaginable to any parent to have something bad happen to their child. Even long after the child has grown up, we still pray to keep them safe. Firefighters, and really *all* emergency services people, are often parents, too. I have to think that the nightmare is made just a little worse when we think that there is a chance that we might just be the ones to respond to a call involving our own child. When our children get old enough to be away from us, with friends and especially driving, we try not to think about it, but it's always with us: the possibility of something happening and things are beyond our control.

Over the years, our fire department tried different ways to keep the stations manned when the ambulance transports a patient. Most often, we called in off-duty firefighters to cover until the ambulance got back. For a time, due to budget cuts, we brought the engine from station 2 across town to cover headquarters and left station 2 unmanned until the ambulance got back to quarters and the engine returned.

It was during this time one night that we got an ambulance call. Engine 2 always responds to all calls, even if it's just for the addition of two more firefighters to help carry a patient. I was not on duty that night, but I was told that the ambulance transported a patient and engine 2 came in to station 1 to cover.

When the ambulance returned, the engine was cleared to return to quarters. They got about half through their three-mile trip back when the dispatcher told them to respond to a reported motor vehicle accident. It wasn't far from where they were at that time, and being already on the road, they arrived at the accident some time before any other help.

I'm told that as they approached, the first thing they saw was a body lying in the road. This person was apparently thrown from the car, which was just up the street a very short distance. I don't remember what that car had hit, but I was told that there was considerable damage.

They parked the engine and the two-man crew got their medical equipment and ran toward the accident, stopping at the body in the street. The EMT on that engine crew started to do a quick exam of that body before checking the second victim, now visible, still in the car. The other firefighter was not an EMT, and in a medical situation, which that was, he would stand back to let the EMT do his job. He would assist, as needed. The EMT found that the first patient was a boy in his late teens with an athletic build, lying unconscious, face down on the pavement. He found that the victim was still alive. He also discovered something else: he *knew* the victim. This boy was the son of that EMT's partner. The EMT did a quick check of the other victim and found him to be dead. He had to tell his partner that the injured boy in the street was his son.

The ambulance arrived and the victim was fully spinally immobilized, placed on oxygen, and transported to the hospital. I'm not sure which hospital they went to, but there is a good chance that due to his severe injuries, they took the victim into Boston to a trauma center. I don't remember if they did.

We respond to too many of these accidents. As I was told the story, aside from the victim being a firefighter's son, there was nothing remarkable that happened. The father of the victim did just what he had to do, just what he would do at *any* accident scene. I'm not sure, after all these years, if the father went with his son with the ambulance. It's highly likely.

The ambulance transported and that engine went back to station 1 to cover. Someone was called in to work the rest of the shift for that father. The boy did recover, though there were permanent reminders of the accident. His speech was slurred and he walked with a very pronounced limp. I guess the main thing though, is that he is alive.

I've been to many accidents, but I just can't imagine the horror of checking a victim and finding that it is one of my children. That has *got* to be our worst nightmare.

That's the Way the Game is Played

As long as I can remember, the job of firefighter has been one that isn't easy to get. With taxes going up and manpower cuts being made in some places, there just aren't that many jobs to be had. There is a lot of competition for the jobs that are available. Many communities take care of filling their own vacancies with their own testing procedures. There is often a written exam, physical fitness testing, interviews, and often an assessment center, where they give you an emergency scenario to see how you might solve it.

The rest come under the state's civil service regulations. They draw their candidates from a list put together after a statewide test given every two years. These days, many entrance exams are general intelligence tests. I guess you can't expect a guy to know too much when he is just trying to get a job. That wasn't always the case though.

Massachusetts civil service used to put out a firefighter manual, <u>The Red Book</u>, and it was available to anyone wanting to study for the fire exam. Unfortunately, back in the early to mid 70s, it was noticed that minority groups were not fairly represented within the ranks of the fire departments. A new plan was developed where <u>The Red Book</u> was abolished and the test was rewritten to be a general intelligence test.

The first time that exam was given, it turned into a fiasco. Minorities were given priority status for hiring. Trouble was, not enough minorities passed the exam with the minimum score of 70%. I don't know the reason. Just maybe not enough of the target group took the test. Well, whatever the reason, they fixed the problem by lowering the minimum passing grade to 35%. With this, they had the numbers that they wanted and the firehouses were quickly filled with undesirables. In this case, they happened to be minorities, but by no means are undesirables limited to minority groups.

That was a generation ago, and those people are all gone, but even back then it created a few problems. I took that test and passed. I never got called. That was the last civil service exam I ever took. I began looking in the non-civil service communities for their tests. I put applications into every fire department in my general area that wasn't civil service.

Finally, there was an opening in one, and I was told that my application was accepted. It turns out that over eighty people applied for that one job. The testing process began with a written exam. Minimum passing score was 70%. That weeded out a good many, and the number was brought lower after the strength and agility test. That part of the exam was tough, but I was young and in good shape and did well. The aim was to reduce the number of candidates to three for oral interviews. I had done well enough, it turned out, to be one of the three finalists. I thought that I had a good chance of getting the job—but it was not to be.

After the interviews, I came in second. I, who had my EMT certification, two years experience as an active call firefighter, and a certificate from attending a cadet basic firefighting course at the state academy, lost the job to a man who had none of that at all. What he did have, though, was a brother on that department. He was from that town and was well known.

I think the whole thing had been a sham to begin with. I was very upset, but if you complain about things too much, you'll get a reputation as a complainer. You'll grow very old before you get a job anywhere. As things turned out, soon after that, there were several openings in another town, the town I had grown up in and where I was also a call firefighter. I got one of those jobs and wound up working my whole career there. I think I was much better off for it.

The whole thing really did stink, but when you've been around for a while, you realize that's the kind of thing that happens. Civil service is not without its problems, either. Some years ago, I knew a man who was up for a job in a civil service town nearby. Turns out that he was going to be passed over in favor of another man, one who didn't score as well on the exam, but had a father who was a fire officer in that town. Once again, it's unfair, but what can you do? You don't want that reputation as a complainer, so you just have to clam up and take it. That is, of course, unless you have friends or the other guy has enemies. Either way, it works.

It seems someone, who remains unknown to this day, made a call to the civil service commission and reported the injustice. It was investigated, and the town was told that they couldn't skip over people to hire their chosen man. They were made to hire the other one. Justice was served. That man got lucky.

Usually things don't turn out that way. Mostly, you just have to be patient, take the exams, and do the best you can until your ship comes in. Love it or hate it, that's the way the game is played.

Reminders

I love to think about fires past, things that happened, and how we used to do things. Many of the tools we used to use have long since gone the way of the buffalo. When I first started on the job, we had an older demand-type of breathing apparatus. The masks had a long hose that you had to connect to a big regulator. They were not constantly pressurized with air, so the wearer had to kind of suck up the air from the tank. As you drew a breath, the sound of the air passing through the regulator made a sound like the hee-haw of a donkey. If, for some reason, there was a problem with the regulator, it could be quite a chore trying to breathe the air from that tank.

I remember one time, back when I was a call firefighter, being called to the station for a house fire. I arrived as they called for another engine and more men. I was on the next engine to arrive, along with four or five other men. The fire had started on the stove in the kitchen and had spread to the cabinets. It wasn't long before it was in the walls and had spread through the house.

We pulled up on our engine and three of us grabbed the SCBA and donned them. There were only three kept on each vehicle back then. Many men worked without them. The other guys went inside, but I was having trouble with my regulator. Finally, I just put the unit on and worked that much harder to breathe. The guys could hear me coming a mile away with that hee-haw. I wasn't getting much air. I got a lot of time out of the tank, but was exhausted from trying to breathe. The guys busted my chops about that for years.

Years later, when I was instructing at the fire academy, I would sometimes work with the students in a training maze. They would have to go inside the maze and find the way out before their air was gone. We used to play a sound effects tape with basic fire ground noises to try to interrupt their thought processes. I would tell the students that if they listened closely to that tape, they would hear what sounded like the hee-haw of a donkey. I explained that this was the sound of an old Scott 2 demand SCBA unit, and that that was what I used when I first started. They would smile, and sometimes laugh.

The memories are fun, but I'm sure glad the SCBA units have come such a long way. They're lighter now. The tanks are smaller and they're easier to put on and take off. Plus, the units are positive pressure. That means that at any given time, the mask is pressurized. You're breathing the air in the mask, not trying to suck it up out of the tank, so it's not so much work to breathe.

One day at headquarters, several years after I had come on the job full time, my partner and I were at the rear of the firehouse when the dispatcher called us to the front desk. This was back in the days when we dispatched our own calls, so the dispatcher was one of our firefighters. We had a rule that said that in the absence of an officer, the dispatcher was in charge. It was his call as to what to send to a call. We came to the front and the dispatcher told us that he was striking a box for a house fire. Since the captain was out on the road, it was up to the dispatcher to decide what to send. The call had come in via telephone. I guess the caller made it sound serious enough so it sounded like we would need more help. My partner and I scrambled to get our gear on and get on the road with our engine. The dispatcher sent the engine from station 2 and notified the captain via radio. Then he set up and struck the box, transmitting it through the alarm system and the radio system.

The fire was on the south side of town. The first due engine would use the water in their tank to start the fire attack. Since we were second due, we would be catching a hydrant so we could provide the first due engine with an unlimited water supply. We got to the area and turned down the dead-end street. The fire was in a house at the end of the street. We had received no call for us to catch a hydrant, and as we approached, we discovered why. Disregarding procedure, instead of beginning the fire attack with tank water, the first engine had laid their own line of hose from the hydrant.

Since they had already connected to the hydrant, we drove right past it and up to the fire. The house was a rather new, split-level, with fire rolling out of the windows from a large room on the right end.

As we got out of our engine, the captain came running out and yelled, *"Who's manning that hydrant?"*

I grabbed a hydrant wrench and started back toward the hydrant. As I ran following the hose, I noticed that the hose was flat, meaning there was no water flowing. I thought they had neglected to open the hydrant. When I got there, I put the wrench on the nut on top of the hydrant and pulled, trying to pull to open it. It turned out that the hydrant was indeed open. I took a better look and found that there was a small amount of water flowing, but nowhere near enough to even think about fighting a fire.

I didn't realize it then, but this was my first experience with what is called a "dead-end" hydrant. The simple explanation is this. The water flows through a continuous pipe, the water main, under the streets. The hydrants are connected to it and have access to all the water in the main. Sometimes, when building a dead-end street or those cul-de-sacs that we're all familiar with, a main is run down and just ends at the end of the street. Water flows in from the larger main. At the end where it stops, there is usually little pressure or volume. A hydrant placed on a main like this isn't much use until the local water utility turns on their pumps and gives us more water at the end of the main.

I ran back and reported what I had found to the captain. He got on the radio and had the water department contacted. They turned on the pumps and soon we had enough water to fight the fire.

I did some research after that fire, and found out that this whole area was full of those dead-end hydrants. This area was developed in the 50s, and for some reason the dead-end hydrants were acceptable. I guess nobody really gave it much thought. Delays in getting water can get costly, not to even mention that at this fire there was a man inside the burning house with a hose, using only tank water. When that runs out, and it will, unless they have tapped into a hydrant, he will have to get out, *if he can*. I don't know how common these hydrants are, but I wouldn't care if I never saw another one.

There is an interesting side note to this, too. We found out later that this fire started in a malfunctioning television set. That was a first for me, too!

Old vs. New

With working at the fire academy, listening to recruit instructors, and finally being one myself, I have lived in the world of modern firefighting a very long time. By modern firefighting, I mean people who understand the science behind their job, including hydraulics and fire behavior; wear the most up-to-date protective clothing, including two-piece turnout gear, hoods, and firefighting gloves; and use modern SCBA. These people are well trained and love to do the job.

I had to think really hard to remember what it was like before this era of modern firefighting. I know that I was with the fire department then. Then I remembered a particular fire in a neighboring town. I had been on the job less than a year when, being off duty, I had taken my wife to lunch from her work in the town next door. When I dropped her off again, I parked along the main street. All of a sudden, the ladder truck from my fire department sped by me. It had a full crew, plus extra men. I looked back to see where they were going, and saw nothing but thick, black smoke up the hill behind me. Well, I knew that our department was at this fire. I should have gone back into my town to report to the firehouse, but I was excited and wanted to be part of what was going on. I had no gear, but walked up the street anyway.

When I got there, I saw the first line engine from station 2 down in the driveway. The house was a big, old, three-story house, and there was smoke pouring out of everywhere. I really don't remember where the ladder truck was, but I'm sure that the stick was not up. I walked up to the engine and saw the deputy chief. I told him that I didn't have any turnout gear, but asked if I could help. He told me to watch the pump. I noticed that there was no apparatus or firefighters from the town that the fire was in. I was told that there was a huge lumberyard fire on the other end of the town and all of their equipment was busy there. I saw an engine company from yet another town arriving at the house fire. They just dropped us some supply hose from a hydrant then sped off to the lumberyard. It seemed that we were on our own.

All the time I was there, I was watching the engine crew working. There were two of them and they were both older men who had been around longer than the SCBA that they never wore anyway. This was the age of three-quarter boots and rubber gloves. There were no hoods to protect your head, and no bunker pants designed to make entry not only easier, but possible. These two men didn't even have their coats completely buttoned up. They were having a terrible time. They got inside the first floor door, turned a corner, and tried to make it up the stairs. Time after time they tried, but with no luck. It was just too hot and the smoke was too thick for them to make it further than the bottom of the staircase. This went on and on, with no real progress.

The fire drew a large crowd of onlookers, as fires often do. In that crowd was a young guy that I knew. He offered to go to the firehouse and get my gear for me. This he did, and with my gear, I was able to do more, but I was still limited. I had a coat, three quarter boots, and some leather gloves. Still I had no hood or firefighting gloves. They did not exist at this time. The gear was substandard by today's standards.

Some two or three hours into the fire, an engine company from the host town arrived. They must have made some significant progress at the lumberyard fire to cut an engine company loose. Up until this time, the crews that had come from my town were fighting the fire alone. That host engine company was able, at some point, to get into the house and up the stairs. The third floor walls were so badly burned that they were teetering and swaying in the breeze. The firefighters got up there and literally pushed them down. They would have fallen anyway. The house was a total loss. It was demolished and another built on the site.

Thinking back on that fire and watching how those two guys tried, without success, to make entry, makes me think how far we've come. We have lighter, modern SCBA, and two-piece bunker gear, made to modern specifications to better protect our people. There are gloves specifically designed for firefighting, and hoods to protect our heads, necks, and ears. We have lighter hose and attack lines that give us more water, yet can be handled by the same number of men as before. Our gear totally encapsulates the firefighter to form a system to protect the whole body.

I'm not saying that the two men I watched at that fire were old-fashioned, heroic smoke-eaters. They came from an era when the fire department was a place to go for a steady job and a paycheck. That check wasn't too big, but it was steady. On-the-job training was the norm, and if the guy who trained you didn't know anything, then neither would you.

Now there have been scientific studies of fire, and its behavior and what it takes to put it out. Fire prevention is stressed. Last, but by no means least, a different kind of person is coming on the job now to wear all that new gear and use those new tools. No longer does the fire department take men off the street and offer them a steady job. The jobs are highly competitive. The men and women—yes, there are women, too—are highly motivated. They compete fiercely for these jobs and are proud of what they do. They are trained *before* they are sent to the line. They are taught how to use the tools and how to wear their gear. They have the courage that comes from a desire to do the job, and the pride in what they do.

I was a part of the tail end of that era. I was a young guy who came on the job just as the old standards were leaving, and I did many of the foolish things that were done then. I'm proud to say that I was a part of the fire service in that era. But I'm prouder when I think of what the fire service has become in the years since then. We've come a very long way since yesteryear.

Reputation

I often told my children, as they were growing up, about how important it is to have a good reputation, and how it takes a lifetime to build one and only a second to ruin it. I have also told this to my students, as well as how that extends to the department they work on. You represent your department every time you go to work. The public often will judge your brothers and sisters by the way they see you act. I have had my ups and downs through the years, but I've always tried to maintain a good reputation, both personally and professionally.

There was one time when my personal reputation bailed me out of a real mess (that was not of my making). As a side job, I worked in the private ambulance service for many years, most of it with the same company. I did my job and got along well with the patients, coworkers, and management. When I first started there, I worked for the owner of the company. His name was on the truck, so he cared about how people viewed his company. He had a son who was in high school. He was a big, sloppy-looking high school kid who worked delivering oxygen on weekends for his father's company.

Some years went by and eventually that sloppy high school kid put on an expensive suit and became president of the company when his dad retired. Around this time, one of the many quality control measures the company took to keep up the good reputation was to create a position of a kind of a regional supervisor. They had a name for them that I can't recall. We called them the "Gestapo." They rode in cars and spied on the help. They went into the medical facilities that we serviced to ask what kind of job we were doing, and they handled any complaints from our customers. They didn't bother me too much. I did my job well and kept quiet.

One day, my partner was another off-duty firefighter. He was an old time EMT who knew his job and did it well. I worked with him often. We were doing a return of a patient to a nursing home. As we moved the patient from our stretcher to her bed, I kept a friendly conversation with her, as I did with most patients. In the middle of moving the patient, a woman came into the room and asked if there was a problem. She wasn't a nurse. She was wearing office-type clothes. We found out later that she was from the corporate office of the company that owned the nursing home. I answered that there was no problem and explained what we were doing in the friendliest way I could. She left the room and we were finished with our patient so we left the nursing home.

Shortly after leaving, we received a radio call to meet up with our regional Gestapo agent at a given location. We met up with him and were asked if we remembered being in the nursing home that we had just left.

I said, "Yes."

He asked if anything unusual happened. I related how that woman had come into the room and questioned us. He said there was a problem and he sent us back to our home station of the company and said he would meet us there. Back at the home station, the field supervisor told us that there had been a complaint from the lady that had come into the room and asked us if there were any problems. She told a tale that had us being loud and profane. She reported that I yelled at and threatened the patient, and when this lady came in to intervene, I supposedly gave her back talk and swore at her, too. I offered to go back with the supervisor to confront the accuser, but he said, "No." He said that they were going to look into things.

Meantime we, my partner and I, were being suspended with back pay promised, if we were found not guilty. I had the distinct feeling that Mr. Gestapo was enjoying all this. This was a chance for him to make us squirm. He came across as a bully who condescended to speak to us, the lower classes, when he had to, or when he could get us into trouble. I never liked people like that, or people like that lady who told lies to get innocent people into trouble.

I was a bit vocal about this suspension and how I didn't seem to have the chance to clear myself. So the field supervisor arranged a meeting with him, myself, and the president of the company in the president's office for the following morning. We went home and I fumed all night.

I am someone who is always early for everything, and this meeting was no exception. I showed up about 20 minutes early. The time went by and soon it was obvious that our Gestapo man was going to be fashionably late to make me sweat a bit.

So right on time, I got up and knocked on the president's door. He told me to come in, and when he saw it was me, he greeted me warmly. The president of the company was the owner's son. I had known him for years. Turns out that he didn't know what the meeting was supposed to be about, so I told him the whole story.

He sat back, looked at me, and said, "You didn't do that. I know you didn't. It's not in your makeup. All day long, I sit here listening to people say they didn't do it, when I *know* they did. But I know you didn't do any of that." He told me not to worry about it.

About that time, there was a knock on the door and the field supervisor came in, slowly, with a "Holy shit! What's he doing in here?" look on his face. The company president told him about our conversation and said that he knew that accusation was false. The super kind of stuttered a bit looking at me sitting there at the president's desk. He said that the lady that had made the accusation had not followed through with a phone call that morning, so as far as he was concerned, there was no problem. I was vindicated.

There was no doubt in my mind that the supervisor didn't realize that I was well known to both the owner and the president of the company. Both knew that this accusation was false. I would never engage in this kind of behavior.

I believe that I was being set up to be fired, to make the company look good by getting rid of substandard employees. The Gestapo agent sure didn't know *me* very well. My own good reputation and work ethic paid off. The president was fair and took care of his valuable people. However, I also had a Plan B. If I had gotten fired, I was going to walk about 200 yards to the law office down the street and file a huge "defamation and wrongful termination" suit. Glad I didn't have to do that.

Nursing Home Troubles

Have you ever wondered what they do in a nursing home if they have a severe problem or major emergency and have to evacuate the building? Neither did I, but I found out. There are many private ambulance companies serving medical facilities. A lot of what they do is transporting people who need to travel by ambulance, usually not for emergencies, but rather for medical reasons. We come and go from nursing homes and never really think about what is in there: invalids, slow-moving elderly, residents confined to their beds, residents with dementia or slow thought processes, and minimal staff.

One day, when working for one of these ambulance companies, we got word of a fire in a large nursing home in the city. It was a place that we went often. The fire was in that part of the building that provided the heat and electricity for the facility. It was not near the patient areas, so there was no immediate threat, but being midwinter in an area that gets frigid temperatures, patients would have to go elsewhere until repairs could be made. They put their evacuation plan into action.

All through the afternoon, our company sent ambulances to assist. They sent my ambulance there, too. My partner and I went in and joined a very long line of ambulances moving slowly up the drive to the facility. There, they would get a patient, do the transport, then return in case they were needed again. There were ambulances from every company that I could think of in the area. The various companies had as many crews and vehicles there as they could send.

I wondered why the line was moving so slowly, and soon I found out. This facility housed residents with various levels of dementia, physical disabilities, and medical problems. Each resident had to have their records pulled and sent with them. An appropriate facility had to be found for each patient, based on their particular needs. Records had to be kept as to where each patient was taken and by who.

We took patients all over the city that night. My ambulance made two trips, taking patients to two different hospitals in different parts of the city. The last patient left by ambulance in the wee hours of the morning.

What an operation! I never gave it much thought up until then, but everything seemed to go smooth. Someone must have put in some serious time in devising the plan. It may be "just a nursing home," but there was nothing simple about evacuating it.

Out of His Way

On any fire department, we have our duty assignment. In a larger place, you'd be assigned to a particular company. For instance, you might be assigned to "ladder 15," "engine 33," "squad 18," or a rescue company. You would go to work wherever that vehicle was quartered. In a smaller department like ours, you are assigned to a shift and a duty station, such as C group at station 1. These might be our assignments, but they are by no means our assignment 100% of the time. Due to sick leave or vacations etc., it sometimes is necessary to shift manpower around to other companies or groups. The firefighters on our department usually will take turns being "detailed out," that is, having a change in assignment for that shift. Often, when someone knows it will be their turn next to be detailed out, they will carry their bunker gear with them in their vehicle, instead of keeping it at their assigned station. That will save time in the morning if they get the call to report to another station.

This personal protective equipment is just as important as any hose, axe, or fire engine. If you have your bunker gear in your vehicle, you have to make sure it's secured: you can't do your job without it. We had one firefighter who had the whole set of bunkers stolen out of an unlocked pickup truck. They could have been held financially responsible for it, but the department chocked it up to bad luck and bought them new gear. You would think the lesson was learned, but not quite.

Some years went by and this same firefighter started spending a lot of time out of state. He almost always carried the gear with him. One day, he discovered the gear missing, once again from an unlocked pickup truck. It was reported to the chief of department.

This was the second complete set stolen. It was much newer than the first set, and so was better and more expensive. They were going to have to order another set and wait for it to come in. The firefighter was going to be held financially responsible for this set. I don't remember if the gear had been ordered or what this person was wearing in the interim: probably loaned gear from someplace.

One day some weeks later, I was on duty at station 2. I was talking to the captain outside. It was summer, the weather was beautiful, and we looked around at life going by. A pickup truck with out-of-state plates pulled in and right up to where we were standing. The driver, an older man, leaned out his window to talk to us. He said that he thought he had something that belonged to us. In the back of his truck were two red gear bags. I opened one and found the coat with the name of our firefighter on the back. I opened the other and found that both bags contained this person's gear. The entire set was there.

The man explained that he was a volunteer firefighter in another state. He had been driving down the highway when he saw the two bags on the side of the road. He knew exactly what they were: fire gear bags. He pulled over and went to get them. When he opened them, he found the firefighter's name and the town name on the coat. He took a chance that it belonged to someone from our department, so he decided to drive the hour or so to our town to hand deliver the gear right to us. Needless to say, we were very happy to see the gear back, none happier than the one it belonged to. He was speechless when he received the call telling him that the gear had been found.

That man, being a volunteer firefighter, knew what he was looking at when he saw the bags. Any firefighter; call, volunteer, or full time; would have known. He didn't have to stop and pick them up. He could have phoned to have us send someone down there to get them. He sure as hell didn't have to go out of his way to drive it up here himself. We thanked him profusely and he went on his way.

Our firefighter got his gear back and didn't have to pay for another set. We never found out what happened to the first set. Hopefully, the lesson was learned *this* time.

Steam Cleaned

The Massachusetts Firefighting Academy provides many different kinds of training and makes it available in different places. Many of these programs involve live fire. Some involve search and rescue. All are very good. For some of the programs, an instructor is sent to your firehouse for a two-hour or three-hour lecture on a given topic. They also have field programs where they will send an entire course, complete with props, to a particular town for practical training. Fire departments from other nearby towns can train together with the host town. By far, my favorite training was the live burns that we did for fire recruits. There was also training for firefighters already working on the job, just to keep skills sharp.

We used to also provide shipboard firefighting training for midshipmen at a local maritime training school. We used a burn facility about two hours away from where I live, but very close to their school. The burn tower was three stories high, and they would set it up like a ship. There were prop hatchway doors, like on board a ship, fastened in place. They would always send the fire teams down from the roof. The aim was to simulate going down below decks to fight a fire on a ship. Because there are no openings in the side of a ship, there were no windows allowed to be opened on the way down. It got pretty hot. Way back, years ago, the poor midshipmen didn't have any firefighting turnout gear to shield them from the intense heat. They would go and fight their training fires with SCBA and rain gear. I used to light those fires so I know how hot it got. I never envied those guys! Things are better today. Now they have gear to protect them from the heat and flames.

The first time I worked with those guys was back in the era of rain gear. I was down on the first floor with another guy who had worked this program many times. The fire team started down from the roof. We could hear them coming and we had something waiting for them. We had one hell of a fire going in the stairway. We were stoking it and feeding more fuel, to keep it going and keep it hot.

The fire team was coming slowly. They made it down through the second floor and turned the corner onto the stairs that we had burning. As they entered the stairway, one of the fire team, the nozzle man, panicked. He opened his nozzle to a full fog pattern, breaking his water stream into fine droplets of water. Yes, there was still a lot of water flowing, but when you break up the stream like that, the water absorbs heat and turns to steam much faster. It this case, it was almost instantaneous. The nozzle opened and the water hit the ceiling. It then turned to steam and rode the hot air back up into the faces of the crew coming down the stairs.

There was a crew of five, plus an instructor, in that stairway. The heat hit them and they all got steamed. They had to withdraw back up the stairs. They regrouped and came down again. By this time, my partner and I had left the building, so things had started to cool off. They managed to put the fire out the second time.

After everyone had withdrawn from the building, the instructor of that crew came up to us and asked who the asshole was that was tending that fire. We looked at him, and saw that he was all red, with splotches of redder red from steam. His crew didn't look much better. He looked a bit angry. The fact was that we had only done our job and given him the fire we were supposed to. It was a loose cannon on his crew who had done things on his own that caused the problem. The instructor was responsible for that. However, judging from the look on his face, we didn't think it was the right time to bring this up. We told him we didn't know who was in that stairway: we had been someplace else. Well, he bought it, and we got away from him fast. No one got hurt, but the instructor's ego and pride was bruised a little. Happens to the best of us!

Why?

This story is a tragedy. Things happened that shouldn't have, and the ghosts it dug up from the past affected many. No matter which side you favor, or even if you try to straddle the fence, you must admit that there is blame, and not for just one, but for all involved in the eventual outcome.

When I was going to school, there was no public kindergarten. There were four elementary schools scattered around town, from grade one through grade six. There was only one junior high school, so all the seventh and eighth graders from all parts of town were put together. Most of the kids you were growing up with you never met until you hit seventh grade.

I remember one kid. He was in the same year as me, but went to a different elementary school. I remember seeing him in school walking through the halls, but I never got to know him. I knew his name somehow, but for no particular reason. I think I had just heard other people use it in conversation. Today, in talking with some of those others who were kids with us, I learned that he was not a very popular kid. He was thought of as kind of strange. I never got to know that about him.

One Monday morning in seventh grade, not too far into the school year, as I recall, word went around the school like wildfire that this boy had been arrested. They said that he had killed someone over the weekend. He was gone and we never saw him at school again.

The years went by, and this boy and his deeds just faded into the past. I never thought much about it, until the mid 80s. I was working with the fire department. I had about ten years on the job then. There were many town employees, and there always seemed to be job openings. I never paid too much attention to town politics. The town was looking to hire a new executive director for the Housing Authority. I guess they did some interviews, decided on a candidate, and hired him. I didn't pay much attention and didn't care. The guy started work. I'm told he was working out well.

Then the talk started, and my vague memories of that kid came back. People were talking and there were articles in the local papers. The story came out that when he was twelve years old, that kid in my memory *did* kill someone. It was reported that the kid I remembered came from a home with an abusive stepfather who drank heavily. He used to beat the boy with little provocation. The reports told how this kid used to think about killing his stepfather, and then thought about killing himself instead. It seems that he did indeed make a suicide attempt, and failed.

After school one day, the boy wound up in the woods with a six-year-old boy, his neighbor. He was doing tricks with a scout knife, making it stick in the ground. One trick went awry and the knife hit the little boy in the chest and stuck there for a second or two. It fell out, but the six-year-old was terrified and started to scream. The older boy couldn't quiet the youngster down and was afraid of being caught and beaten. He panicked. He picked up the knife and stabbed the younger boy twenty-six times in the head and chest, killing him. He left the body there and went home. Later, there was a search conducted and the little boy's body was found. It didn't take too long for them to pick up that older boy for questioning. Soon, it was determined that he was guilty and he went away. So the story went. The stories told of a reform school and a bit of his life after he was released at age seventeen.

At some point, the boy, now a man in his thirties, saw the ad for the Housing Authority director job and applied. Even though his past was known to the hiring authorities, someone decided to hire him for the job. He had come home and lived with his mother in the same house where he had grown up. When the talk and questions started, he at first denied knowing anything about it. Then the papers printed the story, and he consented to an interview with a reporter from a magazine.

The whole story came out. He got hate mail and phone calls. People hounded his every step. He tried hard to keep his job, but when his contract was up for renewal, the town decided not to keep him. He left and secured a job elsewhere, but the ghosts from the past followed him. One day, he hanged himself with an electrical cord at his home. That is the end of the story.

I used to see him in his job as director. I often thought that I might go and introduce myself to him, but I never did. I don't know how I feel about this. How much of the old story about what happened is accurate? Is someone ever really rehabilitated? Should he have come back? I think the answer to the last question is, "No." I think he had some dreams of being forgiven, but there were too many people still around who remembered the incident, like those who took part in the search and found the boy's body. People don't forget.

I think the people who hired him were guilty of acting irresponsibly to the town and to this man by giving him this job. They didn't think about what they were doing. It was inevitable that the past was going to catch up with him and that people would hound him. Did he deserve what the media attention did to him? Whether he deserved it or not, what would any thinking person expect once the media got ahold of the story?

Lastly, did he deserve to die (regardless of whether it was at his own hand or someone else's)? I don't know how I really feel about that, either. I guess he just couldn't live with the past coming back. People, being what they are, are often slow to forgive, and they never forget. I think those that hired him were a lot of well-meaning people who are guilty of letting something happen that should never have been allowed to happen. I can't imagine why anyone would think it would all just go away. He should never have come home.

A Generation of Weenies

Each year, as in many communities, there is a Memorial Day parade in our town to honor those who have made the ultimate sacrifice in the service of our country. Represented in our parade are the police and fire departments, boy and girl scouts, elected town officials, as well as people representing veteran's organizations. There are also a number of bands, including some from the town schools. The parade starts at a school parking lot, marches through a section of the south end of town, and goes into a large cemetery where a service is held. There are usually a number of speakers. When the weather is bad, the speakers never seem to stop talking. It often rains on Memorial Day. I have often thought that the Spirits were against us on that day. Sometimes it's nice, but not often.

One particular year, I remember it was very hot. We marched in our dress uniforms. We just knew that the cemetery service was going to seem long. On top of everything else, our chief of department had us positioned in the cemetery on a road without any shade trees. We stood at attention with the hot sun beating down on us.

All of a sudden, one of our men, a captain, broke ranks and moved quickly to where the high school marching band was positioned. One of the band members had just fainted in the heat. The boy was checked out and the ambulance called. Before we knew it, another one of the high school band members fell down in the heat. And then another. Soon there were several band members sitting down, overcome by the heat.

We, the firefighters, still stood in formation out in the open. The high school band had been positioned in one of the shadiest spots in the whole cemetery. Ironic, we thought, that we walked the same distance as them, and we were dressed in heavy uniforms. We, the old guys, were positioned in the blazing sun and them in the cool shade, yet it was the youngsters who couldn't take the heat and *we* took care of *them*. The only explanation I can give is that we must be raising a generation of weenies.

Lemon House

Years back, a contractor cut in a road off a relatively busy street on the south end of town. The new street ended in a cul-de-sac, as so many others do. On that new road, they build eight or so houses. Before too long, all of these houses were sold and were being lived in. In one of the homes lived a lady and her kids. She might have been in her early thirties and the kids were young, but grammar school age. The woman found a number of things wrong with the house and was always hounding the builder with complaints. I don't know if he ever came and fixed anything. I don't even know if there was anything really wrong with the place. The lady thought there was, and so she decided she was not going to take care of the house or property. She never cut the lawn or trimmed a bush. She had a sign on the house telling people, in large letters that that was a "lemon house," and the builder wouldn't fix it. Needless to say, there was never any doubt about which house was hers.

It wasn't too long before we, at the fire department, became familiar with this woman. I remember the first time I met her. She had called requesting an ambulance, and I don't believe she told the dispatcher what the problem was.

I arrived with the ambulance. This lady, my patient, was outside the house and I went over to talk to her. She told me that she was a nurse and she had been horseback riding that day and had somehow hurt herself. She said that she knew exactly what was wrong. She also said that she had to get to a certain Boston hospital right away for surgery, or else she would be paralyzed, or something to that effect. We didn't know this woman, but she sounded like she knew what she was talking about.

The captain gave the OK for a trip into that Boston hospital, not one that we usually go to. We got to that hospital, and gave our report. Then we returned to quarters, and that was that. The hospital did not have an Emergency Room and was not expecting this patient. The staff seemed confused by why we had brought her there.

That was the first experience I had with her. This kind of thing soon became a pattern. She would call with some injury or illness and we would come. Sometimes we would find her in the house, sometimes upstairs. She didn't take any better care of the inside of the house than she did the outside. There was clutter all over. It was very difficult to walk, let alone maneuver a stretcher in there. She would have herself all self-diagnosed by the time we got there, and would tell us exactly what was wrong, what needed to be done, and where. She picked different hospitals each time.

After a while, the things she said started to not make too much sense. She would talk about ailments we had never heard of. She always said that she was a nurse and knew what had to be done. It didn't take too long before we knew we were dealing with a person with something wrong in the old attic.

This went on for a couple of years, as the grass grew higher in the yard and the neighbors began to complain. I was not working, but I was told that one summer evening, her children went outside to play and she locked the door after them. She filled the bathtub with water, lit some candles in the bathroom, had a glass of wine, and slit both of her wrists.

The children knew something was wrong when they tried to get back into the house and found the door locked. They were yelling to their mother to let them in. Someone called the police. It was apparent that something was wrong when she didn't respond to the screams of her own children to open the door, or the police who yelled for her to open up. Finally, they broke into the house. They found her in the bathtub. She had bled to death.

That is the end of the story of the lemon house. I don't know what happened to the kids: probably went with a relative. Eventually, the place was cleaned up and resold. The new owners didn't have any problems with the house that I'm aware of. I just wonder what was wrong with this lady and why nothing was done to help her.

We in the fire department deal with strange and different people all the time. Some have problems and are in need of professional help. Some get it, others don't. For this lady to do what she did, she must have been deeply in need of help that just never came.

Not one of us, the people who responded to her home so many times, could have foreseen this kind of an ending. It was just a sad situation that ended badly.

More Inhumanity

I've said that the firehouse can be a brutal place to be. We spend a lot of time feeding on each other. You just have to learn to play the game to be a real member of the team. One day after lunch, the captain was in the bathroom. I guess he decided to brush his teeth. He managed to have his toothbrush with him, but he had no toothpaste. He opened the door and yelled over to us in the day room. He asked if anyone had any toothpaste. One guy said he did and told him to wait a minute while he went to his locker. He came back and threw the captain a tube. The captain caught it and closed the bathroom door.

About a minute later, the bathroom door flew open again. The captain was standing in the doorway, holding the door open. He had the toothbrush in his hand and both the brush and all around his mouth were covered with pasty foam. He opened his mouth wide as he yelled, "*It's shaving cream!*"

The room erupted with hysterical laughter. He showed us the tube. It was indeed, shaving cream. He went back inside, cleaned out his mouth, then went into his office.

I don't know if he was given the shaving cream by accident or on purpose, either one is possible. If it were me, I think I would have looked at the tube before I used any of what was inside. Anyway, we all got a good laugh. That is, everyone except the captain.

This same captain, one day, made the huge mistake of letting someone know that something bothered him. In the fire department, only a fool does that. We were eating lunch and the conversation turned to something that we thought was funny, but the captain thought it was a bit unappetizing, and he said so. Naturally, the guys curbed the conversation, right? Not on your life! The captain begged for the talk to be changed, but to no avail. Finally, he picked up his lunch and took it into his office. He had begun to eat again, when the door opened and in came the guys and their conversation. He begged again. Finally, he had to order the guys out of his office. Being ordered, they had to leave, of course, but we all got another good laugh at the captain's expense. If he had only just chuckled or ignored it, the conversation would have changed, and he could have enjoyed his lunch in the comfort of the day room.

There was a situation involving me that I think I handled very well, if I do say so myself. When my son was little, he was a bit different. He liked what he liked and that's all. Once, when he was misbehaving in the supermarket, his mother told him that little boys who don't behave don't deserve broccoli. Then she put the fresh broccoli back on the shelf and he burst into tears. He loved the stuff. Strange.

One day, I took my son to the fire academy to see the fire engines and show him what his Dad did at work. We decided to eat an early lunch to avoid the rush. I got a burger and fries. My son wanted a salad, without any dressing. That was kind of different, but that's what he wanted so that's what he got. I wasn't really thinking about it, when in walked several of my fellow instructors. They came over to say, "Hello" to me and my son. They saw what we were eating and they started on me. The called me a "cheap bastard" for making my son eat salad when I had a burger. They said that if I was going to be cheap, I could have at least gotten him some dressing.

Well, that's how things went for a while as more of my fellow instructors entered. Word spread around about what a terrible father I was, making my son eat a plain salad when I was eating a burger and fries. As soon as I saw those other instructors come over, I knew it was bad timing to be there. They were unmerciful to me, and my son was laughing. I just laughed it off, too. I didn't even offer an explanation. It would have been no use, and would have added fuel to the fire. My son made out well, though. One of the guys bought him a piece of cake. He brought it over, gave it to my son, and said, "There, that's for you. Don't give any to your father." He didn't, either!

Adapt and Overcome

In every group, there are good, bad, and some that are just interesting. At the fire academy, we would get a new class of seventy-two students every twelve weeks. That's a lot of recruits. Most were average, meaning pretty good. Some were exceptional. Some were bad. Then, from time to time, we'd get one that was interesting, on top of being bad or good.

We had one recruit that went around telling anyone that would listen that he had been in the Marine Corps. He was bragging to one instructor about his time in the Corps. He made a statement to the effect that he didn't expect the instructor to know anything about the Marines. A little later, that instructor took the student aside and told him that he, the instructor, had indeed, been in the Corps. He proceeded to tell the recruit what unit he had been with, right up to the divisional level.

Think that straightened that student out? Not on your life! He continued on, not making any friends, with his bragging and mouthing off. I have my doubts as to whether he had actually been in the Marine Corps. He didn't fit the mold. There was too much mouth, too much bragging, and little to show in his performance. The recruit wasn't doing too well in the class, just squeaking by.

When it came time for the live burns to start, we didn't expect too much. I was soon to find that I had judged him correctly. On the first day of burns, we only give the recruits small fires, but still he managed to foul up in a major way. This day is really about learning hose movement. We have five attack lines moving into the burn building, each going to a fire in a different location. We put each fire in a place where the crews have to work hard to get their nozzle into position to put it out. We rotate the crews from line to line to give them a feel for moving line into different places, including upstairs.

I was the incident commander this day. Part way through the day, our hero, the recruit in question, was assigned to a line that was to go into the first floor, turn left, and move down the hall to their fire room. The whole crew knew the assignment, as did the instructor leading the crew in. Near the end of the evolution, the first floor line reported the fire knocked down. A second later, the first floor instructor reported that one of his crew was missing. They tried and couldn't locate him.

I radioed the interior safety men, those responsible for making sure everything goes as planned, to advise them that we had a missing man. As the incident commander, I don't normally go in the building, and so I had no breathing apparatus on. However, having worked in this building for so many years, I was familiar with the layout and went inside. I quickly walked the entire first floor, checking all the rooms as I went, but found nothing. I had just put the radio up to my mouth, getting ready to order an evacuation of the building and a company roll call, when a safety man reported that he had found the missing man on the second floor.

The man was escorted outside and stood there, while I questioned him about why he was on the second floor when he knew his crew was on the first. He said he had lost his crew, and when he found the stairs, he went up. That's all the explanation we got. He stood there while he was yelled at by the incident commander, me, as well as the interior safety instructor and the instructor assigned to his hose line.

In the real world, if a firefighter is missing, we send RIT (Rapid Intervention Teams) in to try to locate him. We would have sent the RIT in to the first floor, where this man's company was operating. We had no reason to believe that he would have been on the second floor. I guess we forgot to factor in stupidity. So we would have risked the lives of an entire crew to search for him, because he took it upon himself to decide where he wanted to work. He got a well-earned, long, subjective report for that performance. More antics were yet to come.

Later, during one of the bigger burns, he was working with a ladder company at the rear of the building. At this point in his training, he should have been well acquainted with the tools, where they are located, and how to use them. They were setting up ground ladders to various floors. His commander sent him to the front of the building to get a 24-foot ladder. Now, a 24-foot ladder is commonly raised by two people, but is light enough to be raised by one person, if the need arises.

The man was gone for a considerable length of time. He came back with a 28-foot ladder, which is always carried and raised by two people. It is the job of the company officer to decide what ladder to use.

When the company commander asked why he had brought a 28-foot ladder, the recruit answered that he couldn't find a 24-footer, so he "adapted and overcame" and brought back a 28. He should have tried a little thought while "adapting" and "overcoming." There were two engines parked out front, as well as the ladder truck. If there wasn't a 24-foot ladder on the ladder truck, he could have gotten one off of an engine, as there is one carried by every engine everywhere. Guess he must have forgotten that, huh? Forgivable, you say? No, it is not. The recruit program is very intense. We try to teach discipline along with everything else: do what you're told. This incident happened well into the program. It was not forgivable at this point. He received another subjective report.

As he went on, he continued to amaze everyone, his fellow students and staff alike, with his antics. He was doing badly enough so his deputy chief had to come in for a conference with the coordinator of the program and the student. It seems that at this conference the recruit went off on a tirade and stormed out of the room. So much for his job. He must have made quite an impression, as the coordinator called the fire marshall's office in the next building requesting two state troopers to escort the man off the property.

One would think that the story ends here. Ahh, it doesn't! I was told by several people who worked on his department that several weeks later, the fire department had not heard from this individual, so they sent someone over to his house to collect department property, still in his possession. When the ex-recruit was asked for his gear, his reply was an astonishing, "I just quit the academy. I didn't quit the fire department." Maybe he should sit down and "adapt and overcome" some more, while he ponders his next move.

Lucky Man

Here is yet another story of people and how they injure themselves with tools. I was working on the ambulance crew when we were called to a residence for a person who had been cut. It seems this elderly man was using a small electric chainsaw in his wooded backyard. It was clear that he wasn't too steady on his feet, and clear that he didn't get around very well. It was also clear that he didn't know how to cut down a tree with a chainsaw. He was cutting down some small trees, four to six inches in diameter. He had already cut several. (I have no idea how he managed to do that.) He was cutting a straight, horizontal cut through each tree.

The last tree he cut was about six inches in diameter. As he cut through the trunk, the weight of the tree pinched the horizontal cut closed, trapping the saw's cutting bar. The saw, being caught and bound in the tree, stopped cutting. The man tried to remove the saw. He reached around the tree, grabbed the cutting bar for support, and put his shoulder into the tree. He pushed up on the upper part of the trunk to release some of the pressure on the bar. As soon as the bar wasn't pinched anymore, the chain started to spin again. Unfortunately for him, the hand that was not on the cutting bar was still holding the saw, with his finger still on the trigger. As the saw started back up, it cut up his hand.

I don't remember who made the call for help, but we arrived to find the man in the backyard with a towel on his hand. The saw was on the ground and the tree he was cutting still hadn't fallen. While we looked at his hand, he told us what happened. Things didn't look too bad, certainly not as bad as they could have been. After all, his fingers were still attached. We bandaged him and took him to the hospital for treatment.

It will never cease to amaze me the foolish, dangerous things people do without thinking, especially when they have power tools and toys. I do hope this was a lesson well learned.

Here Comes the Sun

Like anyplace else I guess, we had some roads that always seemed to have problems. Those busy intersections were always a mess, especially during drive times in the mornings and afternoons. Trouble came and went with the seasons, too. Among the many incidents that we had, one stands out in my mind. There are now traffic lights at that intersection, but before that, there were only stop signs at the side streets. During the busy drive times, it was almost impossible to turn off of the well-traveled side street and onto the main road. Often the police would help move traffic along more quickly through this intersection.

That was only one of the problems. In the afternoon in the summer, going eastbound was not a problem, but headed west, you were going down a small hill as you approached the intersection. As you started down, the big, full, summer sun appeared to be sitting right on the road in front of you. It was impossible to see. This was the cause of many accidents there.

One summer afternoon, a police sergeant had a new police officer riding with him, to break him in. They approached the intersection and saw it was a mess, as always. So the sergeant stopped and directed the rookie to get out and help with the traffic. This new guy did as he was told, but no one thought to tell him about the sun.

He walked into the middle of the intersection to start directing traffic. Sure enough, a westbound motorist could barely see the other cars on the road. There was no way they could see a person standing there. The police officer was struck by the car. The sergeant got out, stopped traffic, and called for help.

I was on duty that day and responded with the ambulance. The police officer was banged up and in a lot of pain. He was out of work for a while, but recovered, and is still on the police department to this day. He got pretty lucky. He could have been killed. The experienced sergeant should have told him of the known hazards in that place. Why he didn't, I couldn't say. But lesson learned, by both the new cop and the training sergeant.

Death Ride

Our fire department has had an ambulance since the early 70s when the first men graduated from EMT school. The first one was one of those old Cadillacs—you know, one of those that looked just like a hearse, only repainted. There was not much room to work in those, but they sure gave you a nice ride.

As the mid 70s came, there was a state grant funding a mass purchase of the type II modular ambulances, the kind that looks like a truck with an ambulance body mounted on it. My town was part of the group purchase and we got the type of ambulance we would have for many years.

One day in the late 70s, our ambulance was on its way back from a hospital when it was hit head-on by another vehicle. It was destroyed. Fortunately, no one was injured. It took a while for the town to come up with a permanent replacement. Until then, we had to do with a rental. The first rental was a modular, just like the one that got demolished, only it had a bigger engine. That ambulance would fly. That's not necessarily a good thing. Some people have a heavy foot, and before they know it, they are going too fast to be safe. The vehicle also leaked oil so bad that we had to add a couple of quarts a day.

There is a road in the next town over that is kind of a well-traveled, secondary road. It is also the shortest route for us to get from our town to a couple of area hospitals. Prior to that time, the road had been narrow and windy. At the time, there was a huge project going on to straighten and widen that road. They had the width dug out, but the road was still dirt. The utilities hadn't moved their wires or poles yet, so the poles were in the middle of the street.

One day, I was working in the ambulance with one of those men with the heavy foot. He was also a very excitable sort of man. We got a call for a man stung by a bee and having a reaction. Being pretty new, it was the first one of those calls I was to see. We got to the address and there was a large man; not fat, just big; unconscious and barely breathing. I looked and saw that his throat was swelled about shut. Paramedics did not exist in our area at that time, and we, being basic EMTs, could not administer medication. The answer was a fast ride. I couldn't even get an airway tube in his throat to keep it open so he could breathe.

So into the ambulance we all got, with me as the attendant and old "Lead Foot" at the controls. To say that it was a scary ride would be the understatement of a lifetime. The patient was unconscious, struggling to breathe, with very little air exchange. There was nothing I could do to help. My partner was all cranked up and his foot went to the floor, or at least that's what it felt like. We went up that road under construction at a high rate of speed, weaving in and out of the utility poles and around construction equipment in the middle of the street. There was dust flying, gravel kicking up, and people were looking at us. We actually made it to the hospital in one piece. I don't remember how our patient made out. I suspect not too well.

I was scared almost to death from that ride. I thought I was going to die. (What a convenient place to be if that happened: in the back of an ambulance. Problem was that I was the attendant. How was I going to take care of myself?) Thank heaven that we got rid of that rental and got a van ambulance. Not as much room, but enough to work. It also didn't go the speed of light. For that, I was thankful.

Adorable

Got to thinking of my drinking days and that reminded me of a story. One Friday night in October years back, a group of kids in their mid teens gathered at the high school. There was no one around and it was very dark, the perfect atmosphere to have a few beers, then a few more, which is what they were doing. It was a small gathering of both boys and girls. One of the girls had her cousin from another state visiting for the weekend. They all got drunk and then someone had the bright idea to break into the high school. They broke into the building where the gym and locker rooms were located. They shot off the fire extinguishers and made a general mess of things. I guess no one thought that there might be an alarm system, but there was, and the police were alerted.

When the police got there, they found the mess inside and started looking around. They found the teens outside in the field behind the building. The visiting cousin, an attractive young lady of about 16, had gotten sick. She had fallen down, thrown up, and rolled in it. She was pretty sick, so the police called the fire department for the ambulance. Lucky me, I was on the ambulance crew!

We got there and brought the stretcher out back to the field. It started to rain as we loaded the sick girl on it. She had stopped vomiting by now. We wheeled her to the ambulance and put the stretcher with her on it inside. Then I got in and we started toward a local hospital. I just knew that the hospital staff would be somewhat less than glad to see us. I was making some notes when the young lady opened her eyes, looked at me, and asked, "Do you think I'm pretty?"

I looked down at her. She smelled, there was vomit in her badly messed-up hair with leaves and sticks other debris stuck in it, and she had dirt and vomit on her face. I looked at her and just smiled and nodded my head quietly, all the while thinking to myself, "Oh yeah, you're adorable." Drinking can make you sooooo attractive!

All in the Family

I don't know for sure if habits and behavior are strictly learned from parents and other adults. Based on my experiences, I have to think that while many things are learned, some things are in the blood and passed through families. We had an interesting, yet dangerous, family that lived on the south end of town. The father had a contracting business and was an excellent stonemason. He was a little older than my parents. He had grown up in the city and learned much about life on the street. He talked tough. Even the sound of his voice made you reluctant to get on his bad side. He walked, talked, behaved, and carried himself as we think a gangster does. He didn't look the part, though. He looked every bit the working man. He was short, stocky, and strong-looking from years of hard work.

This man had a reputation in town of being a man you didn't mess with. There is a story that when his son was in elementary school, he waited after school one day for a teacher who had disciplined his son. The word is that he slapped the teacher around in the school parking lot.

He once had some words with a man who worked with me at the firehouse back when I first started. I remember that that firefighter carried a handgun around with him for a while, until he was told not to wear the gun to work anymore. That was the kind of effect this guy had on people.

People either liked him or hated him. He was the kind of guy who would tell you straight what he was thinking. He used to keep his business equipment in his yard. I remember hearing that people in the neighborhood complained to the town. He got told to remove the equipment from the residential zone where he lived. I never could see the harm. I think people just wanted to mess with him.

Oddly enough, I always got along well with this man. He had two girls and two boys, all quite a bit younger than me. They were all tough guys, even the girls, and they were all bad news. I stayed away from his kids, and so I never had any reason to show him any disrespect at all. He must have liked that. He always treated me very well and respectfully, even when I was a kid.

His kids were something. I know from talk around the neighborhood that the girls were very tough. There was a car accident one night that the fire department responded to. I wasn't there, but it was reported that one of those girls was involved. She wound up kicking a fire officer in the knee.

As the years went by, those kids got worse. The oldest ended up being sent to prison, as was his girlfriend, for armed robbery. Rumor had it that they were both on heroin. A few years later, his little brother joined him after he shot up the parking lot of a local restaurant with an Uzi submachine gun. After a while, the girls just kind of faded away, and I never heard anything else about them. I heard one of the boys got out of prison some years ago. They said he was around town for a few days, then he left. No one seems to know anything else about him or his brother.

The guy hated African Americans. He used all the well-known, derogatory names when making reference to blacks. At some point, he and his wife had problems. I heard he came home one day and found that his wife had run off. Word was that she ran off with a black man. That must have really eaten at him.

His wife left, his kids went to jail or moved away, but he stayed around town. He developed some medical problems, as many people do as they age. I had occasion to take him to local hospitals with the fire ambulance. Each time I saw him, he remembered me and treated me very well and respectively. He always called me by name.

After a while, he must have been on meds for neurological issues: head meds. It was interesting how, when he would go out drinking on some nights and he hadn't taken his meds, he would come to the police station and ask them to lock him up for the night so he wouldn't hurt anyone. They would oblige, and before long, as the fire department shared the same building with the police, we'd hear him screaming and yelling all kinds of things. We could hear him banging on his cell door, trying to get out. This would go on most of the night. Not every night, but often. The next morning, when he calmed down, they'd let him out and he'd go home to sleep. I was always reminded of Otis, on the old Andy Griffith show. Remember him? He was the town drunk who would come into the sheriff's office drunk and lock himself in a cell. This went on for some years until he finally died.

Knowing this man and the way he spoke and sometimes acted, I'm not at all surprised that his kids turned out to be troublemakers. He had always worked hard all his life, so I don't know where they got the idea for armed robbery or using guns to shoot places up. It's that age-old argument: heredity vs. environment. Are some people just destined to be bad and only get worse with time?

All Mouth and No Guts

For about the first half of my career, the fire department shift schedule was two days, followed by two nights, then four days off. After a while, the 24-hour schedule started to become more popular. My department adopted a 24-hour schedule where we had 24 hours on, 24 hours off, 24 on, then five days off. One complete cycle took eight days, so the schedule shifted forward by one day each week. I never really liked that 24-hour schedule, which put me in a small minority. We worked scheduled shifts on a 24-hour schedule, but everything else (like sick leave, vacation, personal leave, etc.) was counted in days and nights. For example, if a firefighter was out sick for the day and went to work that night, he was charged one sick day. If he stayed out for the whole 24 hours, he was charged two sick days. For vacations, you had so many days or nights off, depending on how much vacation you were entitled to.

One day I was working a 24 with my regular shift at station 1. There were three of us, plus the captain. Station 2 had a lieutenant and one private. I stayed at headquarters for the day. The private at station 2 was going out on some type of leave for the night. That required one of the privates at headquarters to go to station 2 to relieve that man and spend the night there with the lieutenant. The lieutenant and the particular firefighter who were working at station 2 that day did not get along. They spent their shifts together in silence and in different rooms in the firehouse.

Well, it was my turn to be the one to go over to the other station if someone was out. I got in my car and left for station 2 at 5:40 and arrived there at about 5:50, about ten minutes before shift change. As I got out of my car, I could hear the house gong alerting us that someone had pulled a box from the street. I grabbed my gear and hurried into the firehouse. I could hear the voice of the man I was to relieve. He was sitting in the driver's seat of the engine, very loudly calling me every insult that he could think of. I had no trouble hearing him from the doorway. I came over and slapped the engine door with my hand, startling him, and he looked over and saw me. His eyes widened as I told him to go. I got my gear on and we went to the call. It turned out to be false, so we were back in quarters very shortly. The lieutenant told me that his partner had already put all his gear away at 5:30 and was upset that he had to get it out again to respond to the box alarm. He felt that I should have been over to relieve him at 5:30. Oh well.

When the captain came over to visit that night, I told him about what had happened. The next time we were on duty, the captain made it a point of telling the guy that I had heard everything that he had said that night. Very shortly after that, the lieutenant announced his retirement. I was next on that promotion list. When the lieutenant left, I got the promotion. I was assigned to station 2 where I would be working with this man. Right away, he started to use sick leave, then vacation, and then he retired himself. He never worked one day with me as the lieutenant. He was all mouth and no guts.

If you're going to shoot off your mouth, you should at least have the guts to stand up and face the music. It worked out for the better for me, though. I wound up with some really good partners that worked well and were a pleasure to be with.

Around the World

Several years ago, I was working at the gas school with the recruit class. In this class was a very petite female recruit. She was an ex-Marine and had been deployed to Iraq and into combat. She was small, but tough, and could do the job as well as anybody. At the gas school, we always had water in coolers available for drinking. We also had a rubber hose that we would connect to a spigot near the classroom. We would turn it on and let it run all day. We'd use this for drinking or washing sweat or extinguisher powder off of us. I usually used the hose for my drinking water.

This day, we had been through some of our evolutions. We gave the recruits a break and they were all sitting near the classroom. I was thirsty, so after doffing my coat, helmet, and hood, I went around to the hose to get a drink. It was then I found that whoever had hooked up the hose that day had neglected to turn it on. The main valve for that spigot was located on the wall in the ladies room. This was a very small room with only a toilet and a sink. I walked to the door and reached for the door handle. The recruits all started yelling and talking at once. I couldn't make out what they were saying, so I just took the handle and pulled the door open. There, in front of me, was the female recruit ex-Marine sitting on the toilet. She looked up at my "Holy shit" face, and I quickly shut the door. As I turned to face the recruits, they all started to laugh, as did some other instructors who had witnessed

what I had done. What could I say or do? I laughed it off and apologized to the young lady when she came out. She didn't think anything of it and laughed it off. I *did* tell her to make sure that she locked the door the next time she went in there, in case there was another unthinking numbskull like me working. We all got a good laugh and went back to work.

We use real product in the gas school and it gets dangerous up there. We keep the gate closed so people can't just wander into the gas area when class is in session. I saw no one enter or leave, yet when we broke for lunch a short while later, I walked into the instructors' lunchroom and everybody already knew about what happened and ate me alive. By the time I got done hearing all the versions of the story, I wondered if I really had even been there! The only thing I could think of was that the story had completely circled the globe and beat me back to the lunchroom. Bad news does indeed travel fast. From that day on, I always made sure to tell all female students to make sure to lock the door. I don't think our ex-Marine harbored any ill will, though. On her graduation day, she gave me a hearty handshake and a kiss on the cheek. I was flattered.

Miracle Workers

Years ago, I was coming to work for my night shift at station 1. When I arrived, the day shift was still out with the ambulance. I was told that they had gone to a really bad motor vehicle accident. When the crew got back, they looked a bit shaken. As we all worked together to get the ambulance cleaned up and ready for use again, I got the story of what had happened.

It was rush hour and the roads were busy with people coming home from work. All too often, people are willing to take chances or drive faster than normal to get home. There was a car waiting to make a left-hand turn from a busy street onto a side street. The young lady driving misjudged the speed of oncoming traffic and how fast she was going as she made the turn. She was hit head-on by an oncoming car. She was the only one injured, but her injuries were severe. Whatever she hit inside of her car had torn off her face just below the eyes. There was no damage to her eyes, but her face; cheeks, lips, and everything below the eyes and in front of the ears; was just hanging on. She didn't completely lose consciousness, but remained groggy and somewhat responsive. She kept raising her hands up to feel her face. That was about the *last* thing they wanted her to do. Who knows what her reaction would be if she found how bad the injuries were. They did manage to keep her hands down. Her face was bandaged as well as possible, and she was taken by ambulance to the hospital.

The story ends there...until about a year later. One day, a young woman came to station 1. She said that she had come to thank the firefighters who had helped her after her accident. It was indeed the same young woman who had such severe facial injuries a year or so before. She was very pretty, and the only hints that she had suffered any injury at all were the two, thin scars, one on each side near the jaw line. You had to really look hard to see them. I'm not sure which hospital she had been transported to, but those doctors put her back together again. Her life could have been ruined, but for those doctors. They were true miracle workers.

15-2, 15-4, and 8 is a Dozen

My fire department, being a rather small one, was once an all part-time department, or as we call it, "all call." They had some system of manning the firehouse, but there were no full-time firefighters in our town. As full-time positions were created over the years, the call department became smaller. When I came on call, there were eight of us young guys appointed at one time. The call department was still quite large and many of those older guys were still there. As those older guys left, they were not replaced, and over the years, the call force was eventually whittled down to ten.

There was one particular man I remember from that older bunch. Looking at him, you'd never peg him as a firefighter in any way, shape, or manner. He was older and quiet. He never moved too quickly. He'd just walk around, smoking his pipe.

When the department would strike a box for a fire, the tone recalling us all to the firehouse would be transmitted over the radio. This man always made it back. He lived right behind the firehouse and so he usually got there first. The rest of us would arrive to find him walking around in his fire boots, (back then we wore those high, pull-up boots), and making coffee. He would always make two pots of coffee. Maybe they used to drink a lot of coffee at night back in the day, but in *my* day, we threw out a lot of the coffee he made.

One night, shortly after I came on call, a box was struck, so I returned to the station. I came inside the firehouse and there he was: boots on, coat in hand, and he had already made the coffee. We younger guys listened closely to the reports coming from the fire ground. We heard the call for another engine to the fire. There was a stampede as we ran to the gear rack. Helmets went on heads, boots were pulled into feet, and coats were donned. A bunch of us hopped onto the rear step. Yes, we rode standing on that step back in those days. The engine pulled out with about five of us on the step, but our older cohort was not one of them. He had gotten pushed aside in the rush and hadn't been able to get on the step.

That was the beginning of the end for him. He stayed around a few more years. This was just long enough for me and others to save his life. We'd be riding on the step, holding on, and he'd suddenly let go of the bar and bend over to pull up his boots, or get out his gloves, or maybe pick his nose, I don't know. We'd get ahold of him so he didn't fall from the speeding engine. I never counted how many times this happened, but he let go often.

He was still there when I was appointed full time. I remember one time when he almost stuck a pick head axe in my head at a fire. He was swinging the axe while standing on a ladder and didn't look behind himself. I almost got hit on his backstroke. Another stampede to the engine a while later made him decide to retire.

Retirement didn't keep him out of the firehouse though. He would often come into station 2 to chat, have a cup of coffee, and to play cribbage. There was a lot of cribbage played in that firehouse back then. We used a board that had been there so long that no one knew where it had come from. We had some pretty good cribbage players in the firehouse back then, but this man wasn't one of them. A good player can move very quickly counting his hand and moving his pegs. Two good players can go through a game in no time. Since games could move quickly, we'd often play two out of three. It came to be expected that we would play two out of three, unless we got a call.

Our friend knew how to play reasonably well, but his weakness lay in the fact that he seemed to have trouble with the counting of points. In the game of cribbage, you only have to be able to add and count to thirty-one. It took this guy forever to count his hand, and even longer with all his double-checking. Then you'd lay down your hand and call out your points. He'd look over to check *your* hand, too. It was maddening! I wouldn't have expected this guy to have so much trouble with it, especially when I found out what he did for full-time work: he was a math teacher in a local high school. Games with him seemed to take forever, not to even mention a two out of three.

When he retired, he had more time. We could expect to see him at the firehouse at any time. He would always ask if anyone wanted to play a two out of three. We did play him at first, but it got so maddening after a while that we started to avoid playing. We would do things like drive the engine out for "training." We weren't trying to be cruel. We just didn't want to play him. It took too long. After a while, cribbage faded away and became a thing of the past. His visits became fewer, also.

After years of retirement, he developed dementia. After a while, they took his driver's license away. Then he'd walk around town. Sometimes he'd stop by, but not often. There were many newer guys he had never met, but he didn't even recognize people he had known for years. Eventually, they had to get him into a place where he could be cared for. His elderly wife couldn't do it anymore. I never knew if he had any children. So, he became just another memory at the firehouse.

It's sad, but I guess that someday we'll all just be memories. But it still intrigues the hell out of me how a man could teach math for thirty years, but couldn't count his way through a game of cribbage.

Name Counts for Something

Back a couple of years, a few years after I retired, I found need to visit the fire department in a neighboring town. I had to discuss something with their chief and get some information. That town is quite a bit bigger than mine, and had a bigger, busier fire department. I wasn't sure the chief would even be in quarters, or if he might be tied up at a meeting. This chief was a man that I had known for quite a few years, both on and off the job. We were not really friends, but always friendly.

Well, I drove over, walked in the front door, and up to the window in front of his secretary. She was not someone I knew. She looked up and asked if she could help me. I told her that I would like a word with the chief, if possible. She stood up and started walking toward his door. She had an expression, like she knew he was going to be busy. As she walked, she asked my name, which I told her. She still didn't have a hopeful look about her. She opened the door and went into the chief's office.

The next thing I heard was the chief's voice booming from his office, "Oh him? Absolutely, I always have time for him. Show him right in!"

The secretary walked out of the office with disbelief on her face. She looked at me as if to say, "Who the hell are you? You must be someone special." Then she smiled and let me into the office, where I shook the chief's hand. We greeted each other like we had known each other for years, which we had.

I finished my business and bade goodbye to the chief. As I left the office, I looked at the secretary and smiled. She smiled back, but she still had that "Who the hell are you?!" look on her face.

The moral of the story is: Always be ready. You never know when royalty will walk through the door!

See How They Live

In the fire department, we handle all kinds of calls. At a fire, things usually are a mess and there is no time to concentrate on much else but the fire, but other calls give us the chance to see inside people's homes. It's interesting to look around and see how some people live. In our town, we have older homes, as well as some very old ones. We have large, high-end new homes. We have elderly and handicapped housing.

We've found hoarders in both new and older houses. These people throw nothing away and constantly add to their collection of everything you can think of, until there is no more room to put anything down. Then they pile it higher. There is often no furniture visible, no place to sit, and no way around, except to walk through the rooms along little narrow paths. Sometimes we can get lucky and find out in time to intervene before something happens, like a fire. We pass a report along to other agencies stating that these people are a danger to themselves and possibly others. Once the ball starts rolling, things can get cleaned up. But we don't always get lucky. I've been to fires in the homes of hoarders. With so much junk, it's hard to find the fire and put it out. It's hard to search for victims. It's hard to move around. There is a very real chance that one of us could get hurt or killed.

I've been inside some very expensive homes and found no furniture. They spent all their money on the house. There might be a mattress and a couple of kitchen chairs or maybe a kitchen set, but nothing else. It seems strange to me. I'd rather spend a little less on the house and get something to sit on inside the house. But that's me.

I went into a house once, a ranch house, where almost every room had handmade shelving units all around the walls, from floor to ceiling.

Apartments in elderly housing are usually cluttered: not dirty, but cluttered. The resident is trying to hold onto a lifetime of memories in the form of belongings that they won't part with, even after downsizing to a small apartment. There are the sad situations found in the homes of elderly people who have stayed in their homes and as they got older, they get less and less able to care for the house and themselves. Things get cluttered and dirty, including the resident, as often as not.

Then there are other people to whom their belongings seem to mean nothing. We've seen expensive homes that aren't cared for: they are not painted, have broken screens, and toys and other items are scattered all over the yard. Others are nice and neatly painted, with nice lawns and trimmed trees and bushes. There never seems to be a pattern. Rich or poor, some people don't care and others do.

The people, themselves, are interesting, too. We've gotten calls for "someone on the floor," and have shown up to find a person, not always elderly, on the floor unable to get up. Sometimes they are bleeding. On the way in, we might notice that the trash consists of mostly beer cans, wine bottles, and/or liquor bottles. It's easy to tell what these people do in their spare time.

There was a man once who called us about his wife one morning. He had been gone out of town for three days. As soon as he left and for the whole time he was gone, all she had done was drink. At some point, she fell and struck her head on a wrought iron railing in the house. Her head and face were still crusted with dried blood from the fall. She hadn't even cleaned herself up. When we arrived, she was alive and conscious, but she was still intoxicated. She tried to be nice, even sexy, in the ambulance. As an added treat, she even grabbed me by the crotch while en route to the hospital. Needless to say, I moved her hand away quickly and sat further back and out of reach.

There are more of those type of closet drinkers than I ever thought. If they keep it up, sooner or later they will need the fire department for something. Then we find out about them.

Older people can be interesting when their mental status has started to deteriorate. Then we could have something strange to deal with. But the elderly housing in our town is open to handicapped people as well. I remember one female who had a mental disability who lived like a slob and positively hated the police department. She swore that the lieutenant from the police department had put sperm in her milk once, and she never forgave him. All I'm going to say about that is that I think it's highly unlikely that that ever happened. Another woman accused the duty fire captain of slapping her across the face. I know that that didn't happen because I was there. That same person also accused the fire chief of raping her digitally. These are good reasons for never going into those places alone.

There was a man in one housing apartment who didn't like us at all. More than once, someone called the fire department and reported that they were worried because they couldn't get in touch with him. We'd show up and he would curse and swear at us and order us to leave.

One of the times we got a call for a well-being check at this man's apartment, we had the police with us. He was yelling inside. We went and got our master key and opened the door. His place was trashed: everything was thrown around and furniture was tipped over. We found him on the floor. He ordered us out of his home, and not too nicely, either.

I asked the man if he wanted us there. He ordered us out again, loudly. I turned to the police officer and said, "He's your problem. He doesn't want us to touch him or to come inside." He seemed to be in control of himself, so we left. I guess the police got things straightened out.

That same man had a visit from a nurse one day. She couldn't get in and he wouldn't let her in. He was yelling swears. She called the fire department and we got the police again. We met the nurse there. We were all at the door when we opened it. The place was trashed again. There was the resident, lying on his mattress in the middle of the floor. He was completely naked and covered from head to toe in his own feces. The smell was horrendous.

The nurse looked horrified and said, "Well, aren't you going to clean him up?"

I, as the lieutenant, said, "No Ma'am. That's your job. He doesn't want us in here." We left him in the care of the nurse.

Not everyone is as bad as that, thank heaven. These are just a few of the many interesting things I've observed when working with people. The stories abound, and every day brings something new.

Just Legs

In our town there was once a dairy farm, well actually there were two. One was very small and was on the south side of town where I grew up. The farmer was kind of a cheapskate. We would go there and hang around and play in the hayloft. Whenever a truck full of hay bales or feed sacks had to be unloaded, the farmer would get whoever was around to do the unloading into the loft. Sometimes we'd have a lot of kids. Other times, not so many. That was hard work, and when we were done, sometimes the farmer would buy us a soda out of his machine. Well, I guess that was better than nothing, and he did let us play around the barn.

But this story is about the other dairy farm in town, the big one. I never knew just how big it was, or how many cows there were, but it covered a lot of area. That farmer was kind of a cheapskate, too. I'm told that he used to hire a bunch of guys with alcohol problems to do all the jobs around the place. Among the buildings on the property was a bunkhouse for these guys. I didn't really know much about this farm growing up, and I didn't realize that it was the bunkhouse that I responded to one gray afternoon in winter. There was heavy smoke showing on our arrival. I was a new guy and pretty much did what I was told. There were two of us on the first engine, and my partner, a much senior man, told me to take the booster hose and go in with it. Booster hose is that hard, red rubber hose you see on reels on the sides of engines. It is useful hose for certain applications, such as brush, roadside trash, or other small fires. It was never designed to be taken into a house on fire. The fact is that it simply didn't supply enough water to fight a building fire effectively. However, because it was easy, there was a lot of booster used to fight these fires back in the bad old days. Booster is being phased out now because of that.

Anyway, I took the nozzle around the house and pulled it inside and up the stairs where the heavy smoke was. We couldn't see at all and crawled around until we found the fire. Another engine showed up, and before long, the fire was out.

To be honest, it was a very long time ago, and I don't remember exactly what was burning. I think it was bedding: clothes and the like. It wasn't a big fire, and was easily put out once we found it.

It was after that that the older guys started talking. It seems that this building had a fire history to it. They told me that this was the bunkhouse and explained to me the kind of guys that normally would be found there. I was told that the guys often would be drunk and set accidental fires inside.

They told me about one fire where there was very heavy smoke showing on the fire department's arrival. They had pulled a hose into the building. There had been no one around to tell the firefighters anything, so they went upstairs with the hose. As they crawled through the smoke, the firefighters began to bump into things and heard voices. It turns out that the place was full of men. They were drinking in their bunkhouse and somehow started a fire. The smoke, as it thickened, didn't bother them in the least. The men inside just went right on drinking, and no one bothered to leave. It wasn't a very big fire, but it was very smoky when the first engine arrived. The firefighters had to yell and clear everyone out before they could do their work. I was told that the farm workers didn't want to leave and gave a lot of argument. They were all eventually gotten out and the fire was put out.

As a new guy, I don't know how I would have reacted if I had made entry alone and started to bump into legs and then have them start swearing at me. I can only imagine that I would have been surprised. No, I think I would have soiled my pants!

Snots

As I've said before, just about all of us have some job we do on our days off from the fire department. Among the many things I did was paint houses. The man I worked for was on our department, too. He was a great guy and fun to work for. If there was any problem with him, it was that sometimes the thought process broke down somewhere between his brain and his mouth resulting in things totally unexpected.

One day, I was on the roof of an attached garage. We were getting ready to take the shutters off the window so we could paint that wall of the house. My boss was standing beside his paint bucket on the roof. The brush was in the paint. We were using "fire engine red" oil paint. This job was something less than a pleasure to do.

Suddenly, we heard the loud buzzing of bees inside the wall. It was clear that they had built a nest in the wall and were probably entering behind the shutter. As we stood, thinking about what we were going to do, a bee landed on the boss's ear and started to sting him. Then the man did something that I wouldn't have thought of. Without hesitation, he grabbed the brush out of the paint bucket, swung it at the bee, and hit himself in the head with it. There was red oil paint everywhere: all over me, the house, the roof, the window—everywhere.

His ear swelled up to the size of a saucer. I don't know whether he got the bee or not. Having to clean up the mess and almost have to bathe in paint thinner wasn't fun, but seeing him hit himself with the brush and snap paint everywhere sure was funny.

Another day we broke for lunch. We were in line at a local sub shop. It was busy there and my boss was a few people ahead of me in line. After a while, he made it to the counter. I was about four people behind him in line when I heard him order a "chicken salad on cesarean."

Well, I lost it. I started to laugh and choke and I had snots hanging out of my nose. People were looking at me, so I had to leave and go outside to regain my composure. The boss came out with his chicken salad on Syrian bread and asked what was wrong. I couldn't even tell him. I would have busted up laughing again. I did get back in line, and after a while, I got my lunch.

Lunchtime took a little longer than usual that day. It's a good thing my boss and I went to the same place for lunch, so he could understand the delay, though I'm not so sure he realized what he had said. Every day was a new adventure!

CPR Instructor Class

The state firefighting academy is very conscious of the duties of the various levels of employees. You do not work outside your classification at all. I can understand that, but sometimes I think it gets carried to an extreme. The instructors are to teach the students. The people from support services are to drive the apparatus, and provide and operate the equipment. They also assist the instructors, when needed. They are supposed to do all this without talking to the students at all. I've seen support people getting spoken to and yelled at by instructors and coordinators for talking to the students. Sometimes the students, not really knowing who to speak to about a question, will ask a support person. Heaven help the support person who attempts to help by answering the question. It doesn't matter that the support people are firefighters, too, often with more experience than the instructor.

I worked in support for about twelve years. I loved the work. I could set up and run the equipment and listen to the instructors. I learned a lot. During the time I was working support at the academy, I was also an EMS Instructor. This had nothing to do with the academy. It was done through the state Office of Emergency Medical Services. I had certifications to teach many things and years of experience with teaching. I was also a CPR instructor-trainer. That meant that I could train and certify other people to become CPR instructors themselves. In fact, I was the *only* instructor-trainer in the whole academy at that time.

Several years back, there was a civil service exam coming up for promotion to lieutenant and captain. On these exams, extra credit is given for a certification as a CPR instructor. There were many who were going to take the test, and some of them asked me if I could hold a certification class for CPR instructor. I agreed and the wheels were put in motion. First, we needed a place to hold the class. These people came from all over the state, so there wasn't really any middle ground, except the academy.

I had all the equipment I needed and sent for all the appropriate paperwork, books, etc. Then I went to ask the director of the academy if we could use a classroom for our class after the academy's programs for the day had ended. He did agree to let us use the room, but not until he had put me in my place. He reminded me that I was *not* an academy instructor, and in *no way* could this be called an academy-sponsored class. He had to make sure that I knew that I was one of the bottom-feeders: good enough to certify some of his instructors to teach, but not good enough to call it an academy sponsored class. I had more years teaching EMS than many of the instructors had in the fire service, but apparently, that didn't matter. Well, I wasn't really bothered by all that. I already knew how the administration felt. I also knew that I could provide something that no one else at the academy could provide. That was satisfaction enough for me.

The class went off OK and I guess those guys got their credit. I got a thank you from some of them. Others never mentioned it again. No matter. I knew what and who I was. I walked with my head held high in spite of the the director's reminder that I wasn't one of *them*.

Modest and Afraid

We have many people who call us for assistance. Often this involves nothing more than picking someone up after they've fallen, or helping them get from one place to another. Sometimes, someone has just gotten home from the doctor or hospital, and needs help moving to a chair or getting into bed. This is the kind of help we provide, and are glad to do so. Since these usually are not emergencies, we have plenty of time and try to make things as smooth and comfortable as possible. The years I spent in the private ambulance business have been a great help here. I learned the easiest ways to move people while keeping them happy.

There was one lady who used to call regularly to have us help her into a car. She didn't need ambulance transport; she could sit in the seat of a car easily. She had one leg and was in a wheelchair. With no ramp, we would have to carry her down about five or six steps and help her into the car. I don't remember why, but she had to go see a doctor regularly. She had a friend who would drive her and they'd call us for the needed help.

The lady was a widow, lived alone, and was petrified of nearly everything. She was afraid of us at first, and always remained apprehensive of those who came to help her. She was scared of being carried. The first time I went there, she asked how we were going to get her out. To me, moving her out is easy. I explained how the patient faces forward in the wheelchair. One of us is behind her and tips the chair back on its big rear wheels. Another person holds firmly onto the small front wheels, and we carry the whole package down the stairs. She was still afraid, so when I asked her to trust me, she asked "Why?" I told her that I did this for a living and I was good at it. I had never dropped anyone.

She got used to me after a while. She always tried to help by grabbing onto things, so we kept having to ask her to keep her hands in. She was a nice lady and I enjoyed talking to her. She always wore a dress or skirt, and being very proper, she went to great pains to make sure that the dress was not riding up as we carried her.

One night when I was on duty at headquarters, we were dispatched to this lady's house. She was supposed to go out to dinner with a friend. The friend went to pick her up, but no one answered the door. Cell phones were not too common then, so the friend went home and tried to reach her by phone. When no one answered, the friend called the fire department. The ambulance, an engine, and the police responded. No one answered the door. We started to look around in the yard and in the windows to see if we could see her. Nothing was visible from the street side of the house. I went around back with a police officer. The house was built into a hill, so in back, the basement was at ground level, and the first floor was one level up.

The whole house was locked up tight, but there were lights on. Not knowing what her habits were, she could have been out, but left lights on. We didn't want to break in unless we absolutely had to. The basement was dark and the first floor was too high to look in. I bent down, cupped my hands together, and called for the police officer. He put his foot into my cupped hands and I gave him a boost, lifting him up so he could look into the first floor windows. Sure enough, there in a bedroom that we could not see into from the other side, the police officer saw her sitting upright in her wheelchair. She was not responding to all the noise we were making. We told the others that we saw her and they would have to break in.

The house had a typical wood entry door, with nine small panes of glass. The easiest way in would be to break a pane, reach in to unlock it, and then open the door. The cop reached for his expanding, metal baton, said, "Get back!" and swung at the glass—only to hit the hand of a firefighter who had not moved fast enough. Well, with that man's hand broken, we were down a man. We broke the glass with a flashlight and reached in. The door still wouldn't open.

We looked in and saw that she had a 2x4 wedged between the door and a cleat on the floor. This locking system did the trick. We had to beat down the door. It really wasn't hard to do, though, and we were inside quickly. We ran into the bedroom and found her in cardiac arrest. She had been getting dressed to meet her friend. She had on a skirt and bra and was putting on a blouse when she was stricken. We moved her out of the wheelchair and onto the floor. Off came clothing that was in the way as we hooked up the defibrillator. We shocked and did CPR all the way to the hospital, but sadly, she did not survive.

We knew she was proper and modest and scared. From the way she had had the door secured, she must have been very afraid. I think she would have been mortified if she had known what happens in an emergency when we are trying to save someone's life. There's just no room for modesty. We just go to work and don't worry about that. If all goes well, the patient can worry about it later.

What Else Could I Do?

A "section 12," or "pink slip," is the legal document that orders an involuntary committal of an individual to a psychiatric facility. Dealing with section 12s is never much fun. I've done it a lot in the course of all the years I've worked in an ambulance. I've had a lot of success with dealing with these people, but I was always on guard for a sudden attack. You just never know what someone will do. Of course, most of the time I had plenty of help to back me up in case something went wrong. If you have to go into someone's house, we would make sure that the police were there. It's the same thing with going into a jail cell or a hospital. It's a different feeling when you're all alone with the person. You have to reason with them, gain their confidence, and yet be prepared for something unexpected.

One day years back, I was on duty at station 2 when we were dispatched for a medical call not far from us on the south end of town. There had been some kind of domestic problem. A boy (as I remember, in his early teens) had put his hand and arm through the glass on a storm door. It was unknown how badly he was cut. The ambulance was coming from station 1, and we were first due.

We got there, went into the house, and were told that the boy had had a fight with his sister. It was more of a severe argument than a fight, as there were no punches thrown. Apparently, he had ended the argument by putting his fist through the window of the rear storm door and run off. His sister said that she had no idea how badly he was cut. I didn't see any blood as I looked around, but even with that, you just can't tell. The police arrived and told us that the boy in question was known to them, and had some emotional problems.

The search was on. We had to find him. It was thought that he hadn't had enough time to have gotten very far. We split up. The police, my partner, the ambulance crew, and I spread out to cover more ground. Well, I headed off into the woods behind his house. I walked about 10 minutes, and then I saw him a little ways ahead of me. He was down in a kind of swampy area. I looked around, and wouldn't you know it; lucky me, I was alone. I called out, and he stopped and looked at me. I walked toward him and kept talking, but he didn't answer. He looked like he was wound up like a spring. I got closer. I thought he might run or let loose on me at any time. I was ready for either. If he ran, I sure as hell wasn't going to tackle him! If he came at me, *I* was the one who was going to run. But it turned out that he did neither.

He watched as I approached. I inched closer and kept telling him that I was there to help him, to make sure that he wasn't injured. I told him I knew about the window and asked if he was hurt. He looked at me and slowly held out his injured hand. There was a laceration on it. I told him that I was going to dress it. He stood and let me bandage his hand. All the while, my eyes were on his other hand, which was clenched into a tight fist that just might come at me any time.

My partner was there, watching from a distance, as were the police officers. I'm glad they kept their distance. If they had tried to get involved, I might have gotten my ass kicked. When I finished bandaging his hand, I asked if he would follow me. He said he would, and we slowly made our way out.

I don't remember much of what happened afterward. We probably took him to the hospital for stitches. The domestic situation belonged to the police. My partner told me later that a police officer sang me high praises for my handling of this situation. If only they had known that I was scared half to death. I had no way of knowing what this kid was capable of. I walked into a situation and just did what had to be done to get out unhurt. What else could I do?

Awestruck

Working for all those years in my fire department, I worked with many good people. We had some bad also, but every group has those. As a group, these guys came together, put on the uniform, and did the job. Most were proud to do the job that they did and were very good at it.

I also spent many years working at the state firefighting academy. It was there that I met those most dedicated to the job. These people worked their shifts on their own departments, then came to the academy, put on another uniform, and taught others how to do the job. I worked in support services at first. That is an often-overlooked group of very good people that set up the equipment, drive the apparatus, and operate equipment, as needed. They also build and light all the fires so the instructors can concentrate on teaching the students. We'd report for work, find out what needed to be done and we'd go set it up. We did our job and had a great time doing it. I made some good friends and had a lot of laughs. We had a respect for each other. Of course, we had some deadwood among us, too. But we got to know each other and what we could expect from each other. Eventually, there developed a good core group of people in support that could be depended on. I was proud to be a member of that group.

After a while, the time came for me to change jobs and become an instructor. Instructors are the people who directly teach the recruits or other students, depending on what program we were working. I worked mainly teaching recruit firefighters. The people I worked with came from all over the state, from all different sized fire departments. We didn't get paid all that well, and still we had people that came from the far corners of the state several days a week. They had in common their dedication to training. They could have made more money doing something else, but they wanted to teach. They were very good at what they did. I knew where each one came from and what their jobs were, but I never really thought about it any more than that. I was proud to work with them.

After a while as an instructor, I was senior enough to be the lead instructor at my stations. I would organize the station and assign jobs to other instructors. We taught recruits the basics of fire behavior, hose movement, fire attack, search and rescue, and self-rescue, among many other things.

After some time, I was setting up and running the fires as the incident commander. I loved doing that. I asked that I be able to assign my people to the jobs that I wanted them to do. That way, I could use the best person for each job. I'd take a man who did ladder work at his own department, assign him to the ladder company, and let him teach the students his field of expertise. It went the same for the rescue companies and engine companies. We often take some of the best men and assign them to interior safety instructor. These people maintained safety on the inside of the building and made sure that things went the way that they were supposed to. I usually had just the right people for the jobs to be done. If I didn't, there was a group of people who were very good at just about anything you asked them to do. I could assign one of these people to a job and know it was going to get done right.

I really never gave it any deep thought until one day. We were doing a large burn with fire recruits. Everybody did well and worked hard and lessons were learned. At the end of every burn, after the building clean-up, we would hold a critique with the students and all the instructors. Each instructor would rehash the day and comment on how his crews had done and the lessons learned. The students would have the chance to ask questions and make comments.

There was an instructor who wasn't doing burns with us that day. I think he was assigned to one of several staff jobs for the day, but he came up for the critique. After the burn staff had spoken, this guy stood up and asked to say a few words. He said to the students that he hoped they were learning and listening to all that went on that day. He said that as he looked around, he was awestruck by the staff that was there that day to teach them. He asked if they had any idea how many years of firefighting experience there was in that instructor staff that day. He pointed out how the burn staff was a Who's Who in the

Massachusetts fire service. He went on to mention a few names, where they worked, and how long they had been doing the job. Many were officers at their respective departments, and some were not. No matter officer or not, they were the best of the best. He said he hoped the recruits realized the quality of the staff and were taking advantage of the knowledge and experience. It gave the recruits a feeling of awe, too. I could see it in their faces. But no one was more awed than me, as I listened to this man speak.

It was then, and days after, that I thought about those men and women I worked with. I was awestruck myself, and felt so humbled next to those guys. I was just honored to be able to work with them, to be counted as one of them. I had an officer of the day tell me once that he always liked it when I was there. I was always squared away. He said he could assign to be my assistant someone who was the biggest bag of shit, and I would make it work. I also had a man once tell me that he would follow me down the barrel of a gun. That was a meaningful statement, especially coming from him, a man with extensive military combat experience. Another once said that he'd follow me into hell with an empty water pistol. I was highly complimented by these things said by my peers. I had never really thought about all of the experience and knowledge of the other instructors until that day when it was pointed out to the students. I still, somehow, have a hard time believing that I was so honored as being thought of as one of that group, that I belonged. The recruits listened when I spoke, and I never heard any one of them criticize anything I said. They seem to think that I knew what I was talking about. I hope that's enough. I guess it will have to be.

Minor Injury

One thing that nearly all fire departments do is to provide mutual aid to fire departments in other towns as back up when they have multiple calls. It wasn't usually too bad to go on these calls, except at certain times, like late at night when our department was quiet and we were trying to get some sleep.

One night quite late, when I was working at headquarters, we got a call from a neighboring town requesting mutual aid. They needed our ambulance to go to a residence where there had been some kind of domestic problem. Nobody likes this kind of call, especially the police who have to go in first and make sure the scene is safe.

We responded and arrived at the address in about five minutes or so. The police had the scene secure and the fire department from that town had an engine company standing by. I don't remember whether anyone was under arrest or not, but we were directed to the patient. It was a woman in her mid to late twenties. I guessed that she was the lady of the house and had had an argument with her husband or boyfriend, which one was never made clear. We didn't see any children.

I approached the lady and asked what was wrong. She showed me a small cut on the index finger on her left hand. She said that she had cut it on the broken window of the storm door. I looked over and saw that the window was indeed broken. Well, this was a simple matter. The cut had all but stopped bleeding. This lady did not want to go to the hospital. I told her not to worry: this was minor and she wouldn't have to go anywhere. I bandaged the wound, said my goodbyes to the lady, and went outside.

I walked up to the officer on the engine company and said things were all set and there would be no transport. He looked at me with an appalled look and said, "You're not going to transport?"

I said, "No, it was only a minor wound." We had cleaned and bandaged it. The fire officer, the firefighters, and the police all couldn't believe that we were not going to transport. It was my opinion then, and it is now, that this would have been a needless trip to tie up the ambulance with. I told them that and we left.

Since I was the ambulance attendant and in charge of patient care, it was my call and I made it. I don't know what their procedures and protocols were then in that town. They probably would have taken this lady to the hospital even for something this minor. I've never believed in tying up the ambulance for something silly without any mitigating circumstances. They probably thought we just wanted to return and go back to bed.

A Little Help

I was working one night at station 1 some years back, when we had a line of severe thunderstorms move through. Sometimes we get lucky and nothing happens and the storms just end. Other times we'll get a lightning strike, or many strikes, and get a lot of calls where we have to check for fire or damage. Sometimes we'll get a fire started by a lightning strike. I remember several times when towns near us had multiple fires from those strikes all at the same time. They had to call in a lot of help to handle things.

We had a strike once that actually didn't hit the house at all. The lightning hit a tree in the yard. That tree just happened to be where an electric spotlight was mounted. The lightning followed the wire all the way back to the house, leaving a small trench in the ground. It then hit the breaker box and blew out the whole electrical system. That started a huge fire that ultimately destroyed the house.

On this particular night, the storm wasn't quite finished when we got a call from a residence not too far from station 1. They reported a loud noise and now they had a smell of smoke from their basement. There was no visible smoke, just an odor. The captain ordered a full response to the house. We were about two minutes away. Our engine got there quickly with the captain in car 2. The family was outside and directed us into the basement. There was no outward sign of any problem from the outside.

Entering the basement, there was indeed an odor of smoke, but it was not strong. What we did notice was a leaking water pipe near the ceiling. We walked over and looked at it. This was an older house without a finished basement. There were floor joists above with the plumbing and wiring running along them. The leaking pipe was at a joint and was squirting a small stream of water up onto the wooden joist above it. There was a wire that ran along this joist also. The joist had charring on it. It had been burning.

Investigation reached the conclusion that the «*BOOM*» had been lightning striking something. What it struck, we never found out. It followed the wire, eventually igniting that joist. The fire didn't spread very far, but it got hot enough to melt the solder in a joint in the water pipe. The joint separated a little and the water sprayed out, putting the fire out.

    I never saw that happen, before or since. It's nice to get a little help from Mother Nature once in a while, but if fires keep putting themselves out, we could be out of business!

Luck

Everybody has runs of luck from time to time. The luck runs in two forms: good and bad. In the fire service, that good luck might involve a good save or a rescue, or maybe a narrow escape from injury for yourself. The bad luck might mean a tragic loss or a near miss during a rescue attempt. The truth is that it could involve any of a thousand scenarios. We've all seen them and had them. A run of luck could be something that will lift your spirits or just send your morale into the sewer.

I worked for an officer once who had transferred to our group. There seemed to be more fires when this man was working than when the other groups were on duty. We thought that was a run of pretty good luck. We were a bunch of young guys and this was what we had signed on for. Nobody got killed or injured, so we were in heaven. But all good things must come to an end, and when that run of fires was over, so were the good times.

We had a run of motor vehicle accidents lasting a couple of years. It seemed that whenever someone got killed or maimed in a car, our group was on duty. We couldn't even escape it on mutual aid calls. Other towns kept calling for our ambulance for MVAs. Since then, I haven't had what I would call a run of luck, good or bad. Thinking back though, a few times when I was out of work for one reason or another, I missed some really tough calls.

In my first year on the job, while I was on vacation, there was an MVA involving a motorcycle. I guess the bike had been following too close to a car that stopped suddenly. The bike rider was thrown over the bars and over the roof of the car. His girlfriend on the back didn't fare too well. She just slid forward and hit the handlebars of the bike. She had some severe internal injuries and did not survive. That would have been my first real messy accident. There were others to make up for that.

I missed two suicides involving firearms. I've seen some of them since. They are never good to have to deal with. There was an incident in a wooded area in town where a man attacked two people with a lineman's axe. No one was killed, but some people were hurt badly.

I was on vacation the night of a fatal fire. There was a suspicion that a teenage boy in the house was doing something drug-related in the kitchen. The kitchen caught fire and the boy jumped out of a window, leaving his mother and grandmother in the house. The first responding firefighters did a search. They brought out the mother, but she did not survive. I always regretted not being there that night. Who knows what difference an extra pair of hands might have made.

There was one shift of our firefighters who saw a string of very bad calls in a very short span of time. Two of those calls involved children. I'm thankful that I was not a member of that group. I can't recall the order in which these calls happened, but it really makes no difference.

They were called to a residence in a neighboring town for a medical emergency involving a baby. They arrived and found a three-month-old girl unresponsive. The child had been abused. She died from massive head injuries. It was suspected that she had been held by the feet and swung at a wall and hit headfirst. Autopsy reports said that there were many injuries in various stages of healing. The baby's father was sentenced to prison for a very long time. Any punishment given out is not enough to make one forget having to go to a call like that.

There was a divorced father who had picked up his young son for a weekend visit. Father, son, and the boy's mother were all from a town not too far from ours. Sunday night, when he didn't return the boy, his mother notified the police. They managed to track the father to a wooded area in our town early in the morning. The man had the boy with him. When he saw the police coming, he took a knife and slit the boy's throat. Then he turned the knife on himself, stabbing himself several times. As luck would have it, the father lived and the little boy died. Just the thought of something like that makes me want to cry.

The same group that had responded to the baby girl in the other town had to handle that call, too. Add to this two fatal MVAs that happened in the same location just over the town line into a neighboring town. Our ambulance was called for mutual aid. That same group was on duty again. They happened a week apart. Those that were killed were young adults who couldn't negotiate a turn in the road and hit a bridge support. These two almost identical accidents happened a week apart.

This was quite a run of some very bad calls for one group of guys to handle in a short period of time. It takes a very strong person to keep his sanity having to deal with that. But we had then, and still have, our ways of coping. Perhaps we weren't really sane when we all took this job.

Only a Candle

In our town, we have mostly single-family homes. Some are very high-end, new homes, but we have very many older homes as well. There are a few places where one could rent an apartment or a room. One of these is a three-story, wood frame building. It has several apartments—I'm not sure how many—over all three floors, with an open central stairway going all the way to the third floor. There is a wooden fire escape staircase on the outside rear of the building. If you know this building and think about it, it would be a nightmare if it caught fire.

I was working at station 1 one night when there was a phone call to dispatch. It came from a resident on the first floor of that building. They reported that on their way out, they could see a flickering glow from under the door of the apartment across the hall. They said they had knocked but got no answer, and they said that they were sure the resident of that apartment was not home. There was no other problem reported. Just that flickering light under the door. It was unusual.

The captain sent the engine from station 2 and an engine from headquarters. He had me stay back at headquarters. The station 2 crew got there very quickly and saw the condition that had been reported. When the captain arrived, they decided to force the door. They did and found no one home. The resident had left a candle burning. The candle had burned down low and unevenly. It had tipped over and fallen off the table where it had been left. It had landed on a small rug on the floor and the rug was starting to burn.

The problem was quickly taken care of. We have no way of knowing how far it had progressed when the neighbors made the call, but it wouldn't have taken too much longer before we had a very real problem on our hands. Thank goodness for busybody neighbors who have the sense enough to speak up. Sometimes—often—I think candles should be outlawed.

Man, What a Ride

In the course of their duties, the police pick up and retain, as "guests," all kinds of people for a great many reasons. There are quite a few who get picked up for their misbehavior for being "under the influence" of some substance or another, commonly alcohol. For some who are not arrested but placed in protective custody, the "reward" for their excessive celebrating is a night in a cell. They get released in the morning.

Of course, there are sometimes mitigating circumstances and the "guest" gets their visit extended. One of these was the young man who was picked up drunk one night and placed in the holding cell, where he proceeded to vomit all over the place. When morning came and he was going to be released, the cell was a disgusting mess and the smell was just heinous. It was decided that the young man in question should clean up after himself. He felt positively terrible. You could see in his face and the way he walked. He was given the proper equipment and made to clean his cell, from top to bottom. I always thought that it was appropriate for him to clean up the mess that he made. I don't know whether or not he ever complained about it, but there are a great number of people who like to yell and scream about police brutality. Some just sit in their cell and do just that: scream. Others seem to know just what buttons to push.

No one really wants to spend time in a cell, so some people will try to convince the police that they have been injured and need to go to a hospital. This sometimes works and the fire department is called for the ambulance to transport our troublemaker to the hospital. Since the police own him at this point, there has to be a police officer accompanying the patient. The officer must stay with the patient until their release from the hospital, after which, the patient goes back to a cell. So the whole thing, if you really think about it, just delays the inevitable.

One winter night, I was part of the ambulance crew when such a person was arrested by the police and brought to the station. It was after midnight and it had been quiet, so we had gone to bed. The police arrested this man for misbehaving in his car while intoxicated. This guy was well known to the police, and I knew him well also. He was being his usual uncooperative self and the police had to use a little force to get him to come along.

In the police station, the man started complaining that the officer hurt his already-bad back. He must have put on a good show, because the police called for the ambulance. We got up, went to the other side of the building to the police station, and saw who it was. I was very sure that he was only complaining because he didn't want to spend the night in a cell, but he did complain about a back problem.

We decided to take full spinal precautions for this man. We put him on a long backboard with a cervical collar. Then we secured him to the board. This is not really comfortable, but he did say his back was hurt. We put the board, with him fastened to it, on the stretcher and secured it down with more straps. Then we left for the hospital.

These modern ambulances are set up for providing emergency care to patients. They are not designed to provide a really comfortable ride. It was winter. It had been snowing and the roads were covered. Not being able to see the pavement, it seemed we hit every bump in the road. By the time those bumps worked their way to the patient on the board, they were really rough.

He swore at us all the way to the hospital. When we got there, he couldn't get away from us fast enough. We left him in the custody of a police officer. That guy was glad to see us go. Imagine, after all we did for him and not one word of thanks. When I see that man from time to time, he still talks about the night we tried to kill him. What an ingrate!

Locations

With the coming of computers and the statewide 911 system, at the touch of a finger, emergency responders can have all the information that we need about a certain residence; things like special needs individuals living there; and even more importantly, the exact location of the residence. If the town was cut up into a square grid and everything was built in square blocks, finding an address would not be a problem. But we have no streets that run in straight lines, and houses are built all over. Some houses are set so far back that they can't be seen from the road or from their common driveways. This is bad enough in the daylight, but at night, finding an address when there is no information about the specific location can be a nightmare.

I don't think that it was our idea, but even before the high tech came in, we had a system for finding locations. We had three drawers near the watch desk. It was divided up alphabetically by street. Each residence on a given street had a card with information and location. These were filed by house number. When a call came in, the dispatcher would get the address, pull open the proper drawer, and get the card for that address. It was a little slower, but it worked well. One must remember however, that any system, manual or high tech, is only as good as the person who's using it.

One night, when I was the duty captain, we were dispatched to a residence for someone having a diabetic problem. There was no other information. Since this type of problem can be quite serious, we needed to get there fast. We knew by the address that it was very close to station 1. Trouble was that there were several long, windy driveways leading to houses we couldn't see. Some of these were common drives, with more than one house on them, and sometimes smaller driveways would branch off of the main one. If we took the wrong driveway it would waste precious minutes, especially if there was no place to turn around, since then we would have to back out to the street.

Thank heaven for the house location system, right? Not really. I was first out of the firehouse in car 2. The ambulance was behind me. The dispatcher was slow and hadn't given us the information yet, so I asked for a location. The dispatcher gave me the address. I asked for the location again, and once again, I was given the address. I said that I knew the address, but I need a location for the residence. The dispatcher paused for several seconds, then repeated the address. This dispatcher wasn't really new. They had been around long enough to know our procedure and what I needed, which in this case, was information about where the house was located. This went back and forth for another couple of minutes. I was getting not only flustered, but angry. I couldn't get anything else out the dispatcher but the address. Finally, the ambulance crew radioed that they had gotten to the residence. I guess they took a chance on one of those driveways and guessed right. I followed.

It was a narrow, windy driveway leading up to a big house. This was the home of a prominent businessman in the area. His daughter was going to be married within a day or two. The bridal party was having a sleepover. There was one woman there who was unconscious, and the others, five or six young ladies, were all running around in a panic in baby doll nighties. Under other circumstances, this might have been amusing, but this patient was having a medical emergency. We packaged up the patient, got her into the ambulance, and off to the hospital. I returned to headquarters in a rage. I waited a while to cool off before going to speak to the dispatcher.

When I got down to the dispatch center and spoke to the person who was dispatching, I had cooled off enough to be nice about things. Angry and disgusted as I was, I took the time to explain procedure and why we needed that location. I guess she was having a brain cramp and screwed up. OK, all was forgiven, but never forgotten.

Sometime after that, the deputy chief and I were talking. He told me that he had spoken to some of the dispatchers, and they were of the opinion that I was a bit impatient and intolerant. He said to me, "You're a teacher. How do you account for that?"

I said, "It's very simple. When I go to teach, I don't expect my students to know anything. That's why they're in the class: to learn. But when I come to work and I have people who never seem to come to the training that is made available to them, and they say they know their jobs, but can't do it when I need it done, I get impatient."

The deputy said, "Oh, OK."

Nothing was ever done in my time to improve that dispatch center. We had good and we had bad. No one ever addressed that which was bad in order to fix it. The system is only as good as the operator.

Lessons in Scouting

Though I, myself, have never been a Boy Scout, I know many who have, as well as many adults who have been involved in scouting. It is said to be a rewarding experience with much to be learned. One Saturday morning many years ago, I was off duty and getting ready to read the morning paper. As I got up and went into the kitchen to get my shoes on, I looked out the window. There, very near my house, was a group of Boy Scouts working on a project. There was a bunch of boys and a couple of adults clearing brush from an intersection to make it easier for the traffic to see as they approached. I watched for a few minutes. I recognized the two adults as scout leaders and I guessed that this was a Boy Scout community service project. I went outside to get the paper from the driveway and stopped to talk to one of the leaders.

My guess had been correct. They were cleaning the intersection of brush. They must have gotten a special permit to burn the brush that they were cutting. It was kind of a wet, dreary day. It wasn't raining, but it had rained and the air was misty. I could see where they were trying to burn. There were some glowing embers and a little smoke, but they were not having any luck getting the fire lit. As I walked back to my house, I saw one of the leaders hand an empty one gallon milk jug to a scout and tell him to walk to a gas station around the corner and get it filled up with gasoline. I was surprised. This man had been involved in scouting for decades and should know better than to use gas, but I really didn't know for sure what he was up to, so I went inside.

About a half hour later, I was sitting in my living room reading the paper when there was what sounded like an explosion that shook the house. The windows quite literally rattled in their frames. I leaped up, ran to the kitchen window, and looked out. There was that scout leader who had given the milk jug to the boy. He was surrounded by fire and was holding the milk jug, now only half-full of gasoline, in one hand over his head. The brush pile was burning fiercely, as was all the tall grass nearby. The scout leader was dancing around trying to get out of the ring of fire. He was a large man and it surprised me that he could be so agile. But I guess given proper motivation, he was able to dance very well. It was a miracle that he, himself, was not on fire. The boys were standing around watching and not knowing what to do. I ran outside just as the man was able to dance out of the burning area. The brush was burning very nicely now.

It seems that the scout had brought back the gas. The leader had taken it and poured some, about half, right onto the glowing embers. The result was that explosion that had shaken my house. All the brush erupted in flames and that leader found himself in a tight spot. After this, they decided that they didn't need any more gas and put it away somewhere. The fire died down somewhat and nobody got hurt. I walked back to my house, shaking my head in disgust. Here was a well-seasoned Boy Scout leader teaching his charges about public service. I think there was a lesson about safety inadvertently thrown in there, too.

I just can't believe that the leader did that and didn't get hurt. Lady Luck was with him, or maybe it was divine intervention. I hope the boys were watching and learned something.

Motivation

Back quite a few years I was working a night shift at station 1, when the captain was called to the phone. There was a lady calling from her home. She told the captain that she had had a fire in the house a little while ago. It was out now, but she thought she should call and tell us so we could check it out. She must have been convincing about the fire being out because the captain went alone in car 2 to investigate.

He was gone a short while. When he returned, he left the car outside and walked into the station to get the camera out of the chief's office. He told us he needed to take some pictures. He said we wouldn't believe this. He took another man with him in the car when he went back. They took a bunch of pictures, talked to the lady, got whatever information he needed, and returned.

It was a Polaroid camera, so when he got back he was able to show us the pictures. It *was* incredible. The fire had been in her kitchen. The counter tops and the undersides of the kitchen cabinets were not only just burned, but had deep charring on them. The fire had been intense and hot. The walls had some heat and flame damage, too.

It seems that the lady was cooking dinner. She left the kitchen and while she was out of the room, something on the stove caught fire. When she came back, the fire had already spread to the cabinets and counter tops. It was between her and the room where her baby was. She picked up a small, kitchen fire extinguisher and attacked the fire. I don't know what she was thinking, or even *if* she was thinking about anything else except the baby. She did a fantastic job!

Those small, home fire extinguishers don't hold a lot. It takes skill to get as much as possible out of them without wasting the powder. It was incredible that she managed to extinguish that amount of fire with that tiny extinguisher, especially with her lack of experience using it.

I never saw the fire in person, but the pictures showed me that it had been a hot, intense fire. Many people would have panicked, but with the motivation of protecting her baby, she did what had to be done. I guess when properly motivated, almost anything is possible.

Equipment Delivery

A few years before I became an instructor at the academy, I worked in support services. That could have meant I'd be out in the yard working with student programs, fixing extinguishers, or making deliveries. The academy held many field programs in the far reaches of the state. It was our job to deliver any equipment needed for the program and pick it up after the class was over.

Making deliveries to the western part of the state was interesting. We'd have to go out to towns that were way out there. You know how when you're way up high and you look out, and even on a clear day, you can only see so far because of the curve of the Earth? Well, I often made deliveries to the small towns well beyond that! With few exceptions, it's all very small towns, with call or volunteer fire departments. You could usually find someone around at the police department, but there was never anyone in the firehouse.

I was delivering some equipment one time for a class when I went to the firehouse and, as expected, no one was there. I made a phone call to the fire academy, and they got ahold of the chief who said he'd be right there. Meanwhile, a Cadillac pulled up with an older couple in it. It was very clear that they were from a place with a full-time fire department manning the firehouse all the time. The man got out. It was apparent from the start that he had to use the bathroom badly. He came to the door. I told him there was no one home. I guess he didn't believe me, or in his desperation, he was hoping that I was wrong. He grabbed the door handle and pulled. The door was locked. He said something like, "You've gotta be shittin' me." He ran for his car and laid rubber up the street as he left in search of a bathroom. Oh boy, it sure sucked to be him.

A few minutes later, the chief arrived on his John Deere farm tractor. He'd been working on the farm and took time out to let me in to drop off the equipment.

Another time I found no one home at the police station, firehouse, or the town hall. The town hall was open, so after checking the building, top to bottom, for people, I left several boxes of the books I was delivering by a desk near the door with a note. It must have been OK. I never heard anything about it.

Another time, I showed up to pick up equipment at another small town, and was waiting for someone to come and let me in. I saw a man walking down the street toward me. I had seen guys that looked like this all through the 70s. He was kind of heavy. He had on long baggy shorts, a baggy shirt with no sleeves stretched over his belly, and flip-flops. He had long, kind of ratty hair, and a beard to match. The guy stopped. It turned out that he was the representative of the fire department. I sure wasn't used to a guy who looked like that representing the fire department. He looked like he could have just crawled out of the mud at Woodstock. We talked, and it turned out that the guy was a couple of years older than me and had gone to high school in the next town from me. He had even dated a girl that lived on my street. Who'da thunk it? I went way out, beyond the curve of the earth, to meet a guy who grew up next door.

High among the funny days spent making deliveries, was a day I went out with another guy, a friend of mine, to deliver ladders to a town way out near the northwest corner of the state. It was a long trip and took about three hours to get there, especially in the truck we were driving. When we got into the area, we looked around. The country was beautiful out there. We missed a turn, but no problem, we just went up the road, into the next state, and turned around. We came back, made the turn, and drove way up to the top of a hill to the firehouse. Man, the firehouse was built into the woods with only a narrow grass strip between the building and the forest. It was strange and quiet. I thought I could hear the banjo player from the movie, *Deliverance*. There was no one around and the firehouse was locked, so we got back into the truck and drove back down the hill in search of a phone.

When we got to the bottom, a man stepped out and flagged us down. I looked and saw that behind him was an auto body shop. It was called *Bona's Auto Body*. Well, it turns out that this man was Bona, himself. He was a slouched, dirty-looking man, with one tooth in the front. We stopped and Bona held out a key on a large tag. He said, "Thought you'd be back for this!" He told us that the fire chief works in another town and leaves the key with him.

So, getting this straight in my mind, we had to drive to the auto body shop and see a guy named "Bona" to get the key to the firehouse. Gee, why didn't we think of that in the first place? OK. Well, we took the key, went up and dropped off our ladders, and returned the key to Bona.

I never really liked making these deliveries, but experiences like this made it all worth it. Needless to say, it made for some interesting conversation on the return trip.

Everyone Treated Equal

For most of its existence, the fire service has been staffed by men. That would be males. Once it would have been white males, but other groups made their way in, but for many years, it was still the men's club. There are many in our ranks who think it should still be that way. However, some years back, women started to infiltrate our ranks and now they're here to stay. That's never been a problem with me. Just about all the places I've worked, I've worked with women. In the ambulance business, I spent many a day with a female partner and those were some of my best days. The truth is, I don't have a problem working with anybody, no matter what race they are; religion they practice; sexual persuasion; or gender; just as long as they do their job. If they don't know something, I tell them to ask and we'll get along just fine.

On my fire department, we had two female firefighters. We were all a bit apprehensive when the first one was appointed. It was a big change for us. She worked out fine. She just kind of blended in. She was one who didn't have much to say and just went about her job. She did what she was asked to do and wasn't afraid of work.

When the next female arrived, things were different. For one thing, this woman was not afraid to express an opinion. She was much more outspoken. She'd sit right in the middle of the guys talking and telling stories and joking and the like. Many of the guys were sort of afraid of her. Where she was so outspoken many were afraid that they'd say something wrong in front of her and be called on the carpet for sexual harassment or something like that. I had worked with this woman a few years back in the ambulance business. We both worked for the same private company for a little while. I left shortly after she was hired, so I only had a little time to get to know her. I knew her well enough to know that I had to censor very little of what I said in front of her. Some of the guys would tell me that I'd better watch what I said to her or I'd get in trouble, but I wasn't worried.

Before this woman was appointed to the department full time, she was a call firefighter for a while. The training officer at the time didn't like her for some reason or other. Maybe he thought she didn't belong, I don't know. The call department would drill in the evening once a month. This would happen on a night when the training officer was working. I worked on the same group, so I often assisted in the drills. One month, the training officer was not going to be in on drill night and asked me if I would take over the drill for that night. I love to train, so I agreed. I decided on an SCBA drill for that night. I put them on air, blacked out their face pieces, and sent them into the darkened basement of the firehouse with a goal: either find their way out or find a victim. It was a very successful drill on search and rescue without the benefit of eyesight. They were all very pleased with the drill.

After the drill, the female firefighter came up to me with a request. She asked if any new equipment, specifically turnout gear, had come in. I said that I didn't think so. I didn't know that we needed anything new. She showed me what she had been issued. She had no hood or helmet, her gloves were too big, and her boots were huge on her. She did have a coat that was acceptable. I asked why she was issued that gear, and she told me that the training officer had said that there wasn't anything else. Well, I knew that that wasn't true. I took a chance that no one would object if I issued this call firefighter the proper gear. I told her to follow me and we went to the gear storage area. There was a whole box of new helmets. I gave her one. I found boots that fit her, and gave her a hood and the right size gloves. When we were done, she had everything she was supposed to have. She was happy and left.

The next day when the deputy chief came on duty, he called me aside and asked me how that female firefighter had done the night before. I told him that I had no problem with her and she did everything that I asked, just like all the guys. The deputy told me that he'd been getting some bad reports about her from the training officer. I said that I didn't see any problem with her. Then I told the deputy about the gear she had been issued in the beginning and how, on my authority as training officer du jour, I had issued her equipment that fit and some things that she didn't have before. He asked me why she hadn't been given the right equipment from the beginning. I didn't know and told him so. Then I said that I knew that some of the guys were apprehensive about her. I said that if people were worried about being accused of discrimination or sexual harassment, the fastest way to get in trouble would be to treat her differently than everybody else. A good place to start was to give her the same gear that we issued to everybody.

It Can Happen Anytime

After a snowy winter comes a rainy spring, and if it's rainy enough, the river that runs through our town will overflow its banks. The whole center of town is usually under water and traffic has to be routed around the center. Right near the center of town is a typical country road. It is windy and a bit hilly. The river passes very near this road as it feeds into a pond. When the river overflows, most of this road can be under several feet of water. One part of the road is up higher than the rest. Even during the deepest flooding, this section, as well as the side streets that run off of it, always stay above the water. There is water on all sides, cutting it off from all other streets. The area is called the "island," of course!

There are a large number of houses on the island, with people who have to get off to go to work in the morning and come home at night. They also need the protection that the fire department provides. Usually, before the water is too deep, we will drive an engine out to the island and staff it 24 hours a day.

The last several times the floods have come, the Army National Guard has provided 2.5-ton Army trucks. They have the ground clearance to drive through the high water, and can hold quite a few people. It's not very comfortable, but what the hell; it's not a cruise after all.

Before the Army stepped in to help, we used the fire department boats. These were pretty small boats that couldn't hold many people. They were staffed by firefighters. During one of those times, I came on duty for a day shift at station 1. We had been running the boats for a couple of days. The boats ran on a schedule. During the time between runs to the island, the boat crew came to the firehouse to rest and warm up. One of these men was an older man. I couldn't say how old he was, but his son went to school with me, graduated the same year, and was on the fire department. In fact, he was working at station 2 that day.

During a break, the man came into the firehouse. He started across the apparatus floor and stopped to talk to me as we stood behind the ambulance. As we talked, I noticed the man was getting very hard to understand, and he had a kind of faraway look about him. I thought he was just tired. All of a sudden, he started to shake, then convulse. Then he started to fall. It was like his feet were frozen in place and he just toppled over. I caught him before he hit the floor. He wasn't conscious as I laid him on the floor and called for the ambulance crew. The two guys working on the ambulance that day were just in the next room. They came in and evaluated him, then got him on a stretcher and into the ambulance. Then they pulled out the door, heading south, toward the nearest hospital. The engine from station 2 was dispatched to meet the ambulance on the road and supply another man for the transport. It seems that the patient had stopped breathing.

When the engine and ambulance met, the spare man from the engine got off to join the ambulance crew to help with their patient. It was then that someone realized that that man was the patient's son. They told him to get in and drive, while the ambulance driver got into the patient compartment to help with the patient. As he got into the driver's seat, he asked if it was his father. He was answered, "Yes."

Well, the transport went smoothly. They were able to restore the patient's pulse and breathing. It was found that the patient had some form of clot or obstruction that had made its way to his head. As the clot passed through his brain, that's when his breathing and heartbeat stopped.

The crew did well with the patient care, and the driver did very well, also. It's the mark of a professional when you can separate yourself from the situation and do what has to be done.

The patient got lucky. He did recover, but he had to retire after that. I guess we never know what can happen. A man is seemingly healthy, and suddenly this happens, ending his career. I guess it can happen anytime, but at least he survived to tell about it.

Square Peg

I guess everyone has known someone at some time in their lives that just didn't fit in. The fire service is no different. I've seen many who had dreams of being a firefighter. There are also those that just want to wear the uniform and don't care for the work. Hopefully, these people are found and weeded out before they get past their probation. Like everything else, though, firefighting isn't for everyone. Some people just don't fit in. My department has had several over the years that I can think of. Two stand out. One of them wanted to jump right in and be one of the guys, but he didn't want to listen. That doesn't work. You have to come in and keep your mouth shut. Listen to what's said and learn. I think this guy wanted to be the boss and had dreams of glory. Well, it didn't take this guy long to get weeded out, although he stayed loosely affiliated with the fire service. He ended up selling fire apparatus and equipment.

The other square peg that I remember was a guy who just came one day and got a job as a part-timer, a call man. I really don't know why he wanted to come on the fire department. He didn't really seem to have an awful lot of interest. This guy stood out in a crowd. I don't know what there was about him, but he was different. He lived in an apartment in town with his girlfriend, and they both were strange. She would come in with him and be wearing all black, with black lipstick, and hair that looked like it hadn't seen a comb, brush, or a wash for some time, as well as the rest of her makeup that was, well, bad! He always seemed to be kind of lost in space and talked the way we associate with the drug culture: "Like Wow, Man. Far out," and things like that.

Well, right or wrong, a guy like that labels

himself as strange, and the guys pick up on it and don't want him around. He did some odd things. He called the ambulance to his apartment early one morning, because he had cut his finger on that old type of pull top from a beer can and he needed a Band-Aid. Another time, he called up early in the morning to say that his dog had just come home and smelled like smoke. He said that there might be a fire somewhere. Things like this really endeared him to the guys.

One night during his time with us, we had a house fire. I was off duty and came back when recalled. I caught one of the first engines responding and ended up at the fire. This fire was strange. It seemed to be all contained inside the walls. No furniture got burned, unless it was up against the wall. Two inside staircases had burned away. We spent a lot of time cutting holes and opening walls and ceilings, chasing the fire to put it out.

At one point, the incident commander called for another engine company for more manpower. At the firehouse, a bunch of guys started to get onto the engine, including our square peg. He was told to get off and stay behind to man the station. I was at the fire, but I heard that that the guy yelled and threw a tantrum. He finally stood in front of the engine so it couldn't leave the firehouse—or so he thought.

As he stood there, the captain in the front seat told the driver to go, and go he did! Our square peg friend had to jump out of the way.

Since this was at night in the winter, we were all cold. Finally, it was decided to send coffee to us at the fire scene. Guess who wangled his way onto the coffee truck? That's right: our buddy! I was working inside the house when he arrived. I remember seeing him run from the coffee truck into the house. He ran through the house and right up where the stairs had been. The stairs were gone, but we had a ladder lying in the stairwell for access to the upper floor. I watched as he made his way, at a run, all the way to the attic. He then stopped and looked around, with no idea of what to do next. He was told to assist in setting up lighting, so out he went.

A little while later, I decided to get a cup of coffee. Since I was on the first floor, I climbed out a window. I was right next to that window: it was faster than the door on the other side of the house. I really needed that cup of hot coffee. When I got out of the window, I looked up and there was our pal, screaming an order at me to go get him another length of extension cord. He was standing there, holding onto the plug at the end of the cord that was stretched to its full length. In his other hand, he held the end of a cord that was attached to a portable spotlight that was teetering on the sill in an attic window above. He was looking down at his hands and at the cords, as if he were trying to figure out how to stretch the cords to get the two more feet he needed. I looked at him, shook my head, and went to get coffee. He should have put the cords down and gone to get another length. Or better yet, he could have made sure he had enough when he left the truck. Then again, we didn't need a spotlight in the attic anyway, so if he had done what he was told in the first place, he wouldn't have run out of cord.

Anyway, after that fire I never saw him again. There was still the dread that he'd show up again, but he never did. He must have lost interest. I remember hearing, some time later, that he had died. I never heard from what. Eventually, he faded from memory. There's no one there now who would remember him. He was just a square peg.

Some Never Learn

One winter night when I was the duty captain, things had been pretty quiet. There was a light snow falling, just enough to make the roads slippery. With nothing happening, I went to bed around 10 p.m. Not too long after, we were awakened when the house lights came on and the bell started tapping out a box number. This is what happens when a fire alarm box is pulled from the street. The box was on the south side of town.

I got dressed, put on my bunker gear, and responded in the car, while the other firefighters on duty got dressed and prepared to respond with the ladder. The streets were slippery, but almost no traffic was on them. I made good time getting across town. When I got to the location of the box, there was a car up against the pole that the box was mounted on. The car had slid off the road and into the pole, tripping the box.

The crew from the engine company was talking to the driver of the car. I radioed back to cancel the ladder and have them respond with the ambulance instead. The police were there also. I seem to remember that they had detained the driver of the car. I don't believe he was hurt too badly, but he went to the hospital to be examined.

As I walked around, I noticed that the passenger side windshield had been hit very hard and pushed out. It looked as if someone's whole body had smashed into it. I asked who the passenger was. Out of the small crowd of people gathered to watch, a young man stepped out. He told me that he had been the passenger. He had not been wearing a seat belt and the car had no airbags. Though he said he didn't have any injuries, the mechanism of injury told us this man could have some very serious injuries that might not become apparent until later. I tried for all I was worth to get this man to go to the hospital. He kept refusing. I can't *make* anybody go. He seemed to be perfectly aware of what had happened, and he understood everything I told him, including what I said might happen later. I told him that if he had any problem later, to try and get himself to an emergency room. He signed the release papers.

Just then, a pickup truck pulled up with a woman inside. She told us she was the young man's mother. I pulled her aside, showed her the windshield, told her what her son had told us, and that he signed a release form declining our advice about going to the hospital. I said that she would be doing him a favor if she could convince him to be checked out. Then, he got into the truck with her and they left. I later heard that she drove him right to the hospital and told him to be examined. I guess he was more afraid of his mother than anything else.

I have seen many windshields pushed out by heads, but I'd never seen one quite like this. So much of it was pushed out, like it was hit hard by something large. I heard that they didn't find any serious injury with that man who hit the windshield. He was very lucky. Not very smart, though.

One night about a week later, his luck ran out. He was the one driving this time when he got into another accident. I don't remember whether he hit another car or a tree or a pole, but he this time he hit his head and lost consciousness. The car burst into flames. He burned to death before anyone could reach him. It's too bad the lesson was wasted. That's about all that can be said.

The New Guy

Usually when one leaves a job for one reason or another, a two-week notice is customary, if one wants to leave in good standing. It's not a good idea, usually, to burn bridges. New employers know this too, and will usually allow any new employee the chance to give notice to the employer that they are leaving. Fire chiefs certainly know that, and also give any new hires the chance to leave their former job in good standing. However, that isn't always the case.

We had a chief a few years ago, that did everything by the seat of his pants. He lived for the moment and never gave a thought to any repercussions. We had an opening for a full-time firefighter once. The chief wanted the slot filled right away. He called the next person on the appointment list, one of our call firefighters, and told him that if he wanted the job, "Be there tonight." So much for leaving in good standing!

Imagine putting the kid in that kind of a situation. Well, he wanted the job, so he made a call, did some talking to his employer, and quit. He reported for work at station 1 that night. I don't know who else knew, but I didn't find out until I came to work that night. In walked this guy, in uniform, and said that he was starting work that night. That kind of put us in a bad position, too. Here was a new guy, coming to work for the first time, and on a night shift. Yes, we all knew him, but he hadn't really been trained or briefed on station procedures or anything else.

I said to the kid, "Come with me." He followed me out to the engine. I pointed to a seat and said, "If we go out, you sit here. Follow me and don't touch anything, and do as I tell you." He was also to be third man on the ambulance crew. What a way to break in. Talk about throwing a guy to the dogs.

When he finally did go for basic training, he went to a different academy than everyone else on our department. It was a private academy, run by a city for their own firefighters. Our chief was mad at the state fire academy for some reason, and didn't want to send our man there. He used some influence and got him into that city's training academy. At the city academy, training was geared toward that city's fire department and how *they* did things. He got an education, but not the well-rounded one he would have gotten at the state academy. He was a good kid and caught on and eventually did well, but he got off to a rough start, thanks to a boss that just wanted things done "right away."

Training Burn, July

There is no substitution for experience on our job. The next best thing is training, a lot of it. Training burns are great. I had done many over the years, but the ones we held in an acquired structure, like a house that was going to be torn down, were the best.

A few years ago, we acquired a small house to use for training. It was on a corner of two busy roads. It had an unfinished, workshop-type basement. Next door to the house, there was an old fruit and vegetable stand, and behind it was a large cornfield. The farmer lived in the house, grew his corn out back, and sold it in the stand on the corner. He was retiring and had sold his land to a developer who was going to build condos. We got the house to have fires in for training, but we were not going to burn the place down.

I was asked to be the official igniter. My job was to build and light the fires. I could rest while others put out the fire, then back in I went to set up the next one. For fuel, we used straw and pallets. The straw burns hot and fast. That makes it possible to do multiple fires in a short period. We use pallets for keeping the straw up off of the floor as we spread the fires around the room.

Being the diabolical bastard that I am, I like to get creative with my fires. I like to stuff cupboards and cabinets with straw, then load up the rest of the room with pallets and more straw to make the fires big and hot. We had to be careful though. Since we were not going to burn the house down to the ground, we had to make sure the fire didn't get into the walls. If it did, we'd have a real house fire on our hands, and all the inherent danger that goes with it.

We scheduled two evenings of controlled burns. One big problem was that it was July and it was as hot as anyone could remember. Everyone had to make sure they drank water and rested, or we could have problems with people dropping from the heat. This drill was for only our department. Often neighboring towns will be invited to take part, but where this was located, there wasn't enough room for more than our own guys. There was a lieutenant who was to be incident commander, I was to be igniter, and other people were designated as safety officers. We had another man who was to do nothing but run the pump. He was wearing his bunker pants with no coat or helmet.

I remember the first fire was a basement fire. I did that one right. The crew's entry was delayed until the fire really got going, then they were sent in against a wall of flames. After lighting it, I managed to get out through a staircase that took me into the house. The door to the outside was full of fire.

Things went along like that for the first night. We had all kinds of fires, big and small, in different rooms. The heat was brutal. Every time I came out after setting a fire, I'd drop my gear and air pack, then sit and drink as much water as I could in the time I had. It never seemed like enough time, but this was fun learning.

If that first night was tough, the next night sucked all the strength out of everybody. Funny how heat can do that. By the second night, it was tough to build the fires, put on all my gear, light the fire, go on bottled air, and then make my way out. I couldn't get my gear off fast enough. Everybody was dragging from the heat, both from my fires and the weather.

Finally came time for the last fire. It was to be in the kitchen. This gave me a lot of opportunities to make the fire big and hard to fight. I took my time building it. When it was done, I was proud. It was a thing of beauty. I was dead tired and hot, but it was done. I lit the fire and bailed out. Then I quickly dropped my gear to cool off, and watched the attack on my handiwork. It was looking good: heavy smoke pushing out and flames following. They pushed out from around the door. I knew someone was going to wet their pants when they opened the door.

Then, all of a sudden, the officer in charge of that attack line panicked. He threw open the door, opened his line, and went right in. This was way before the fire had reached its intended size and intensity. At least one third of the straw that I'd so carefully laid out, got soaked. Thanks to one panicked officer, they missed out on what should have been one hell of a fire.

Well, the training was over and we started to pick up. Suddenly, there was a commotion. It seems that the man who did nothing but stay outside the building to run the pump, who wasn't even wearing his turnout coat, was overcome by the heat and passed out. Guess it's a good thing he didn't have to go near the fire.

After what seemed like forever picking up, I went home to shower. I could hardly move. The heat had sucked all the strength out of me. My joints ached. Even my hair was tired and sore. Those live burns are great, but maybe next time we can avoid doing them in mid July.

Sorry, We Can Help

In our fire department, each shift has always been run by a captain or the deputy. In later years, we added the rank of lieutenant and put him at station 2. Whoever is running the shift commands two stations, so they have to visit station 2 at least once during the shift.

One afternoon, back before we had lieutenants, I was on duty at station 2 with another guy. He was a little younger than me, but we were of the same vintage. The captain was over to visit and we were all in the day room talking, when in walked a young lady looking for help. It seems that this lady had just had her car worked on at a local car repair shop where they had fixed a tire for her. She had driven as far as our firehouse when the tire went flat. She put it up on the jack, but they had put the lug nuts on so tight that she couldn't get them to budge. She asked if we could help her. The captain turned to speak. He was in command, so we stayed quiet. The captain told her that we could get her a police officer if she wanted, or she could make a call, but we couldn't help her change her tire. I was completely embarrassed. She turned and left the firehouse, and the captain just went right back to our conversation.

Soon, the captain decided to head back to headquarters. He got up and walked to the door. We followed and looked out through the glass of the door. There was the girl, by the edge of the road, having a horrible time. The car was up on the jack and she was using that crappy lug wrench, the kind that gets supplied with the car. They're junk and almost never do anything but round off the lug nuts. She was in tears as the captain got into car 2 and drove right past her.

As soon as he was gone, my partner and I went outside. I got a big four-way lug wrench out of my car. We went over to the lady and said that the captain was gone. We could help her now. She stood up and dried her eyes, as my partner and I had her tire changed in about three or four minutes. She was grateful, and I think a bit confused, as she got into her car.

I have to say that I have never felt so ashamed and embarrassed in all my career as when the captain said we couldn't help her, without at least looking at the problem. Once left on our own, my partner and I managed to serve the public and at least preserve the image of the firehouse as a place you could go for help, a place where people cared. Sorry Capt., but I guess we *can* help, after all.

To the Rescue

I have been asked many times through the years, what made me decide to become a firefighter. I usually answer that I really don't know. I had friends whose fathers were firefighters, and I used to chase fire engines with them. I guess most little boys will chase fire trucks, but I got to know something about what was going on when they got to the fire. This kept on until long after most others stopped chasing the trucks.

At several points in my early adulthood, I wondered what I was going to do with myself. Firefighting sounded interesting, so I thought I'd give it a try. I did well on the tests and finally got a job. And the rest, as they say, is history.

But there is another story that may have unconsciously influenced my decision. From the time I was a little kid, my family used to go to a place up north that belonged to a friend of my Dad. This place was in the wilderness. It was an old farm from the 1700s. The original house had burned down, who knows when, and the new house, which was quite old, was on the other side of the yard. The house was full of antiques, from the furniture to the old newspapers and all the other interesting things we would find in the attic.

If you went for a walk in the woods, eventually you'd come to the stone walls that are so common in New England. Generations ago, farmers cleared the land and stacked the stones they had removed to make walls around their fields. There was a spring where the cows used to drink, long before anyone alive now remembers. It's all kind of grown over now, but it's still there. There is a family cemetery in a clearing in the woods, not far from the house. The marked graves are from the early to mid 1800s. There are several unmarked graves, too. There was no one around for many miles. If you went for a walk in those woods, you brought some kind of protection, usually a gun. We did a lot of shooting there. There were all kinds of wild animals in those woods. The only rattlesnake I ever saw in the wild was in those woods. I loved that place. That was where we would spend our vacations.

Sometimes we would go there with the people who owned the place, sometimes it was just us. My Dad would get the key and we would spend time having fun. Dad was very strict about how we left the place. Of course, we'd leave it clean and orderly, but Dad always said that if we left anything out, animals might get into the house and do some damage.

At the end of one trip, we put everything in order, packed up, and got into the car. It was a 1966 Chevrolet Bel Air. It was a four door and had seatbelts. No one used them in those days, though. Dad was driving and I was in the right front seat, with my little sister in the middle. Mom and my other sister were in the back. We started for home. The first few miles were on a long dirt road. This area was so isolated that hardly anyone ever traveled on that road. You could sit and watch all day, and see only two or three cars.

We had been on the road home about a half hour when Dad asked if everyone was *sure* that everything had been put away. I don't remember who it was, but someone wasn't sure that they'd put the butter away. Well, Dad having the temper that he did, lost it. He made a quick U-turn and started back, all the while yelling at us for forgetting things.

We finally turned off the highway onto the dirt road where the house was located. Dad was still mad, still yelling, and driving too fast. What were the chances that there'd be another car on that road? Well, as we went speeding around a turn, Murphy's Law kicked into high gear. In the middle of the road there was another car coming the other way. Our cars met, left fender to left fender. My little sister slid off the front seat, into the dash, and split her head open. Dad told me to hold my sister and keep pressure to her head, while he got out to check on everybody else. Nobody else was hurt, but it seemed that my sister was hurt enough for everybody.

I said Murphy's Law kicked into high gear because a few minutes later, along came another car. I never could have imagined it. In this car was just a father and his son. That car stopped and the man and the boy got out. He said to my dad to bring my little sister and come with him. He told his son to stay with us and he would be back. Dad and my sister got into the man's car and they took off, driving fast toward a town, and hopefully a hospital.

My Mom, sister, and the people in the other car just waited around for the police to come. We thought Dad would call them from the hospital. I was walking up and down the road with the son of our savior. He was a year or two younger than me. He saw the look of concern on my face, and he said something like, "Don't worry. My Dad's a fireman. He'll take care of things and everything will be all right."

After what seemed like a century, the police came, and a while later my Dad got back with the fireman. My sister had a bunch of stitches in her head, but was otherwise all right. With a little work with a crow bar, retrieved from the farm where we stayed, both cars were drivable, so we all were on our way again.

I never forgot what that boy said, "Don't worry. My Dad's a fireman..."

That was the summer of 1968. I was fourteen. Six years later, I got on the call fire department, and two years later, I was appointed full time. I worked 33 years for that department and retired as a captain. Do I think this incident may have had something to do with my decision? I don't know, but it's never left my mind.

It Ain't Gone Yet

It's interesting to see some of the things that go on at the firehouse. I remember seeing one guy scoop salad out of a bowl with his bare hand. You know he doesn't do that at home. We had a guy take great pride in washing his coffee cup. He would turn on the hot water, tip the dish detergent bottle over, give it a squeeze, and let the cup fill. The result was more water than he needed to use, enough dish soap to wash a whole sink full of dishes, a sink absolutely full of soap suds that spilled out onto the floor, and a cup that still wasn't clean.

Funny how the sink could have dishes in it, since no one would admit to leaving dirty dishes there. In the past, we had a person who started to throw away dishes and silverware that other people left in the sink. When we ran out of things, that person was told to stop.

I cleaned the kitchen one morning at station 1. Right after I was done, another guy, a newer guy to boot, had his breakfast and put the dishes in the sink. He was going to leave them there until he finished his housework. Never mind that I had just cleaned the kitchen. I spoke to the officer and he told the man to clean them up *now*. The guy did, and he was pissed off at me. Tough.

There is a funny thing that happens all the time and seems to be indigenous to the firehouse, any firehouse. I've talked about this with many firefighters from all over, and it's always the same story. We've even laughed about this at the fire academy. I'm talking about the firefighters' unwillingness to eat the last piece of anything. Or maybe it's just that they don't want to wash the plate.

There can be a cake that someone brought in or that was donated. The guys will eat it, possibly over days. When it's almost gone, people keep taking smaller pieces. Soon, there might be a piece left that's so thin you could almost see through it. Still, the guys will cut pieces off of that small piece. When told that maybe they should wash the plate, the answer is, "It ain't gone yet. There's still some left."

It works that way with cake, pie, cookies, ice cream, leftover dinner items, or whatever. It's amazing how small a piece you can cut off a crumb, and you'll hear the guy taking it say, "There's still some left." It's the same phenomenon in every firehouse. No one wants to be credited with having eaten the last morsel—then you gotta wash the plate!

The Assistance We Provide

When the very first assisted living facility opened in our town, it was a new concept to many of us. We had been to nursing homes and elderly housing projects, but this was different. This facility had apartments for elderly people, with medical staff right on hand. It was like a combination of nursing home and elderly housing.

"Assisted living" was what it was called, but we soon found out *who* provided most of the assistance. They would call the fire department for every little thing. It didn't seem like the staff did any assisting at all, or at least, very little. They cut down the duty staff at night, as do most places like that, including hospitals. Just enough staff was there to take care of the residents, except that *we* took care of the residents. Every little bump or complaint resulted in a call to the fire department for the ambulance. One night, a resident asked a staff member for a Tylenol for a headache. The fire department was called. On our arrival, that staff member found out that we didn't carry medications on our ambulance. No problem. The ambulance returned.

When that facility first opened, we were called one night and found the door locked. There was an electronic lock on the door with a key pad. We needed to know the combination to get in. Often, places like that will give us a key or combination in advance. This time, we didn't have it, so we banged on the door. A man appeared, not at the door, but back a little way from the door. We could see him and he saw us. All he did was wave and smile at us. Finally, someone arrived who knew the number and let us in. It turned out that the man waving at us was a non-English speaking assistant who didn't know the number anyway.

The next time I came to work, we had the combination number on a note pad in our vehicles, with orders not to give it to the staff who worked there. Sounded strange to me then, and it still does. I thought maybe they locked them in like guard dogs.

Well, it wasn't too long afterward that those locks were gone. One afternoon, we got a call for a "man lying in the middle of the road" in a neighborhood not too far from this assisted living facility. Engine 2, the ambulance, and the police responded. The man was face down in the street, just like the caller said. He was conscious, but unable to tell us anything. He had clearly fallen on his face. His nose was bleeding and his face was pretty scratched up. The man cooperated, though. As we were securing him to a backboard for transport, a car pulled up and a woman got out. She explained that this man had "escaped" from the assisted living facility from the Alzheimer's unit. She was responsible for the patient and went with him to the hospital.

It was shortly after that that I found out just where the Alzheimer's unit was. Ironically, it was called the "Reminiscence Unit." We were directed back to that part of the building when someone had fallen down and gotten injured. I thought it was interesting that an electronic lock with a number pad was on the door to enter this unit. The door swung inward. There was another door to exit that swung outward. That door also had an electronic lock with a number pad. The number for the exit door was different from the number for the entry door.

Any time we went there, we would always hear soft music playing throughout the unit. The residents would all be sitting and staring off into space or shuffling around. I always got an eerie feeling going in there. We were locked in and had to rely on a staff member to let us out. One could easily dream up a nightmare that involved being trapped in that place.

There is a second floor in the assisted living facility where residents also live. The elevator has got to be one of the slowest on the face of the Earth. We were often on that second floor for calls. When our patient was almost ready for transport, whenever possible I would to try to go down the hall in advance and capture the elevator for our use. I had to. One can understand that the residents move very slowly. That, coupled with the slowness of the elevator itself, might let rigor mortis set in while we waited for the elevator to return.

All in all, it's kind of an interesting place. With all of the assistance we provide, it sure increased our number of calls per year since they opened. As I sit and think about it, my mind drifts back to the Alzheimer's unit again. I told my kids that if they ever put me in a place like that, they had best be on their guard. All I'd need is one lucid moment to escape, and then there would be no place on the globe they could hide.

The Principle of the Thing

A year or two before I retired, we had a big lightning storm one night in late summer, just before school was about to begin. Lightning struck the high school and burned out their fire alarm system. This system is required by law to be up and operating when school is in session. Without it, a fire department detail has to be present. This firefighter would walk around the campus with a radio, prepared to call for help, if needed. Since it was going to take some time to fix the system, the school department hired a firefighter to be present in the school for each day that school was in session.

After turning down a few chances to work this detail, I finally decided to take one. The money was good and there wasn't too much to do. I walked around all morning and talked to people that I knew. When lunchtime came, I went into the teachers' cafeteria. They were serving pizza. I got two slices and went to pay. They told me I didn't owe them anything. I asked what they meant. The pizza wasn't expensive but there was a cost. This banter went on for a few minutes. I kept saying I wanted to pay, and they kept saying I didn't have to.

They looked at me like I was crazy. Finally, I asked if the teachers had to pay. I was told, "Yes."

Then I said that I was getting paid well for the day and I was going to pay, just like everybody else. They finally relented and took my money.

Maybe I'm nuts, but it didn't feel right, kind of dishonest, to take the lunch for free. Many times, I have enjoyed hot coffee, given to me free on a cold night, while fighting a fire. Sometimes, we would even get some food. That was different. We were working, and tired, cold, and wet. Here, I wasn't doing anything but walking around and getting paid well for it. I didn't care what other people had done on this detail. There is a time and a place for everything, and this wasn't the time or place for this. It was a small thing, but it's the principle that counts.

The Unexplained

Over the years, I've seen people do a lot of stupid things. Sometimes they weren't paying attention or didn't read the directions. Sometimes they just plain didn't know what the hell they were doing, and didn't care. Often they were young people who, as we all know, are going to live forever and so they do as many foolish things as possible. Add being under the influence of alcohol, or something else, to that youthful behavior and often we have disaster in the making.

One thing that still remains a mystery to me in several ways happened on a New Year's Eve. That was one of the nights of the year when things could get very busy in EMS, and sometimes very interesting. We were called with the ambulance to a large residence in town. There was a big party going on. They were all young people attending the party, mid to older teenagers. That led me to believe that the adults were out of the house for the night, and Junior, whoever that might have been, decided to have a party. The house was so full of partiers that we found it hard to find, let alone get to, our patient. Many people tried to tell us where the patient was, but with various degrees of intoxication and all the noise, we had a hard time understanding them.

Finally, we found our patient in the large entryway in the home. It was a boy, between sixteen and eighteen, who was semi-conscious on the tile floor. He was not able to tell us what happened to him. Someone told us that he had jumped from up above where he had landed. I looked up. There above us was a kind of balcony on the second floor that looked down on the first floor, just inside of the front door. I guess he just got up on the railing and dove off onto the next floor down below. Luckily, he didn't land on anyone.

We brought in our c-spine immobilization equipment and started to package him up. As we worked, the crowd started to push in close. It seemed that everyone who had had a few drinks, and *that* was nearly everybody there, wanted to offer help. We asked several times for the crowd to move back. No one listened and the crowd pushed in closer. We finished as best we could, loaded the patient onto the stretcher, and started to push our way out.

    I don't recall if the police were there or not, but I can't see that they could have done us much good. When we made the outside, there was a feeling of relief. I felt like we had had a narrow escape—from what, I don't know. But it felt good to be outside. I don't remember how the kid made out. I have always wondered, though, what had made him do something so stupid.

The Way You Taught Me

When I was a lieutenant, I became training officer. In our department, each officer was responsible for commanding a shift, as well as having another duty. One was the EMS coordinator. One was responsible for keeping track of our turnout gear, and ordering more as needed. I was responsible for making the training schedule for the entire department, and for training our ten call firefighters. As a lieutenant, I was second in command of my shift. On those occasions when the captain was out, I was in command.

I still kept the training officer job when I was promoted to captain. In addition to my training officer responsibilities, now I also had command of a shift. The schedule for the call firefighters' training sessions varied through the years. Training sessions were held on weekends for a while, and at a later date, the training was changed to weeknights. Whenever it was done, I always believed in practical training. I wasn't going to put on a video telling how to do something, when everyone would get more out of it if we went outside and *did* it. We raised ladders, ran pumps, drove engines, practiced water rescue, and a host of other things. I always believed in showing my guys how to do something. I may have talked a lot, but as I talked, I got down on the floor and *showed* them what I wanted them to do, and how I wanted it done. They saw me do it first. Then they did it, whatever "it" was.

For a while, we had a chief who for some reason seemed to hire call firefighters from distant towns. They were really too far away to respond to a call for assistance from our town. I worked with what I was given, and they were all good men and one woman. They just lived too far away to be useful to us. After a while, most of the ones that lived far away left us for full time appointments elsewhere, and our newer call men lived nearer.

Finally, it was down to just one guy who lived far away. He was a good kid, very quiet, and tended to keep to himself. You never really knew what he was thinking. He would just be there and watch. Then he'd do what he was told, and most often, did it right. Finally, there came a time when this man told us that he had gotten a full time appointment in another town and would be leaving us. The department who hired him always sent their new people to recruit training at the state firefighting academy for their initial training. Since I was a recruit instructor at that academy, I knew I'd be seeing him again.

Sure enough, some weeks later a new class started and my old call man was in the class. I didn't get any real chance to talk to him for a while. Personal interaction with the recruits by the instructors is discouraged. However, some weeks into their training, I was walking down a hall and along came my man. They were on a break and he was wandering the halls alone, looking at the pictures and plaques from past classes displayed on the walls. There was no surprise in seeing him by himself in the hall. He was still a bit different, always someone who seemed to be happy with his own company.

As I approached him in the hall, he looked up. I stopped and asked him how things were going. He told me that things were going fine and he was doing well. Then he said something that made me feel good and proud. He said, "Whenever they are going to show us something new, I already know where they're headed with it because that's the way you taught me."

That's the way I taught him. He listened, learned, and remembered. He used it to help himself in his further training getting ready for his career. I was very proud of him, and I guess I must have done something right, too.

Surprise!

I was on duty at headquarters in the early evening in the summer, when we were dispatched with the ambulance to the next town over for an MVA. This town has a lot of pastureland with horses and cattle. The place we were going was about a three mile run for us. When we got close, we saw that a car had gone off the road, knocked down a fence post and the attached fence, then continued on into the pasture. There were no animals in the pasture at that time.

The host town had an engine sitting on the roadside and the crew was with the patient, about 75 yards into the field. We were not going to risk driving the ambulance into the pasture, so we parked and started to get our tools and the stretcher ready to take them out to the patient. The officer from the engine company was standing with his crew and yelling something to us. At that time, there weren't too many portable radios around, like there are today. We couldn't hear him or understand his hand signals. We thought maybe he was telling us to hurry.

My partner led as we pushed the stretcher out into the pasture. We were following the path of the car. As we got near to where it had knocked over the fence post, I saw my partner start to twitch, then slap at the air. It was then that I noticed specks in the air around him. The specks turned out to be bees. Their nest had been in the ground, next to the post that was hit, and they were angry. My partner danced for a second, then broke into a run, dragging the stretcher behind him. I willingly followed.

We got out to the patient and the crew from the host town, where the officer was laughing. He said that he'd tried to tell us about the bees. He got a kick out of it when I asked how the hell we were supposed to hear him all that distance away.

Well, the patient went to the hospital and wasn't hurt too badly. We gave the bees a wide berth on the way back to the ambulance. What luck, of all the posts in that fence line, the car had to hit that one, and we walked right into it. Well anyway, I found out that day that my partner could dance. I don't know what step he was doing, but it was interesting.

Lesson Learned, Hopefully

As recruit firefighters progress through the weeks of basic training, there are many things learned. Many of these are not part of the written curriculum, but important nonetheless. One day during live burn training, it may have been phase-3 burns, I had command of the rescue company. Our job was to go onto the floors above the fire, ahead of the lines, to check for victims and report on conditions and fire extension. The rescue company was talking about what they'd do if trapped by the fire and how careful they needed to be in making sure they had a way out.

Some of these students seemed just a little cocky, so we set up a scenario for them (and didn't tell them about what was going to happen.) Multiple fires were built on all floors of the burn building. The evolution started with fires on the lower levels and crews sent in to fight them. The ladder company was setting up their aerial ladder in preparation to open the roof, if it should be ordered. The rescue was ordered to the top floor to check for fire extension.

My rescue company advanced up the interior stairs to the top floor, where there is just one room. It was a big room to search, so I sent two of my guys to the left and I went with the other two to the right. They didn't see the instructor hiding up there, waiting for us to pass, or the straw ready to be lit. We felt our way along the wall in the dark. When my crew met up again at the center of the wall at the far side of the room, the other instructor lit the fire. It was between us and the stairs. We were simulating a fire coming up the stairs behind us and blocking our escape. Of course, this was a controlled exercise, and we were never really trapped.

I got my crew together and we started backing toward a window with a balcony. I got on the radio and called a "mayday." "Rescue to command." When command answered, I continued, "Rescue is on the top floor. We have fire between us and the interior stairs. We are backing toward the window on the bravo side, division 3. Requesting a ladder for extrication."

Command acknowledged our transmission. "Rescue is on the top floor, fire between them and the stairs, backing toward the window on the bravo side, division 3. Requesting a ladder for extrication."

This was going to take a couple of minutes, but when you're waiting for something, one minute seems like ten. I was about to take the crew out onto the balcony when I noticed two of them missing. I saw them working their way back toward the interior stairs, toward the fire, and opening windows along the way. This training scenario was working better than I had hoped. They were making grave mistakes that we could address when the evolution was over.

I let the two guys continue, and when the evolution was over, we got together to go over their performance. I always remind the students that this is a controlled evolution. They must envision something bigger. We talked about what happened:

> We went up the stairs and split up to cover both sides of the room quicker.
>
> We met and started back.
>
> Then we found that our way was blocked by fire. Presumably, the fire came up the stairs after us, cutting off our escape.
>
> We knew our relative position in the building, and so we began to back toward a window where we could be rescued.
>
> The "mayday" was called in properly, with our position and actions made clear to command.

It was then that things took a bad turn.

> Two of the crew decided to make their way back to the stairs via the outside wall. They never told anybody

what they were going to do. They went off on their own: never a good thing to do.

They made their way toward the fire. In the real world, that probably would have cost both of them their lives.

As they moved along, they opened the windows. This would have fed air to the fire, allowing it to burn freely. With no hose operating on that floor, the fire could easily have taken off. That would have killed the remaining members, waiting for rescue by the window.

All this was explained to the recruits: what was done right, what was done wrong, and why it was wrong. I think it was an eye opener for them, especially the two who left the group and opened the windows.

Recruit training is more than just basic firefighting and hose movement. A big part of it is survival and doing the right things to reduce your chances of getting killed or injured doing a job that is fraught with dangers. I hope this lesson hit home. I believe it did.

Recognition

For a number of years I was the department training officer, responsible for any and all fire training within the department, including a small call department. Whenever possible, I tried to get houses that were slated to be torn down for us to use for training. Training did not necessarily mean live burns. Houses can be used for search and rescue, ladder and ventilation operations, as well as a whole host of other things. However, when one came up that we *could* use for burns, I would jump at it.

To use a house for burns, everything had to fall into place just right. The house couldn't be a rickety old place ready to fall down. It wouldn't be safe to send people into a place like that to train. We had to have permission from the owner and the neighbors. The hydrants had to be on the proper side of the road so we wouldn't block traffic and inconvenience anyone. The timing had to be right so we could get the burn in before the scheduled demolition. There was a lot to do to arrange a live burn.

Back a few years, we had a chief who didn't pay attention to details. He had a different way of looking at things. He called me into his office one day. He told me that he knew of a house that was going to be demolished. He said we could drill in it and even hold burns there. I was excited!

He gave me the address and told me to check it out. I drove to the address and couldn't believe my eyes. All the houses in this neighborhood were big and relatively new. This one was a large, modern house with plenty of access, a walk-in basement, and three floors for us to work with. I couldn't understand why anyone would be tearing it down. Things didn't make sense. The house was out of the way and the hydrants were on the correct side of the street. Still, something wasn't right. The place was vaguely familiar. I got out of the car and walked around, through deep snow, looking in the large windows. The place was vacant, but there was some debris lying around. It just looked the way you would expect after the people had moved out.

As I walked back to the car, it came to me. I had seen this place on the news just recently. They had done a report on a house that had a severe mold problem. Try as they might, the homeowners just couldn't get rid of the mold, and it was getting worse. They tried everything they could think of—and failed. Finally, the homeowners decided to move out, tear the place down, and rebuild. This was the house. I had seen it on the news.

Now, I don't know much about mold, especially this kind that seems to have a mind of its own. I just don't think it would be too safe to set fires in this kind of atmosphere and then send people into it. No one knows how the mold might react. I didn't think it would be safe even for non-fire training. If someone got sick, there would be hell to pay.

I drove back to the firehouse and went to see the chief. I told him what I had remembered about the house. He said, "Well, walk around and look in. If you don't see any mold, then go ahead and use it."

I guess, knowing him, I wasn't really surprised at what I heard. I just said, "Thanks," and shook my head as I walked away. There would be other houses. I took a pass on this one.

Not a Close Family

When I was working in the private ambulance business, I was always a part-time employee. I sometimes worked a great many hours, but I was always part-time. I never had a regular shift to work. I took what was available, from day to day.

Well, one day I was working a 6 a.m. to 2 p.m. shift. We got out on the road on time and were given a 7:00 call. It was to pick up a patient at a local hospital and take them to another hospital for radiation treatment. The patient was at a hospital that did not have the facility to give this kind of treatment. Then another ambulance would transport them back to the original hospital.

We got to the hospital, took our stretcher, and went up to the floor. I was the attendant, so it was my job to go to the nurses' desk to get information on our patient and do the paperwork. I looked down at the patient's information. I knew the name. However, some people have the same names as others. Then I looked at the address. I knew that, too. The patient was my uncle. I was surprised, to say the least. I felt bad that I had to find out like this. He and his family only lived a couple of miles from me, and I didn't even know he was sick.

As it turned out, he had been pretty sick for some time before he finally went to the doctor. When the doctor looked at him, he saw an advanced stage of cancer of the esophagus. The medical office building was attached to the hospital, so he could ship my uncle directly from the office to the hospital, and that's what the doctor did.

This was to be his first radiation treatment, and would require additional time for some marking and other things to be done. I went into the room to see him and we talked a lot, both then and during the trip to the cancer care facility. It was mostly just small talk about family and things.

My uncle lost this battle a couple of years later and I attended his funeral. Funny how someone can live that close and you never see them. No one even told me he was sick. I guess I can't really blame anyone but me. I just don't come from a close family.

Hurried Up and Left

Back before I became an instructor at the fire academy, I worked in support services. That meant we did just about everything else, except actually teach the students. Back in the 80s, the original fire academy buildings burned down, the result of several arson fires. Training had to go on, and so it was kind of taken on the road. Different places were found to conduct different parts of the training.

When I first went to work for the academy, training burns for the recruits were conducted in two places. We did smaller fires at a burn training building that was fairly local. There were quite a few houses in that area, so the fires had to be small and smoke-free, or the locals would complain and we'd be shut down. The larger burns were held at a facility on Cape Cod, where there was a small burn building. Each half of the class would spend two days there. Without a lot of houses around, we made some big fires.

We'd go through a lot of air bottles for our SCBA during these burns. Since there was no compressor for filling the air bottles, a very large number of bottles had to be brought down from the academy by truck. Arrangements had been made to refill all of our air bottles at a firehouse not too far away from the burn building on the Cape. They let us use their compressor and we did the work. At the end of training for the day, it was the job of us, in support services, to take the truck full of empties and fill them. Then we'd drop the truck off at the training area to be ready for the next day.

One day, it was my turn to go and fill bottles. It was a lot of work and time consuming, not a one-man job. Even with two people working, it was tough getting it done in a reasonable time. But on this day, there were only two of us. At the end of that day's training, we took the truck and drove to the firehouse where the compressor was. When we got there, there was no one in the firehouse. Apparently, that fire department had a fire in progress. However, the place was open and we could go in and do our job.

As we worked, firefighters kept showing up there, getting on the engines, and leaving. Mutual aid companies started to show up, too. Then they'd leave, having been called out to the fire. We were listening to the local fire radio. There was a major fire at a power plant in the town where we were. We continued our job, which seemed to be taking forever.

As we were nearing the end of the job, the commander at the fire scene put out a call for more air bottles. There was oil soaked insulation burning in the walls of the power plant. Many air tanks were needed for the firefighters to get inside and do their work.

Suddenly, my partner and I had a horrible thought: what if someone found out that we had a truck with a couple of hundred full bottles on it? Would they commandeer it? *Could* they commandeer it, being state property? We didn't know, and we sure as hell weren't prepared to attempt to withhold them and maybe get arrested, or worse yet, have to explain to our bosses that our bottles were taken after all our work, and we couldn't have training the next day. We did the only logical thing we could: we worked like demons and got the job done as quickly as we could and left quietly. We didn't stop to talk to anyone. We were really beat by the time we got back to the hotel, but at least we had all of our bottles and we had saved training for the next day. A job well done!

Evidence Tampering

One night, not too far into the evening, although it was dark, we were dispatched to a residence for an attempted suicide. I was the ambulance attendant that night. When we got to the address, we found that the house was set back off the road a long way. The driveway was flanked by hedges on both sides, making it really narrow. It was so tight that as we attempted to back the ambulance down, the hedges were rubbing against the vehicle. It was going to take some time to get the ambulance in, so I got out, got my medical jump kit and portable oxygen, and ran down the driveway, while my partner continued to back the ambulance down the driveway.

The police were already on scene, and the first person I saw when I got up near the house was the duty sergeant, standing near a car. There was an unconscious young lady in the driver's seat of the car, her head leaning against the left front window. The car was running and the doors were locked. I seem to remember a hose from the tail pipe leading into the car through a window. I don't remember which window it was, but it was not the left front window next to her. It was rolled up as far as it could be with the hose in place. With the doors all locked, my first instinct would have been to break the rear window and unlock the front door. As it turned out, I didn't have to. I remember somebody running from the house with a set of keys.

Anyway, we unlocked the door and I opened it. I took the woman out and put her on the ground. Her body was moveable when I took her out of the car, so that meant that rigor mortis had not set in yet. But when a person's heart has not been beating to circulate the blood, you can see discoloration where the blood has pooled at the lowest point. This is called lividity. I think I remember seeing that. Since this takes a bit of time to happen, when you see it, it means that the person has been gone too long for us to help. CPR would have no effect and is contraindicated in this type of situation. There were no paramedics in our area at that time, and with the presence of lividity, it was clear that we could not work the patient, as she was already deceased. It then became a police matter. We packed up our things and returned to quarters.

We found out later that the police sergeant was very angry at us and had filed a report. It seems that he said that we had opened the car and removed the body, thereby tampering with and destroying evidence.

Interesting thought, but let me respond with this: how the hell were we to tell if our patient was deceased if we hadn't done what we had? No one ever answered that question. Someone must have agreed with us, because nothing else was ever said about it. The sergeant had stood by and watched as I opened the door and removed the victim. He never said anything then. If he thought there was something wrong being done, he should have spoken up, not that it would have done any good. It was my patient and I was going to check things out.

Car Lock Outs

People sure do some funny things that often don't make any sense. For example, they take all the keys for their car and put them in the glove compartment, just in case they ever need them. Then they manage to lock the one key they're using in the car, sometimes with their small children and pets in the car. Other times they leave the car running when they shut the door, only to find out that now it's locked. Who do you think they call when they're locked out? That's right: the fire department. Oh, there are a few organizations and auto clubs that sometimes people can and do call, but mostly they call the old FD.

Back in the old days, we were not much better than the auto clubs. We used the same tools, but we did it for free, where they would have to pay for someone else to come. You might have gotten back into your car without damage, but that depended on who showed up to help. Some guys were real crackerjacks with the Slim Jim, while others just couldn't make it work. For a short time, we wouldn't try to open someone's car unless it was an emergency. There was a concern about liability because of the damage that happened all too frequently.

Eventually, the fire department got a tool that worked great. It was based on that trick that everyone knows, involving inserting a straightened-out coat hanger into the door jam. Then you'd see if you could use it to catch the door handle or the door lock. This new tool was a bendable metal rod that was plastic coated. The end was bent into a sort of hook. The rod was about five feet long. The kit included a wedge that you forced into the doorjamb to create a gap. It was plastic, so it wouldn't scratch the paint. An inflatable bladder, like the one in a blood pressure cuff, was inserted into the gap and pumped up with the little bulb on its hose. The gap would widen. Then you would bend the rod so it could grab what you wanted inside the car. It was simple as hell: no more Slim Jims.

This new tool worked fantastically. I can't speak for everyone, but I never failed with it, and I never spent more than ten minutes trying. It got so I enjoyed responding to car lockouts.

There was one very popular organization providing roadside help that many people belonged to. They paid for their membership and they could call any time of day or night, from anywhere, and help would come. At least, that was the theory. The fact was that you would never know who would be sent out to help. It all depended on which garage had a contract with the club. Sometimes they would come and successfully help. Other times, the people that the club sent couldn't help, and there were several times that I know about where they never showed up and left the people stranded.

One day, when I was working as the duty captain, I took car 2 to a call for a vehicle lockout. It was at an address not too far from the firehouse. I arrived and met a young lady who was visiting a friend. She and her friend were standing next to a black SUV. She had the keys in the ignition and had shut the door, which was now locked. She told me that she had called the auto club first. It had taken them a long time to get there. The man who showed up tried to help. He worked for a while, but in the end, he wasn't able to open the door. He told her that there was nothing he could do, so he left. He just left!

Well, that's when she called the old FD, and out we came, or at least, out *I* came. I looked and saw that it was a nice looking car, a black Lexus SUV. It seemed to me that the owner tried to keep it clean, inside and out. I got out my tools and looked inside to decide what I should try to hook to open the door. It was then that I noticed a hole where a lock button should have been. I looked across, and the other lock button was missing, too. I asked her what happened to her locks. She was very surprised when I showed her. The buttons had been there before the guy from the auto club had worked on the car. Then I noticed that the paint was chipped and scratched all along the door where it meets the bottom edge of the window. It was the same on the other door. It was clear to me that the man from the auto club had gone to town with a Slim Jim. He nicked and scratched the paint each time he shoved the tool inside the door. He then grabbed and pulled at anything he could find inside the door. He managed to damage the locks and the window operation mechanism. I pointed this out to the lady.

She was angry, and who could blame her? I'm glad I had taken the time to show her *before* I touched the vehicle. It was clear who was responsible for the damage. It took me about five minutes to open the door. I told her she should have called us first, and she agreed.

I don't think I would have wanted to be on the receiving end of the phone call that I knew she was going to make. I've heard too many stories about negative experiences with those auto clubs. I think I'll take care of things myself. Of course, that is just my opinion. I guess those clubs can help, sometimes. However, the fire department never fails, and *we* stay until we get the job done.

Santa Pants

Our fire department has sponsored an annual visit from Santa Claus further back than most of us can remember. We mount his sleigh on top of the fire engine. For three nights, we make scheduled stops around town so the kids can talk to him. One year I helped build a new sleigh and paint all new signs to put around town, advertising the ride. Things usually went pretty well.

Most years, we get the real Santa, but there have been occasional times when Santa couldn't make it, for one reason or another. When that happens, we need to have a volunteer, usually from the fire department, fill in. We keep a Santa suit in the firehouse, just in case. There have been some obstacles over the years, some bigger than others, but nothing we couldn't overcome in order to bring Santa to see those kids. We've been out in freezing rain, driving snow, and pouring rain. We've even had an occasional nice night, though it's usually cold. That's no problem if you dress for it. If you don't, well, go find another shoulder to cry on.

Once we even had a report of a house fire while we all were waiting around for the ride to start. We managed to fight the fire and still get Santa out to visit with the kids on time.

Another time, we had a man pull the engine out and run over a battery charger that was boosting up the engine's batteries. «CRUNCH» It was smashed flat. The mechanic almost had a stroke. He couldn't yell too loud though; he was the one that told the driver everything was clear for him to pull out.

Even when things went wrong, we always managed to get Santa out to the kids. One near catastrophe happened years back on a night when Santa couldn't make it. We got a volunteer. It was cold and he was going to dress for it. He put on his bunker pants. (We called them quick hitches back then.) They were made for speed and warmth, rather than protection. Then he pulled the Santa pants on over his bunker pants. It a very tight squeeze, to say the least, but everything held together, so out we went.

At each stop, Santa arrives in his sleigh on top of the engine, but he always gets down off the engine to visit with the children. We got to the first stop of the night right on time. There isn't really any time to waste. We have a tight schedule to keep. I was standing on the rear step getting ready to help Santa down. He got out of the sleigh all right, but as he swung his leg over the bar at the rear of the engine, I saw the whole backside blow right out of the Santa pants. *Holy shit! What do we do now?!*

We were committed to that first stop. Thank heaven it was a small one. The next one, however, always had a lot of kids and the pants would never last the night like that. We decided we had to sacrifice some time and be a little late for the second stop. On the way there, we stopped at station 2 and we all went in, including Santa. We looked everywhere we could think of, even in the medical kits, and got as many safety pins as we could find. Then we went to work doing a hasty, creative repair on those pants. In about ten minutes of frantic work, we had a pair of pants that were useable for the night, as long as our Santa fill-in took off the bunker pants, which he did. The rest of the night went well, though we were a little behind all evening long.

The next night, the *real* Santa Claus made it and saved the day. The guys had to scramble to get a replacement pair of pants for our Santa suit, just in case Santa got double booked again.

It's in the Blood

I've always said that it takes a certain type of person to become a firefighter and stay with it for a career. Fighting fires is dangerous, but that isn't the only thing that presents a danger to the people who choose firefighting as their career. It is this kind of person who will stop and get involved in situations that can cause trouble off the job, too. I don't mean to say that firefighters are the only ones who ever stop to help. I mean to say that it's in their nature to stop and lend a hand when they can. This can put a person in danger.

One day some years ago, two men I know, both off duty firefighters from the same town, were going home from the part-time job where they both worked. They were traveling together in the same car that day. They were just getting onto the highway when they saw a car stopped in the left lane with the hood up and pushed back over the windshield. There were two older teenage girls and a six-year-old girl in the car. It seems that they had been driving along when something made the hood latch release and the hood blow upward. The girls couldn't see to drive and didn't know what to do.

The two off duty firefighters pulled up to the disabled car to assist in getting the car to the breakdown lane. One of the guys got the girls out of the car and off the highway into the breakdown lane. The other firefighter got into the car and was able to drive it to the right to be mostly in the breakdown lane. There was a guardrail there, but the car wasn't right up against it. There were several feet between the car and the guardrail. He then got out and got ready to pull the hood back down. Just as the man pulled down on the hood, he saw a flash of activity out of the corner of his eye. A car was coming down an off ramp and onto the highway. It was bouncing off the guardrail. Before anybody realized what was happening and had time to react, it went in between the disabled car and the guardrail, and struck those who were trying to get to safety off the road.

The impact killed the six-year-old girl instantly. One of the firefighters was not injured, but the other one suffered severe injuries, with a fractured pelvis and multiple long bone fractures in both legs. It's a miracle he wasn't killed as well. The injured man needed surgery to put him back together again. He was out of work for about eighteen months before he healed and was able to return to work. He *did* return to the fire department and worked for years until his retirement.

We heard what had happened was that there was a female driver, alone in her car, driving on that highway. She had a seizure disorder of some kind and had not taken her medication. She started having a seizure and lost control of her car as she came to the ramp near where the disabled car was. I heard that that woman was well connected to people in high places at the state level. They circled the wagons around her. She neglected to take her medication, but somehow was never prosecuted for her actions.

A little girl was killed, a man lending a helping hand was almost killed and suffered through a long recovery, yet the person responsible was never held accountable, thanks to her contacts. Quite a tragic story, but I'm sure they wouldn't hesitate to stop again if someone needed help. It's in the blood.

Lucky Shot

I am not a golfer. I've never played the game in my life. But I have been out on and all over the golf course in the course of my job with the fire department. I've seen lightning strikes, chest pain, dehydration, heart attacks, and cardiac arrests, but the biggest hazard on the golf course has got to be the ball. The golf ball is hard. It bounces well and can be hit a long way. It also travels at a high rate of speed and hits hard. I've seen bruises, lacerations, and broken bones from ball strikes. I've seen people hit in the head at a distance, and even that created an open wound.

The first time I ever saw a golf ball strike was a couple of years before I came on the fire department. I was working for a department of public works nearby. We were doing some roadwork near a public golf course. There were many people playing that day. I saw a young man get ready to tee off. His club made contact with the ball, and at that exact moment, another young man walked in front of him. The ball hit the man just above the left eye. I was 50 or 60 yards away, and I could plainly hear the «CRACK» as the ball made contact with the man's head. In no time, the eye was swollen shut. His head had been split wide open. He was only semi-conscious. He was taken away by ambulance. It was a sight to remember.

A rather unique incident that I remember was a man who came into the firehouse one weekend afternoon. There were tears in his eyes as he showed us his hand. On the ring finger was a ring with a yellow stone. We were told that it was an old family heirloom. This man had been golfing with friends and had been struck on that ring with a golf ball, hit from some distance away. The ball all but flattened the ring on the man's finger. The finger was swollen and purple all the way from the ring to the tip. He was bleeding from under the ring. He told us later that he was going to ask us not to damage the ring too much, but by the time he got to us, he was in so much pain that he told us to do whatever we had to, just get it off. It was flattened, so there was no way it was going to slide off. We used a ring cutter and made two cuts, cutting the ring in half. When the pressure was off, the look of relief on the man's face was something to behold. He didn't want to go to any hospital with us and I didn't really think it was necessary. The color started to come back, and though still sore, it was getting better. We gave him his ring back and an ice pack for his finger and hand and he went on his way.

What a shot, hitting him right on the ring! (I wonder if that cost him a stroke.) Were they a real marksman? I think not. It was just a lucky shot for the golfer; and a really unlucky shot for the guy wearing the ring.

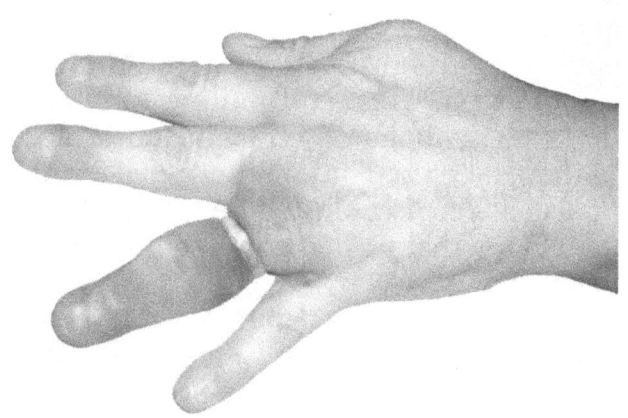

Justice Delivered

Here's a story to show just how cruel I can be to the people who ask for it. We had a police officer in town who was really quite pleased with himself. He had a real case of the "little man syndrome," and on top of that, he thought himself quite the ladies' man. He was also a kiss-and-tell artist. We never really knew how much was true, but I guess anyone who talks about it that much, can't be doing too well. Anyway, that's how the saying goes. This man had quite a reputation as a jerk with most who knew him, and people got tired of listening to the stories of his exploits, in and out of the bedroom.

One day, when I was on duty at the firehouse, this cop parked his cruiser out front and came in to use the bathroom and to brag. He told me that he had just been down to the state park on patrol. There had been an ambulance from a private company parked there, waiting to be assigned a call. He said that the ambulance crew included an attractive blond girl (although he used other descriptive terms). He had stopped and talked to her. I could tell he was quite pleased with himself as he told me that he had gotten her phone number and was going to call her.

Well, as it turned out, I worked part-time for that same ambulance company, and I also knew that blond. He was right; she was attractive. She was also kind of vain about her looks, and had a bit of a reputation. I have no clue whether that reputation was deserved or not. She and I were friends. She had always been nice to me and I just didn't want to see her tied up with that man.

The next time I went to work at the ambulance company, I saw her and asked if I could have a word with her in private. I said, "You met a police officer the other day at the state park?"

She said, "Yes," and looked puzzled that I would know about that.

I told her that what she decides to do or not do wasn't any business of mine, but I thought there were a few things she should know. Basically, I told her the man was a "P–I–G pig," in the worst way. I told her if she did anything with him, everyone would know about it, in detail, within a day. I said further that, even if she went out with him and did nothing, he would make something up and spread it around. Everything I told her was true. She thanked me for the heads-up.

About a week later, I asked that cop, "Whatever happened with that blond?" He said that he had called her and she had refused to go out with him. I walked away, laughing inside.

A friend had been spared embarrassment and a jerk had been deprived the object of his conquest, as well as a chance to brag. Sometimes even I can dispense justice!

Sad Coincidence

One evening in early winter in about 1984, I was off duty and sitting at home watching television, when I heard the fire department receiver upstairs. They were striking a box for a house fire. I ran upstairs, put on some warmer clothes, and left for the firehouse. At that time, my station for recall was station 1. I drove the three miles to the station without any trouble, and when I entered, the radio was transmitting a call for the ambulance to the fire scene. An officer looked at me and ordered me into the ambulance. My partner got in the passenger side. He was a pretty new guy, but no youngster. He was a good man.

Off we went to the fire scene. En route, we were told that they had found a resident inside the burning house. It was an elderly lady, found on the kitchen floor in cardiac arrest. She had almost made it out of the house. The guys had gotten her outside and were doing CPR. This was going to be my partner's first code blue.

We arrived and I was told to back into the driveway. I let my partner out, and with the help of some spotters, was able to back in. Someone opened the back and took out the stretcher and a long backboard. The long backboard was put on the stretcher mattress, to go under the patient, to give a hard surface to press against during CPR. They got the lady on the stretcher and loaded in the ambulance, and my partner and another man got in. I got back into the cab, drove out into the street, and headed for the closest hospital. CPR was kept up all the way to the hospital, and continued for a time in the emergency room, but sadly, the patient did not survive.

This whole scene is not an uncommon occurrence in the fire service. Sometimes, if we're lucky, we can get there and effect a rescue in time to save a victim. Often, it's too late, and the heart had been stopped for too long for us to be able to save them. What made this incident so sad was that the elderly victim was the grandmother of a boy who had lost his life in a fire in his family home several years earlier, just a little way down the street: a sad coincidence.

Memorable Moment

We have all been guilty of not taking care of ourselves as well as we should. With the drinking and smoking and all those hazardous pastimes, besides doing a job that is dangerous, it's a wonder any of us live to retirement. While smoking isn't the same scourge it once was as fewer people smoke, the other vices are going strong.

What about just staying home in bed when you're sick? I know several firefighters who have never taken a sick day in all the years of their career. That's fine if you're never sick, but coming in when sick and spreading it around isn't nice.

Many of us don't even stay at home and rest when we have been hurt or had surgery. I remember one day while setting things up in the gas school at the fire academy, another instructor came up to me and told me that he was going to try and take things kind of easy that day. He was letting all the instructors know. Gas school usually has plenty of help, and even if they didn't, it's usually not much of an issue if someone has to hang back a bit. Also, this man was a senior, well-respected man. If he wanted to hang back, there was a good reason. Well, I asked him what that reason was, just out of curiosity. He told me that he'd had a vasectomy at the end of the week before. He had gone snowmobiling over the weekend and now he was in pain. He said it felt like he had a third nut and it hurt like hell. We all got a bit of a chuckle out of that.

We worked all morning and I kind of lost sight of the vasectomy man. We broke for lunch and he wasn't in my thoughts as I sat in the instructors' room eating. Suddenly, Mr. Vasectomy walked in, wearing a big smile. He said that as he had been walking across the yard toward the lunchroom, he felt a <<POP!>> as that third nut broke. With that, he held up the underwear he had been wearing. Most of the front of the garment was taken up with a huge, watery, bloody stain. It seems that he had had an abscess that had relieved itself. Well, after everyone got done being grossed out and cursing the man for ruining lunch, we all had a good laugh. The man left the room with a spring in his step, pain-free.

I don't know what he ever did with his shorts. I hope he burned them, but it would take something one hell of a lot worse than that to ruin lunch for that group!

Hole in the Ice

We have a hermit that lives in town. He's really harmless, as far as anyone knows. I know people who went to high school with him. He grew up in town, and up until some point in the late 70s, still had family living in town. I was told that he did some time in the Air Force in the 60s. I don't know what he did when he got out, but I remember him well through the 70s.

There were a couple of brothers in town who were kind of wild. This guy used to stay at their house. Back then, there was a lot of trouble between the police and the young adults and teens. The young folks used to hang out in the corner of a ballpark right across the street from the house where those brothers lived. The hermit used to hang there with the young folks. I can't be sure, but I have reason to believe that he was a bit older than most of them. However, he blended in fine.

He spent the summer with the youngsters and slept in a hammock strung between two pine trees in the brothers' yard. Summer ended, it got cold, it snowed, and still this guy slept in the hammock. I can remember looking out some mornings and seeing him start to stir, covered with snow. There was no one left in the ballpark over the winter, so I don't know what he did with his days, but he was back in the hammock at night.

Finally, after a while he disappeared. He turned up living in the woods around a large lake that we have in town. The only trouble he ever gave anybody was that he was an incessant talker, plus he stunk, too. He would never shut up, so people avoided him. He also made a real mess in the woods where he camped. He'd scatter his belongings all over the place. His messes got so bad that the police had to keep moving him out. He always came back, though in another part of the woods.

One very cold winter day, I took an overtime shift at station 2. The lake had frozen pretty solid all over. About midmorning, we got a call for someone possibly fallen through the ice, in a certain part of the lake that we couldn't get very close to. Engine 2 was first due. We pulled the engine into a large cemetery that kind of borders the lake. We could make pretty good time getting to the spot from there. We parked, grabbed our ropes and rescue suits, and through the woods we went, running down a path and towards the lake. This was all reasonably clear of snow, luckily. We got to the area and looked out. Sure enough, about maybe a hundred feet out, there was a hole, and around the hole, there were some things scattered around, but very close to the hole. We could make out a winter knit hat. There was what looked like a bag or a backpack. In short, it was possible that someone was walking, fell through, and dropped what he was carrying.

We started to put on our rescue suits when out of the woods came the captain. I guess things didn't smell right to the captain, (not that he was smelling the man in question), he told us to hold up while he checked this out. Out onto the ice he went in his buoyant rescue suit. We weren't too worried: the ice was very thick. There were holes left by ice fishermen all over. This hole was larger than a normal ice-fishing hole, but the ice was strong around it. I guess the captain's intuition was right on. It turned out that our friend, the hermit, was living in the woods somewhere nearby. He was known to do whatever washing that he did of his body and belongings in the lake. He had come out onto the ice for some reason. No one knows for sure, but maybe he widened one of the existing holes for some purpose. But he left his hat, gloves, and a mess of smaller belongings around the hole and had wandered off. Somebody had driven by the lake and had seen the debris from a distance. It sure looked like someone had fallen through. So the person made the call.

Everything turned out to be fine. The only real problem was the "What ifs." What if the ice around the hole had been thin and someone went out to see if they could help? What if the ice had been thin and the hermit, himself, had fallen in? What if he went under before we could get to him? What if we had gone into the water looking for him and something went wrong and one of us got killed? Almost everything we do has at least some hazard attached to it, and an ice rescue is no different. Even when everything goes well, that list of "What ifs" is always there. Maybe we won't be so lucky next time.

Just Not Right

The debate over the quint has gone on for a long while and it still rages. This piece of apparatus is called a "quint" because it has five functions that used to each require a separate piece of apparatus: it has a pump, an aerial ladder, a hose, ground ladders, and water. Most of these old functions were lumped together into other vehicles over the years. Gone are the hose wagons that used to carry the hose for the engine company's pump. Now the engine companies carry their own hose. Engines have carried ground ladders as long as I can remember, and all pumps now have a tank for storing water on board. Basically, what they did to create the quint was to combine the engine and ladder truck. Now you have one piece of apparatus with the powerful pump of an engine, and the aerial capabilities of a ladder truck. Quints were developed as a cost saving measure for departments buying apparatus. Instead of buying a ladder truck and an engine, they can buy one vehicle that can perform as either.

There have been problems when a department responds to a fire with a quint. If they commit the apparatus to do engine work, it is hooked to a hydrant with attack lines running from it. Sometimes they may find that they need a ladder truck somewhere else at the fire. You just can't move an engine when it's hooked up to a water supply and is fighting the fire. Now, the incident commander has to special call an additional ladder truck, which may be coming from a distance, if one is available at all.

The same is true if the vehicle is committed as a ladder truck with the aerial ladder in use. You may later need another pump or lines run to another part of the fire, but the quint may not be available for this use. In spite of these inherent problems, quints are selling.

My department bought a quint some years back. We have yet to experience any real problems with its functions. One of the last fires I had before I retired was a kitchen fire. The whole shift was at headquarters for training when the call came in. I was driving the car, so I got there ahead of everyone. I saw smoke coming from the open front door and called in, "Smoke showing."

I parked and had my gear on, so I went inside to look. It had been a fire on the stove and had burned the bottom of the cabinets a little. The lady of the house was lucky. She spotted the fire almost right away and called us. When I came out, the engine company was just pulling up. I radioed for dispatch to hold off striking the box. I was pretty sure we wouldn't need all the extra manpower and equipment which would come if the dispatcher struck the box. But since we would be tied up for a while, I ordered them to get people to cover both stations. I had the engine take a line into the house and check for extension.

The ladder/quint, being the slowest vehicle, arrived last. I ordered them to lay a 4" line to establish a water supply in case it was needed. I still wasn't sure there had been no extension of the fire behind the cabinets or into the walls. This was done, and a further check found no fire extension.

Old traditionalists often argue about quints vs. real ladder trucks or engines. I always loved to hear the debate go back and forth. Then I would interrupt them and say, "Do you know what the last orders were that I gave to a ladder company?"

They naturally answered, "No."

Then I'd say, "I ordered them to lay a line!" which is very much the job of an engine.

To this, they would just shake their heads and mutter, "That's just not right."

Loved His Job

There was a man in town that I knew. He was quite a bit older than me. He grew up in town, went to school there, and then went in the service. After his discharge, he came back to town and joined the police department. He eventually wound up as the department's youth officer. He's the only youth officer that I remember who had any kind of decent relationship with the youth of the town. Of course, no one likes everyone, and being a police officer could, and probably does, increase the number of people that don't like you. But I think that this man was generally well thought of. He got in when EMS training was new, and so became one of the town's first EMTs. Although police officers did not work on the ambulance, they did respond to the same calls. It was often nice to have another person with knowledge and training to help out.

Sometime earlier in his career, the man suffered a gunshot wound. I heard that it was self-inflicted while cleaning his weapon. That sounded a bit odd to me. The police carried revolvers at the time. I don't know how you'd clean a loaded, cocked revolver. But I never knew if the story was true. Sometime during his recovery from his injury, he was diagnosed with insulin-dependent diabetes. He always claimed that it was the result of a transfusion that he got after his gunshot injury. Again, I really don't know if that is true or not. What I *do* know is that even though he didn't work in the ambulance and as youth officer his responses to emergency calls became rare, he kept up his EMT certification long after most of the other police officers had given up theirs.

At our training sessions, he talked often about his diabetes and problems that could arise from it. As the years went by, the diabetes took its toll on his health. He suffered from a problem with his feet resulting from the diabetes. This required him to wear special shoes. He began to look sickly as his condition worsened. All the while, he was still working as a police officer and as the department's youth officer. Many people probably would have tried to get a "disability retirement" by this time, but this guy loved his job.

Things finally came to a head when his eyesight started to become worse, another diabetic problem. His eyesight started to fail him so he couldn't work. I would see him sometimes walking around during the day. He always had his police radio with him to listen to what was happening. Finally, he went through some eye surgery to correct his vision so he could drive and return to work. I know he was happy to be back.

He hadn't been back too long, when one day he was driving his police vehicle. He signaled for a left turn, made the turn, and crashed into the side of the fire ambulance as it was on its way back to headquarters from a hospital run. He didn't even see the ambulance. He just made the turn and crashed. No one was hurt, thankfully, but the ambulance was totaled and the police officer was taken off the road. No longer able to perform his job, the man retired from the police department.

I saw him a few times after that, but he never looked too well. It wasn't an awfully long time after that that he died. I heard that it was, once again, due to complications from his diabetes. I really don't know for sure.

I have known many people in my long career in the emergency services. I've seen many who would jump at the chance to retire. I've seen people try to get disability retirements using the flimsiest of reasons. Most didn't get them. But I've rarely seen a man who tried so hard to keep the job he loved so much.

Abuse of Power

I was on duty one Saturday afternoon years ago at station 1 as part of the ambulance crew. That day we were in the midst of a bad snowstorm. It had been snowing since the night before. We had much accumulation and it was still coming down hard, and blowing. It was the kind of day that no one really should be out on the road, unless you worked in emergency services or plowed streets. The town's plows were hardly able to keep up and it was a hazard to drive anywhere.

We received a call, a request for the ambulance to a residence. We knew the name at this residence. The lady of the house was a town selectwoman. We arrived at the home and were greeted by the selectwoman herself. She took us into a bedroom where her husband was lying in the bed. Unknown to us, he was ill. I'm not sure after all these years what his real problem was, but on that day, his catheter came out and he needed it reinserted. This was years before we had any access to paramedics, and we, as basic EMTs, were not able to perform the task that needed to be done. It was a simple procedure that could be done quickly at the nearest hospital, just in the next town over. This normally wouldn't have been a problem, but there was a problem. The selectwoman insisted that her husband be taken to a hospital that was miles away, and well out of the range that we operated in at that time. Even on a good day, that would be something we probably would not do, but on *this* day, in *this* weather, there was no question. We couldn't take him there. The lady was adamant that he go to that hospital. No other was good enough for her husband. It wasn't a question of anything serious that needed to be done. Today, paramedics can perform the task without taking you out of your home, but not then.

The lady started to get rather nasty. The captain arrived and told her the same thing we had told her: we couldn't go to that distant hospital. The road conditions alone would prohibit it. I remember she started to get a bit pushy. I don't remember the words that were spoken, but I remember that she thought that because of the position she held in town government, we should do what she wanted. The captain stood by his decision. As I recall, we made arrangements for a private service to come and do the transport. That was an expensive alternative, but common sense alone said to stay close to home.

I was told that she called the chief of department to complain. The chief was a practical person who did things right. He told her that the captain and ambulance crew had acted properly. We never heard another word about it.

Maybe she didn't make a big issue out of things because she was afraid of criticism of her attempted abuse of power. That's what it was, after all: an attempt to use her authority and position in the town government as leverage to get her own way. Well, she found out how far that was going to get her. Funny how that same kind of abuse seems to be seen at all levels of government, from small towns all the way to Washington D.C.

Gone with the Wind

Working at the state firefighting academy as long as I did, I saw many people come and go. There are very few working there now that were there before I started. Everyone who works as an instructor or support staff is part-time, and either works for a fire department somewhere or has retired. Many people don't end up working at the academy for a long time. The pay isn't great, so some leave for a better paying part-time job. Others live in a distant part of the state. The expense of traveling that far is not worth it. It just gets too expensive to continue working there. Every time someone is promoted to chief of their department, they're basically lost to the academy, as chiefs normally work four or five days during the week. There are also some who retire and just leave.

It's not common for someone to be fired. Usually, if someone isn't working out, they just cut his hours down to nothing, and he kind of disappears after a while. Sometimes, a person will step far enough over the line to get fired. The man in this story did just that. As far as I know, he has the record for the shortest employment with the academy.

This man came to work in support services. He was a well-experienced firefighter and fire officer from a small city in the central part of the state. He was a bit upset over the limitations placed on new employees. It doesn't matter who you are or where you come from, or even how long you've been on the job. All new hires at the academy have to be trained and certified to use the equipment, operate the engines, and even to work in the burn tower.

On his first day working there, this man did some menial jobs. When he came in for his second day, for some reason he went upstairs where the secretaries and administration staff work. This man had a bit of a problem in that he loved women. Usually that's not a problem, unless you just can't leave them alone and aren't smart enough to take "No" for an answer. He saw a woman upstairs that he liked the look of. This woman he spotted was attractive and very well endowed. She was also married with kids, as was the subject of our story. It didn't matter to him, but I guess it did to her.

Well, he homed in on her, hanging around her desk and talking. I guess she told him she wasn't interested, but he kept it up. He'd come in out of the drill yard, call her phone extension, and try to talk to her. I hear that he kept on suggesting that they get together, all the while she was getting more and more sick of his advances.

Later, the woman complained to her supervisor. This supervisor was a nice lady, but definitely a no-nonsense type of person. She held a rather high position in the academy administration. The next time the man called upstairs, the lady patched it through so her supervisor could listen. I'm not sure how suggestive he got, but it was enough to anger the supervisor.

When our friend came to work for his third day, he was met at the door by administration staff and escorted off the property. He was warned that if he came back, he might be prosecuted. So ended this man's two-and-a-fraction day career at the fire academy: the shortest one that I know of, and I've been there a long time.

Homecoming Surprise

This is a sad story, and very short, because I never found out any of the details from any investigation that there may have been. It was strictly a police matter from shortly after we, the fire department, got there. It started for us on a mid-morning on a nice summer day. The ambulance was dispatched for an "unresponsive person" at a home not too far from the firehouse. As per protocol, engine 2 from the south side was also dispatched.

I arrived with the ambulance and was directed by the police to an attached garage with a car parked inside. In the car was the body of a young man, seated in the driver's seat. He was probably in his late teens or very early twenties. He was very pale, stiff, and quite dead. He had been there for quite a while. There was a six-pack of cans of beer in the car. One beer was empty. Another was part full and sat open on the console between the front seats. There was also a large bottle of scotch whiskey on the floor in front of the passenger seat. Its cap was on, but there was a glass, a mid-sized water glass, about half-full of scotch set down neatly on the console. The body sat upright in the seat with the head back and eyes closed, like he was asleep. There were no signs of life. He had been gone too long to attempt to revive him. I looked around the car, but nothing seemed out of place. The ignition key was in the "On" position, and the car was out of fuel.

The residents of the house had been away for three days. When they returned, they opened the garage and found this morbid scene. It turned out that they knew the victim. He was the son of some friends who lived nearby. I don't know what problems he might have had, but he seems to have come up with a plan to bring it all to an end. This young man would have known that these people would be gone for three days and he wouldn't be disturbed. It was figured that the day they left, the young man got his beer and scotch and drove to their empty house. He did nothing else but let himself into the garage. He drove his car inside, closed the door behind him, and left the car running. He had a beer, poured some scotch into the glass, and sipped from it. He finished one beer and opened another. At some point after this, he sat his beer down and put down the scotch. He sat back into the seat, laid his head back, and went to sleep.

So ended our involvement. When a body has expired, it becomes a police matter. It's always sad to think that this young man had problems, and the only way he could see to get away from them was to end his life. Nobody knew of any problems, and there was no indication that anything had been wrong. His suicide was totally unexpected.

This is yet another piece of baggage that I've picked up along the way. I think about this once in a while and wonder what happened. But like so many of the other things we see, it doesn't do us any good to dwell on it. We just move on, and sometimes we remember.

First Big One

It wasn't my first fire. I had been to a few others as a call firefighter. There really wasn't anything special or out of the ordinary about it. These kinds of fires happen every day. But it *was* my first really big major fire. I got to see things in operation there that I had only seen in drill.

I was still a call firefighter at that time. There were going to be several openings for full time firefighters coming up soon. A bunch of us had gone through most of the exam process. Next would be the interviews. They were to be held on a Saturday morning in January. I had done pretty well in the rest of the testing, but I never liked interviews. The day came. I guess the interview went all right, but no one told us anything. After it was all over, I had some lunch and headed over to my girlfriend's house. I spent the afternoon there.

In the early evening, my mother called me on the telephone there. She told me that she had seen a fire engine from a neighboring town heading for our station 2. She didn't really know what it meant, but thought that I should know. Of course, after two years on the call fire department, I knew very well that that engine was coming in to cover our south station because we had a fire somewhere. I said goodbye to my girlfriend and left for the firehouse.

When I got to my duty station, station 2, there was indeed an out-of-town engine in there. I was told the fire was in a popular restaurant in town, a bit north of where I was. I should have stayed at the firehouse, but as an eager, young call firefighter, I wanted a piece of this one. So I got into my car with my gear and off I went to the fire.

The restaurant on fire was the original of what would become a small chain of restaurants that had been around for many years. This was dinnertime on a Saturday, so the place must have been full. I was told that it had been full, but all patrons got out all right.

As I approached, the flames lit up the sky. There were engines and ladders and firefighters everywhere. I was excited beyond belief. Trying to get through the police roadblocks, I was stopped by a police officer. I told him I was with the fire department and he waved me through. I parked in a nearby lot, put on my gear, walked across the street, and reported to an officer for orders.

As I looked towards the building, I saw that there were ladder pipes set up. Sometime before I got there, part of the roof had collapsed and two firefighters had been injured. I didn't find this out until later. Neither had any life-threatening injuries. They were back injuries: serious, but not fatal.

I was told to climb a ladder with a hand line and direct the stream into the window. I did that and spent most of my time there, in the same place. After some hours, they started to relieve some of us to return to the firehouse. I was released and went to station 1, as ordered.

Lord, it was cold! Everything was covered in ice. I remember not being able to unsnap my coat because the snaps were frozen shut. I had to take it off by pulling it up over my head. It was so ice-encrusted that it stood in the corner where I put it until the ice melted. I remember seeing a man with icicles hanging off of his bushy eyebrows. I spent the rest of the time helping put the engines back in service again. When everything was done, we were released. Everything about this fire was exciting. I already knew that I wanted to spend my life as a firefighter, and after that fire, I was doubly sure.

Because the restaurant involved was so well known, this was one of those landmark fires that everyone remembers. Some years later, I was thumbing through a book on local history when I came upon a picture taken at that fire. Though the picture was taken from some distance, it didn't take long for me to find myself in it. I looked right at the window where I had been working and was able to recognize myself, standing on a ladder, directing a hose stream into the window.

My first big fire, permanently part of my memory. Now, here in front of me was a photo, with *me* in it, making *me* a permanent part of the history of this fire. Imagine that!

Blood in the Water...

I've said many times that the firehouse can be a brutal place. Everything is fair game and you check your ego at the door on the way in. One cardinal rule there is never let anyone know if something bothers you. Let them know, and it's open season on you and your feelings. If you get ravaged, it's best to just laugh along with everybody else. Laugh, and it goes away. Get mad, and it stays with you until you give up and laugh. Of course, not everything is really fair game. If a guy is down, he'll be treated right. What is fair game and what is not is sort of a code known only to the firefighters. It's not written anywhere. We just know.

I worked with a man once who said that he absolutely hated those metal coat hangers. Well, where do you think he found them? Everywhere, that's where! They were in his car, in his locker and his bed. Everywhere he looked, he saw those hangers. This was a man who had been on the job longer than me. I would have thought he would have known better than to say something and set himself up, but he didn't, and more was yet to come. He never laughed about those hangers and the guys just kept it up. The man had a temper. He'd get really mad and everyone would laugh.

The same man had a thing about bread. Bread could be anywhere; sandwich, toast, bread and butter; it didn't matter. It just had to be cut a certain way. If you take a piece out of a loaf of sliced bread and hold it up, it has a top which is rounded and a bottom which is square-ish. He had to have the bread cut so each half had the top and the bottom. He let the guys know that, and that was all they needed to hear. They would get his lunch and cut the sandwich up into small pieces or quarters or anything they could think of. They'd get his toast with breakfast and do the same thing. Once, he brought in a whole loaf of bread so he could make toast in the morning. The first chance the guys got, they got ahold of his loaf of bread and cut each individual slice all the different ways they could think of: every way but the way the man wanted.

This guy had a lot of little quirks and everybody seemed to know about them. He got mad easy and they knew about that, too. He had kind of a tough time with the guys busting his chops. He never joined in the laughter, so it just didn't stop.

Childish behavior, you say? Maybe, but that's the way it is in the firehouse and there are reasons for it. It's all part of the culture and we all know it. You'd think he would have known better than to drip blood into the water when the sharks were circling.

Boaters in Distress

Almost every active firefighter has a sticker on his vehicle window identifying them as a firefighter. The most common one is the union sticker, but there are others. Working as I did at the state firefighting academy, I got to know people, firefighters, from all over the state.

One weekend day while on duty at station 1, we received a call sending us to a pond on the south side of town for boaters in distress. The dispatcher told us that the caller said there was a canoe tipped over near a beach area, and there were people in the water. There isn't supposed to be any swimming at this beach area, but people swim there anyway. They also launch canoes and small boats.

Responding to the call was engine 2 with their boat, and from station 1 came car 2 with our boat, as well as the ambulance. We arrived in the ambulance to find the engine 2 crew talking to two or three young ladies who were watching a canoe that had indeed tipped over. There were two men and a younger boy in the water. The ladies had come with them to this pond, but elected to stay ashore. The men were laughing and swimming toward shore slowly, dragging the canoe along with them. It seems that the three of them had taken the canoe out with the intention of turning it over for fun. I seem to remember a life jacket on the boy.

As we waited for them to reach shore, I was looking around. My eyes spotted a car with a fire union sticker on the window. I asked the ladies if someone in their group was a firefighter. One lady spoke up and told me that it was her boyfriend's car. She also told me what department he worked for.

As the trio with the canoe got closer, I recognized one of the men as a man that I worked with at the fire academy. I looked at the lady and I told her what the man's name was. Her eyes widened. Then I told her that I knew where he worked, too. She understood how things work in the fire service, as far as harassing each other. She had tried to save him from some of it by telling us that he worked for a different town than he did. She must have thought we would never know the difference, that we couldn't, or wouldn't, bother to track it down and find out. When I told her that I knew her boyfriend and I worked with him, she knew the jig was up. They guys were just having fun and there was no problem. We all had a good laugh.

    I kept getting a good laugh at that man's expense, even though I like the man very much. Such is the nature of the beast. I did tell him about his girlfriend trying to cover for him. I said that any girl who'd go that far out on a limb for you, you should marry her. He laughed. Sometime later, they did indeed get married. I'm still friendly with them both, though I see them infrequently. But I never let them—either one—forget about that day. They still laugh.

Brain Cramp

The fire department rarely, if ever, buys tools and equipment just for fun. From spanner wrenches through axes, pikes, and power saws, these are the tools of the trade and need to be taken care of. They need to be used with care by a well-trained hand, and cleaned and maintained when not in use, to be ready for the next time they're called upon to help us do our job. This also applies to the vehicles we use.

Our engines and ladder trucks, besides providing the means to get us to an emergency in a hurry, are tools themselves because they have the built-in pumps and aerial ladders. They also carry the smaller tools that we need, like ground ladders, forcible entry equipment, power saws, and the like. If a vehicle is driven recklessly, is involved in an accident, isn't maintained, or is driven and operated by someone who is not trained in its use or has a bad attitude, the vehicle just might not arrive on scene. If that happens, the tools on board do not arrive either.

My fire department had only one ladder truck. The old one was replaced about halfway through my career. The new one was quite large and needed presence of mind to operate safely. Most of us did pretty well with it. We took it out for training, not only driving, but operating the aerial ladder, too.

One day, when the truck responded to a call, the driver got out and placed the chock blocks under the wheels, as per protocol. It turned out that there was no fire. The crew got back onto the truck to go back to the firehouse. The driver placed the transmission in gear and pushed down on the gas. The vehicle did not move. He pressed harder on the gas. The engine revved up, but the truck still did not move. Instead of getting out and looking at what the problem might be, the driver just pushed the gas pedal to the floor. This time, the truck slowly moved.

It had a rough start at first, going up and over a bump. Had the driver gotten out, he would have noticed the chock block that had been left under the wheel. But the driver never got out to look. Instead, he forced the truck forwards, up and over the chock. The block was caught up in the dual wheels and got wedged in there. In the process, it punctured the inner tire and flattened it, as well as an air bag in the suspension system, effectively putting the truck out of service.

Knowing the driver, I don't think a bad attitude was the problem. The problem was a lack of thought, or possibly inadequate training. The truck told the driver that there was a problem, but the driver didn't listen. The result was that our only ladder truck had to be taken out of service for repair.

This incident cost the town some money, but it could have been far more costly. What about the fact that we might need the aerial device, hand tools, ground ladders, or the built-in pump that it carried? You can call this an accident if you want. In the absence of intent, I suppose it was. Someone was not paying attention to what was happening around them. This is the kind of accident that cannot be allowed to happen. The effects can be far-reaching and the results can be tragic.

Watch What You Say in the Firehouse

We once had a man working on our fire department who was legendary for being a miser. It was sometimes said that he still had the first buck he ever made. Anyone who really knew him, however, knew that he spent money regularly on himself, but no so often on others. One day, he decided to take his kids to an amusement park. He never did any research before going, so he didn't know how much it would cost to get in. The family got in the car, drove a couple of hours, and got to the park.

They got up to the gate where the sign showed the admission price. The man turned his kids around at the gate, put them in the car, and drove home. He wasn't going to spend that much money going to an amusement park!

Well, I guess the man couldn't keep quiet about it. He must have told someone, and before he knew it, everyone on the whole department knew. People were calling him cheapskate, miser, and a whole host of other things, none of them complimentary. One guy even said that if he didn't have the money at the gate, he would have sold the spare tire to his truck rather than disappoint the kids. Someone among those savages at the firehouse even put up a sign and a collection can to try to collect money to send that guy's kids to the amusement park.

Of course, it was a joke and we all got a good laugh out of it. How he does things with his family is certainly none of our business. I have certain personal feelings about what he did, and I never would have even mentioned it to the kids until I knew how much it would cost. But that's all just my opinion, and nobody asked for it. But he never should have told anyone in the firehouse!

Constant Vigilance

When my kids were small and in grade school, I used to get to go along on school field trips from time to time to chaperone. I remember one such trip when the kids were in early grammar school. (I don't remember where we were going.) While riding on the bus to our destination, there was a little girl in a seat right in front of my daughter and me. Back then, the rules on the busses weren't so strict, and the kids would stand in their seats and turn around to talk. When the girl in front of me turned around, I noticed some heavy scarring from her neck down, starting just below the chin.

There's no mistaking a scar from a burn, and that's what this was. It seemed to have been a really large burn, too. Something about her brought back a vague memory from some years before. I asked and my daughter told me her name. It didn't ring any bells. I asked my daughter if she knew what had happened to her to give her those scars. She didn't know. My daughter did tell me the area where the girl lived. With that, things started to come back to me.

The next time I went to work at the firehouse, I went and spoke to a man who had always worked the shift just before mine. He would always be getting off work just as I came on duty. I asked him about a certain call he went on some years before. The pieces came together. I remembered that day. I came in to work for a night shift and found the whole off-going day shift very quiet and subdued. They just walked around, waiting for their relief to come in so they could leave. I knew the look. I had seen it before after something bad had happened. I asked a friend just before he left. He filled me in.

A couple of hours before shift change, they had responded with the ambulance to a home where a child had been injured. They arrived to find a toddler screaming and badly burned. The mother had been making pasta sauce in a crock-pot on a counter top. She had forgotten to make sure the cord was out of reach of the little one. Sure enough, the little girl walked over, grabbed the cord, and pulled the crock-pot off of the counter. The hot pasta sauce spilled all over the little girl.

I never heard about the atmosphere in the house, but I can only imagine how bad it all was, with the baby screaming and mother coming apart emotionally, as well as the sense of urgency that a call like that produces. Pasta sauce tends to stick, so they had to wash it off of the toddler to stop it from continuing to burn and causing more damage. In a chaotic scene like that, you have to keep your head and concentrate on what you have to do.

After cleaning off the baby as much as possible, they needed to cover the burns to prevent more damage before transporting her to the hospital. One of the firefighters was just about to put a large dressing on the burns when another firefighter suddenly yelled at him to stop. He was about to use a trauma dressing. Although this kind of dressing is good for large cuts and other soft tissue injuries, it sticks to burns. Fortunately, he was stopped just in time. A nonstick, burn dressing was applied, and the baby was wrapped in a burn sheet. Then she was taken to the hospital.

As is so often the case, we lost track of what happened to that little girl after she was brought to the hospital. As the years went by, it became just another memory of a call from the past. But we don't often forget completely. When I saw that girl on the bus and found out a little about her, it wasn't hard to determine that this was the same girl. She was somewhere between six and ten, probably closer to six. She was happy and seemingly healthy, but she was deeply scarred. I can only imagine what it was like for her to recover from an injury like that.

That little girl's mother probably blamed herself often for the mistake she made—and she should. Because of her actions, an innocent child had to pay the price. People make mistakes, right? Yes, they do. But as parents of small children, I believe we give up that right to make mistakes. We owe it to our children to keep watch and keep them safe as long as they are in our care. I know that Mom paid a terrible price, too: anguish, sorrow, and deep feelings of guilt for the hurt her one moment of inattention caused. We need to pay attention. Constant vigilance: without it, the price to be paid by all concerned is far too high.

CPR Save

I was on the job long before there were any paramedics, advanced life support, or SAEDs. We had CPR only, and often you had to work the patient by yourself. We did sometimes have a partner, but even still, to have a save with CPR alone was kind of rare. They did happen sometimes, but not often.

As the years went by, EMS improved. Paramedics came along with defibrillation equipment and meds. We still ran a BLS ambulance, but now we could get also ALS. They were non-transport and would ride with us in our ambulance, and treat the patient.

The town next door to us was very busy. They had two ALS ambulances that were kept going all the time. Sometimes, when ALS was not needed, our BLS ambulance would get called in to help with some of the calls.

One day in the afternoon, I was working at headquarters. We were listening to the other towns on the fire radio. The town next door was busy. Sure enough, we got a call to respond to that town for a male patient with chest pain. My partner and I went with our ambulance. We had both been on the job for quite a few years and felt confident in our abilities. We picked up our patient, loaded him into the ambulance, and then I got in the back with him. The hospital was not too far away and within that town.

As we started off, the patient was conscious and alert, and in discomfort with chest pain. Shortly into our transport, the patient stopped talking and lost consciousness. I felt for a pulse, but found none. I quickly got out an oral airway and a BVM, and called to my partner, "Step on it. The patient just arrested!"

My partner said, "You're kidding me?!" as he picked up speed. He got on the radio to report our latest development.

I knew just what to do, having done this many times before. I carefully inserted an airway into the patient, and started one-man CPR with a BVM. On the way to the hospital, we would have to pass a firehouse. My partner arranged for us to meet up there with one of the ALS ambulances that had become available. The medics would then take over with their meds and equipment.

Before we got to that rendezvous, I felt for a pulse, and found a strong one. The patient then started to breathe for himself. When we arrived at the firehouse, the medics came into the back of the ambulance. I told them what I had done, and that I had gotten a pulse back.

They examined the patient, and said, "Good job!" As the hospital was only two or three minutes away, they told us to continue. They didn't come with us.

We arrived at the hospital, brought our patient inside, and turned him over to the hospital staff. He had a strong pulse when we left him. It was a good, clean save.

A couple of weeks later, I was on duty at headquarters again. I was sitting in the day room, reading. The chief walked through, and as he did, the phone rang and he picked it up.

He listened for a minute, and then he looked up at me and asked, "Did you guys have a save the other day?"

I told him where it happened and said that it was a good save. I added that it was a couple of weeks ago.

He spoke into the phone again. I couldn't believe what I heard. He said something to the effect of, "It was too long ago." Then he hung up.

He had been talking to the local newspaper. They had heard about our save and had called to get the story. Here was a chance for some good publicity, and the boss didn't give them the story because it had happened two weeks before. It was just beyond belief!

DTs

This is story about drinking and it dwells within the realm of the disgusting. One night years back, we got a call for an unknown medical at a residence. Unknowns are a real blast. You never know what you'll walk into. I was on the ambulance as the attendant. We arrived at a large home with a two-car attached garage. We were directed into the garage where we saw a set of five or six wooden steps leading into the house. Our patient, a male in his late 40s or early 50s and dressed in the suit he had worn to work, was lying face down on these steps, his head toward the top, feet toward the bottom. He was conscious, but was convulsing and unable to get up. Much of what he said made no sense at all.

It turns out that this man had been a very heavy drinker for years. I guess he functioned well for a long time. If I remember correctly, he had stopped drinking cold turkey, just a few days before this incident.

As we started to examine our patient, a neighbor, who also claimed to be a doctor, appeared. Doctors who just show up, give a few orders, and then leave, are the bane of our existence in the EMS field. Soon this neighbor-doctor started giving orders. He ordered us to transport the patient in a facedown position on the stretcher. That is almost never the right thing to do. He was adamant, until we asked him if he was taking responsibility for the patient. He said, "No," and disappeared quickly.

We put the patient on the stretcher, on his back, sat him up slightly, and gave him oxygen as we started to the hospital. The man continued to mumble and talk gibberish. At some point shortly into the ride, his body emptied itself. He did not vomit, so protecting his airway was not an issue. However, the most disgusting smell I've ever experienced filled the patient compartment. I opened every window I could get to and turned on the blower fans, all to no avail. It was brutal.

When we got to the hospital, my partner came to the back and opened the ambulance doors. He gasped as the smell hit him. He backed off for a second to catch his breath. We quickly unloaded the stretcher and wheeled it into the ER. When the nurses saw—and smelled—what we had brought them, they directed us into a nearby room. The man had just made a mess of everything: himself, his clothes, the stretcher, the linen, and the back of the ambulance. The nurses worked in shifts, two at a time, to undress him and clean him up. The nurses could only work for a minute or two, then they had to come out to get some fresh air, and two more would go in.

I took the ambulance stretcher into another room to clean it. The sheets, pillow, and pillowcase went into biohazard bags. I used every cleaner/disinfectant that I could find. Eventually, I got things cleaned up, all except for a large, yellow stain on the vinyl mattress cover. It was not removable. That stain was on that cover until the day we replaced it years later.

Of all the calls that I answered over the years, this one has to remain the most disgusting. The man was a major, long-term alcoholic whose body had begun to rebel against what he had been doing to it all those years. It was shutting down. The man did not survive, but the memory of that call lingers.

Dog Struck

Just about all of us in the fire service do something else to supplement our income and to use up spare time. Some of us stay at home and take care of the kids while off duty because our spouse has a well-paying job. I've done many things to make a little money. One of them was painting houses with another man on our department. On days when I was off and he wasn't, I would go painting, so we'd keep the job going and someone would be there just about every day.

One day, when I was painting, I was close enough to home to go there for lunch. When I was done eating, I got into my truck and started back to the job. I got to the end of the street and turned. I looked ahead just in time to see a young girl and her dog on the sidewalk. The dog suddenly darted out into the street and was hit by a car almost right away. The driver couldn't help hitting the dog since it ran out in front of him without warning. The car stopped and the driver got out, but wasn't sure what to do. The girl ran into the street and up to where the dog lay, still alive. The little girl was crying, yelling, and screaming in the middle of the street as the driver looked on.

As Murphy's law would dictate, the traffic picked up. There were a lot of cars zipping around the girl and the dog, and none stopped. What could I do? I stopped on the side of the road and walked out into the middle of the street. I tried to direct the traffic around the little girl and keep everyone safe. There were some nasty words exchanged between me and some motorists who were in a big hurry. There were not too many cell phones around back then. I kept directing traffic, hoping that someone would call the police.

The street we were on was where my fire chief lived. He also had gone home for lunch that day. When he came out of his house, he saw a commotion in the street and looked over at me. He was within yelling distance and asked what was wrong. I called out to call the police, which he did.

A short time later, a police cruiser pulled up in the middle of the street. The officer, with help from me and the driver, put the dog onto a blanket and got it into the police cruiser. He took the dog to a veterinarian's office nearby.

It turns out that I sort of knew the girl. She was a friend of my daughter and had been to our house before. After the police took the dog, everyone else left. The little girl's mother came by and thanked me. I went back to my painting.

The next time I went to work at the fire department, the chief called me into his office. He handed me a letter. It was from the mother of the little girl. She sang me praises and called me a hero. She couldn't say enough nice things about me. The chief just smiled and I left his office.

I still have that letter in my scrapbook. Funny, you can save the life of someone and hear nothing about it from them or their family. Then there is something like this, when all I did was to keep the traffic moving around a little girl and a dog (that turned out to not even be hers). Hero? I think not. What else could I do?

Meet My brother

Most recruits that go through the state fire academy do reasonably well. Mistakes are made and lessons learned. We have a system of demerits used in grading practical skills. Minor mistakes get 1 demerit. Some people make some very big mistakes. Majors get 5 for each different major infraction. So if someone has a bad day, doesn't listen, or just doesn't get it, those demerits can add up. There is a limit, quite a high number, after which you wash out of the program. This doesn't happen often, but it's always on the minds of the students. This is kind of a good thing as it makes them learn to work under stress.

To grade some of these skills, we put together several scenarios called "hose evolutions." The crew drives up to a designated spot, gets off, and each member of the three-person crew has tasks to perform, ending with water coming out the end of the hose. We can grade a bunch of practical skills this way.

One day in late summer 2001, I was grading the person running the pump in a hose evolution. He was not doing too well. This was a kid who thought he knew everything and that we had nothing to teach him. As I stood and watched, this man was having trouble hooking up the right hose to the right place. Basically, this guy didn't know what the hell he was doing. However, this was testing time, not instructional time, so we let him go on.

After a while, the officer of the day and an assistant coordinator came over to watch. It was decided that I would write up a subjective report on this man for his failure to properly get water out of the pump. All told, it took him over 40 minutes to complete his portion of the evolution. It shouldn't have taken him more than three or four minutes.

When he was done, we went over what was wrong and counted up all the demerits. There were a lot of them. Then I informed him that he would be getting a subjective report, also. He got angry. He told me, "I could run this pump in my sleep," to which I remarked, "Well, it's too bad you weren't sleeping because you sure as hell couldn't run it when you were awake."

Well, that did it. This man didn't have any use for me at all. He didn't misbehave or show any disrespect. He just avoided me.

This man's class was still at the academy at the time of the 911 attacks in New York. A while afterward, firefighters from all over the world, myself included, were gathering in NYC for funerals. At one such funeral, I was with a friend in a sea of fire department blue uniforms in front of St Patrick's Cathedral in midtown Manhattan, when I heard my name called. I turned, and walking up to me was a man that I recognized from a previous recruit class. He had been his class's president. (Strange that he was in civilian clothes. I never asked why.) He asked me how things were going and we made small talk for a minute. Then he said something to the effect of, "I think you know my brother."

He turned towards the man behind him, also in civilian clothes. I looked and saw a man trying his best to be as small as possible. You guessed it. It was my friend from the recruit class. Funny thing, this man was supposed to be in recruit class that day at the academy.

He said, "Hi," and I said something like, "Yes, we've met." He looked a bit terrified. I kind of smiled and went on my way. I had him. I could have had him roasted, but the look on his face and his knowledge that I let him off the hook was punishment enough. Also, he was there for the funeral of a brother killed in the line of duty. I sure wasn't going to fault him for that.

Damage Control

When I was promoted to lieutenant, I took on the added role of department training officer, a role I kept through the rest of my career. It was my responsibility to decide on the training topics for the full-time firefighters. Each shift officer made sure this training was conducted for their own group.

It was part of my job to conduct monthly training for our small call department, never more than ten people. While training on basics; pumps, hose, SCBA, and the like; I tried to keep the drills active and interesting. We would use some backup engines and simulate a response to a call at a selected building in town. The call people would drive the engine to that location and they would receive orders when they arrived. Since we drilled on weekends, we often used one of the school buildings because they would be unoccupied. We would raise ladders, pull hose, use hydrants, and squirt water. We tried to make it realistic.

Sometimes we'd get permission to drill in a house slated for demolition. Burning them was usually not an option, but we could use them to practice other skills, like search and rescue and advancing hose into a house. At most of the drills, either myself, the assistant training officer, or both of us would oversee the drill.

Once a year or so, I liked to arrange a special drill. When possible, we would arrange a live burn. Working as I did at the state firefighting academy, I could often arrange drills using their facilities, including use of their burn building and their instructors. I did this once or twice and had very successful drills.

The academy is a very busy place. In order to keep things manageable, class sizes are limited, so I had to try to book certain drills early. One year, I wanted to set up a burn again. I spoke to the proper people and was given a tentative OK for my people to attend a burn class that had already been scheduled.

As the time drew near, the academy got a new director who was just starting to get the feel for his job. At that time, I got a message saying that the class was full and my people would not be able to participate. To say that I was displeased would be putting it mildly. I checked to verify this with the people in charge of those classes. They said it was full and we were out. Well, it is what it is.

I thought about what to do, talked to some people, and then placed a call to a fire department a distance away. I knew that they had their own burn building that we might be able to use. I got their training officer on the phone and set it up easily. It all went like clockwork. A day was arranged. We had to provide all equipment and an engine, as well as supervision and instructors. All of this was no problem.

When everything was all set, I went to inform our chief of what was going on. He was not pleased at all. He said to let him handle it. I didn't know what he was going to do. I found out later that he had called the academy and harshly asked the new director what kind of outfit he was running, and how could he pull the rug out from under us when the training was scheduled!

I tried to tell the chief that I had rescheduled the location of the burn, but he didn't want to hear anything else from me. The new director at the academy was at a loss. He didn't know what was going on, but he was going to find out. He called the man in charge of those burn classes, and I guess he went up one side of him and down the other.

I only found out all this happened when the guy in charge of the burns called me on the phone. I knew this man and had a good relationship with him, until then. He asked me why I went to my chief and complained. He said that he had gotten his head handed to him. He basically blamed me for it. I tried to explain what I thought had happened, but I still don't think he believed me.

I had enjoyed a reasonably good reputation at the academy, but this whole thing didn't make *me* look too good either. I had to spend the next two weeks doing damage control on my own reputation. Since this director was new, I sought some advice from a person I knew in the director's office. Although I had just met him, the new director seemed to like me and we got along well, but I was advised not to talk to him about it. My chief still didn't want to discuss the matter with me.

The day of the burn in that other town's burn building came and went. It was a very good, successful day. Soon, the problems created by the interference of other people kind of drifted into the background. My relationship with the man in charge of the academy burns was never the same after that. We are cordial when we meet, but that's all.

I feel really bad about the whole situation. I guess I should have not involved the chief, but it was part of my job to keep him informed. I never thought he'd meddle like that.

Regarding that new director, he didn't last too long. He had a rather stormy relationship with many of the instructor staff, and there was a problem between him and the state fire marshall, who also happened to be in charge of the entire academy. The marshall told him to do something one day, I don't remember what, but I guess it didn't sit too well with him. I heard that the director told the marshall that he didn't work for him (the marshall): he worked for the training council. The following Monday he was met at the door when he came to work. He was told that he had been fired. He was allowed to clean out his desk and was escorted off the property. I guess he found out exactly who he *did* work for.

Confidence

When I worked at the state firefighting academy, there was a drill station that every recruit had to go through. It wasn't popular with most of the instructors. They didn't want to work and teach this station. It was called the confidence course. The students did not wear protective firefighting gear. They wore class B uniforms and the same shoes they wore for morning exercise and physical conditioning. I guess that the reason that many instructors didn't like it was that they might have thought it was kind of a playtime. It had no tasks that directly involved the fighting of fire.

There were some instructors who liked teaching this, and I was one of them. I thought that the confidence course was very much related to the job, in that it taught the recruits to work together in groups, under a leader. This was done in two different ways. They were taught to work as a group, with each one doing something different, but toward a common goal; and they were taught to work as a group, each doing the same thing, toward a common goal. I would often start off the lesson by explaining why it was so important that we all learn to work together when we come from all across the state. I talked about incidents where crews and apparatus from distant towns have covered firehouses and answered calls. I spoke of probability vs. possibility. It was improbable that they would ever have to answer a call with firefighters from distant cities and towns, but it was possible. It has happened before and could happen again. This was something the students had never thought of.

There were several different tasks we had them perform. First, we would have each recruit, one at a time, stand on a platform and fall backward into the waiting arms of their fellow recruits. In this way, they learned faith and confidence in their brothers and sisters. I often did it first, just to show how it was done, as well as to show that I had faith in them, though I didn't know them. I had confidence in them because they were firefighters, and that was enough.

Another task involved marking off an area on the floor. We called it the "swamp." There were some cement blocks in the swamp and the recruits were provided with a number of 4"x4"x8' posts. They had to stretch these posts from block to block to build a bridge across the swamp. The blocks had been strategically placed so that there was only one way it would work. When it was done, all members of the group had to cross the bridge without falling into the swamp. If anything or anybody touched the swamp, everything had to be dismantled and they had to start again.

From this, they learned to work as a group, each performing a different task. Some would be looking for the right block to use for the next post; some would be handing posts out to members standing on the bridge or blocks; some people on the bridge or blocks would pass the posts even further out to yet other members; and some would be helping other members of the group across. The common goal was building the bridge and getting everyone across. This activity could represent firefighters working at an MVA, or different companies at a building fire, each performing a different task, yet working together toward a common goal.

For another activity, we had two 4x4s that we laid on the floor, side by side. These posts had holes drilled in them, with a short length of rope through the hole and knotted so it wouldn't slip out. We had the group of students stand on these posts, one foot on each, like skis. They all got on, one behind the other. Each one held a

rope from each 4x4. The object was to work together and walk the "trolleys," as we called them, across the floor and down a predetermined course. The course included a turn. They worked as a team to accomplish this, and it was done for time. The recruits had fun seeing how fast they could do it.

From this, they learned to work together, each doing the same thing to accomplish their goal. In relation to the job, it could be a crew all working together to move a big line full of water through a building.

If there was enough time, I had another fun activity. I had four recruits take their firefighting hoods and put them on backward. This would take away their sight. I would appoint a leader and give him a length of rope about 10 feet long. I would tell him to use his group, put them on the rope, and form the shape of a square. That is, each would be holding the rope and standing so the rope made a square when they were done. The rest of the group would watch. Sometimes it went well and the leader knew just how to do things. Other times, it was comical to watch as things were fouled up or orders given that the crew couldn't follow. When they were finished, they would take off their hoods and see how they had done. From this, they learned communication. We would have a talk on how to communicate and give or follow orders in the dark.

From all of these activities, they learned to direct others and follow orders. There were many other things we could have done, but we always ran out of time. Everything done the day we ran the confidence course was a learning experience. I've heard it said that, "Play is the work of children," and there is something to be learned in almost everything we do. These recruits were our "children" to teach. If this was merely playtime, they must have worked hard at it because they did a lot of learning. All it took was a short explanation of what we were doing and its relationship to their jobs. Once they understood, they learned.

Not Showing Off

This is another story about the need to pay attention at a medical call. It's so important to the patient and often there is little margin for error. This happened one night when the captain was out and I, as the shift lieutenant, was in the car commanding the shift. It was early fall. It wasn't really cold, but cooling off at night so the mice and bees were looking for a warm place for the night. Some bees found their way into the attic of a two-family home on the south side of town. A boy of about twelve, who lived on the second floor, got stung. I don't remember whether he went into the attic or the bee found its way downstairs. Either way, the boy got stung one time. As I recall, it was the first time he had ever been stung and his mother called the fire department for assistance.

We sent the engine from station 2 and the ambulance from headquarters. I responded with car 2 from headquarters also. Station 2's engine was first due. A few minutes after their arrival, they reported that there probably would be no transport. The ambulance arrived a couple of minutes before me. When I arrived, the ambulance crew was outside, near their vehicle. They told me the engine crew was upstairs with the mother. They had the "refusal of transport" papers for her to sign.

There was a boy outside the house. I was told that he was the one who had gotten stung. I went up to talk to him. As he spoke, I noticed that he was wheezing a bit. I took him to the tailboard of the engine and had him sit down. I asked him how he was feeling. He said he was OK, but to me, it didn't look that way. He was still wheezing and his breathing was slightly labored. It was getting dark so I took out a pen light and looked at him. I could see hives on his neck. I asked him to lift his shirt. His torso was covered with hives. Either of these is a sign of an allergic reaction to the sting. Together, they could mean something serious is happening. In an allergic reaction of this type, things can go very bad, very quickly.

I told the ambulance crew to watch him and I started into the house. The engine crew met me at the door on their way out. I stopped them and asked if they had examined the patient. They said, "Yes," but with the tone you'd expect from someone who had just been told that he hadn't done his job right. I didn't mean to imply that at all. I told them that the kid was wheezing and was covered with hives.

I said, "He *has* to go to the hospital."

They had a refusal form signed and said that the mother didn't want him taken to the hospital. Something told me that Mom hadn't been told the whole story. I went back upstairs and introduced myself to the mother. I explained what we had found with her son and tried to explain what anaphylaxis is. I explained to her that her son had labored breathing and hives, two classic signs of an anaphylactic reaction. I told her that maybe he would be all right, but maybe not. It was possible that her son's condition could worsen very quickly and become life-threatening if she waited to see how he was later. If that happened, we might not be able to get back fast enough to help him. We had no epi on the ambulance at that time, and there was no guarantee that any paramedics would be available. It might just be a fast ride to the hospital, hoping that we could get him there in time.

After hearing what I had to say, I think she was a bit scared. She never realized it could be so serious. Better to put the fear into her and act now, rather than have her wait until later and maybe have a tragic outcome. Telling her the whole story is part of our job. She agreed to the transport and we tore up the refusal form. The transport went well without any incident.

I definitely got a cold shoulder and an attitude from that engine crew. These were men with a lot of experience and they were talking like I was accusing them of not knowing their jobs. I think that they thought I was shoving my weight around because I was in charge. That wasn't the case at all. That kid needed to go to the hospital right then: our basic EMT training taught us that. Experience, especially having seen severe anaphylaxis, reinforces that lesson.

I don't really care what those guys thought of me. It wasn't me showing off. Lessons learned in more than twenty-five years of EMS experience told me what to do. If they left with that refusal form, they wouldn't have done their jobs right. If I allowed that to happen, then I wouldn't have done my job right, either.

Feels Like Home

  I have never liked a "Bed and Breakfast," though I've stayed in quite a few in my travels. I don't really find myself comfortable. It has nothing to do with the accommodations. They're usually just fine. It has to do with the feeling I get when I stay in one. It feels like I'm in the home of someone that I don't know, which, I guess is true. I like the privacy of a motel or hotel. Then I can be by myself, or whoever I'm traveling with, and not have to try to make conversation with someone I don't know.

  Mealtime is another time things can be uncomfortable at a B&B. I don't go to restaurants where we sit at a long table with people that we don't know. I like the privacy of a private table for just my family and me. I don't like sitting at the table in the dining room with the others who are staying at the B &B and feeling like I have to make conversation. The hosts are usually great and do their best, but I just don't like staying at a B&B. However, there are times when a choice is not available.

  Some years back, we went to a family reunion a couple of states away. The relatives who were hosting certainly did not have the room to put up all who were attending. They had a friend who ran a small B&B who could accommodate my wife, me, and our fourteen-month-old daughter. That was the best that we were going to do, so we decided to stay there. When we arrived, I didn't like what I saw at all. The place was beautiful and the lady kept a very nice home, but as it turned out, they just had a room that they rented out sometimes. It wasn't even a real B&B. It was much smaller. We were guests in the home of an older couple that we'd never laid eyes on before. Uncomfortable as it was, I made the best of it. The lady of the house was very nice and couldn't do enough for us.

  When we got up our first morning there, we were told that breakfast would be ready in a few minutes. We went downstairs to the dining room where there was an older man sitting at the table reading the paper. The lady of the house came in and introduced this man as her husband. Then she went to get the food. The conversation started out slowly and a bit awkward, but when the man said that he was a retired New York City fire lieutenant, all that changed. Suddenly the conversation flowed. When two or more firefighters get together, the shoptalk starts. We could talk for hours about the job. While the lieutenant and I talked, I saw the ladies exchange a couple of glances, but this was no surprise to either one. Both had lived for years with a firefighter and were used to this sort of thing.

When time came for us to check out, I really didn't want to leave. I could have stayed and talked shop all day. A firefighter is at home in any firehouse. When the man told me what he had done, who he was, we were brothers, firefighters with much in common, no matter where we worked. That B&B felt very much like home.

Cold Rain

Many years ago, when I was on the call fire department, we would drill once a month from 6:00 to 10:00 in the evening. During the summer when the days were long and we had plenty of sunlight, we could drill on pumps, SCBA, hose, and anything else we wanted. As the year went on and the days grew shorter, we would drill on the same things, except that now the drills would start with setting up portable lighting so we could see.

One evening, as it started to get cold at night, we set up our lighting. We would be drilling with the ladder truck. We went through just about everything we needed to know about the truck. The last thing we drilled on was the set up and use of the ladder pipe. This was a rather old ladder and so it had an old type of ladder pipe.

The set up involved attaching the gun itself to the end of the aerial ladder, then stretching 100 feet of 3" hose from the gun down the ladder and into a unit called a siamese connection. The siamese allowed two feeder lines to be attached to feed the 3" line, and thus the gun would be in operation. This set up was fed water by an engine that would be hooked up to a hydrant. The fun part of this drill was when we took turns on the ladder tip and got to control the gun.

We were drilling behind the headquarters firehouse, which stood on the corner of two main roads in the center of town. Being in the back of the station kept us free from any problems, or so we thought.

We had been spraying water for a while when the police came out and told us to shut down the water. We didn't see what the problem was. Then they told us that they were getting reports of cars sliding and coming sideways down the big hill on the main road behind the firehouse. There had been several accidents out there.

We couldn't see much of this because there were many trees between us and the road. We also thought there was enough distance. I guess we underestimated the power of our own tools. Apparently, the water stream was shooting over the trees, coming down in a fine mist onto the road, and freezing on the hill, creating a skating rink out there. We shut down and put everything away, confident that we knew about the ladder truck and its equipment—especially what we could expect from the ladder pipe. At least no one got hurt.

Cursed

It always seemed to me that there were certain places in town, streets, or neighborhoods where there have been more incidents than anywhere else. There is a street in town that has had more fires that any other single street. Extend that to the neighborhoods off of that street, and we have a pretty large number of fires in one area. There is no arsonist running around though. I'm just counting all fires that I can remember. My memory extends back to when I was in junior high school and goes until a couple of years after I retired. I was at many of these fires and was the incident commander for one of them. On the street itself, I can count five or six. Include the side streets and the number goes up to ten or so, with three of them resulting in at least one fatality. This isn't a really long street and certainly isn't in a rundown area. I just think the place is cursed.

There is another street where there seem to be more serious motor vehicle accidents than any other single street in town. This road does carry a lot of traffic, but it's just your typical, two-lane residential street, and the problem isn't the whole street, just a certain stretch of it. I remember back in high school, a kid that lived near me got killed, along with his friend, in an MVA on that stretch of road.

One of the most horrific accidents I've been to happened on that same stretch of road. It would have been worse, except there was no sense of urgency, as both of the car's occupants were very obviously dead. The accidents there weren't always fatalities. I treated some bad injuries on that road also. It got so after a while, we would cringe when the call was an MVA on that stretch of road.

What made that road so cursed? Well, there is a kind of long straightaway before some wide sweeping curves. It may present an opportunity for young drivers to show off the driving skill that most of them haven't developed yet. It also is a stretch of road where the town high school is located. A large number of high school age drivers use that road. There was a fatality near the beginning of the stretch of road when a young pedestrian was struck and killed by a car while crossing the street in front of the high school. The reason for that was clear. The youngster crossed the street in front of a car without looking, and the driver of the car was a high-school-age girl with a pretty new license. She was only 16 years old and her lack of experience behind the wheel likely affected the outcome.

Not all of these accidents involved high schoolers. I do remember a single car accident where a young mother had potential for severe neck injuries and much time had to be taken to stabilize and remove her from the car.

The others can't really be explained as to why they always seem to happen here. Whenever I can't explain something, I often blame it on the evil spirits. I think these cursed spirits are at work in these areas, and have been for many years. If you have a better explanation, I'm all ears.

Beauty and the Beast

Working for all those years at the state firefighting academy, I met firefighters from all over the state. I made some very good friends and met some very interesting people. There was one, a friend of mine, that comes to mind now. He was definitely descended from white, Irish catholic working-class people. He was also a bigot. Usually there is nothing funny about bigotry, but the way this guy acted and talked, we all just had to laugh. Even those African Americans that we worked with over the years, the ones who might sometimes be targets of bigotry, had to laugh.

There was a female firefighter who came to work with us for a while. She had come from one of the smaller cities around Boston and had come through the academy as a recruit. She was short, overweight, loud, had a large bust, and a sense of humor that had everybody in the room laughing. As a worker, she was no ball of fire. She was also African American. Back then, we said she was black. This made no difference to anyone but my friend. He wasn't the type to be openly hostile to a black person. He would just be kind of quiet and would talk to them only if he was spoken to. I'm still not really sure that he had anything against African Americans. Maybe it was just something he had heard all his life and had been practiced by his family and he never really thought about it. I don't know.

What I *do* know is that this woman found out about his feelings and decided to have some fun. She would stand next to him and try to kiss him, then watch him run away mumbling to himself. She would follow him around, call out to him, "Come here and give me a hug!", and blow him kisses. She and the rest of us got a big laugh out of it.

After a while, she took it up a step. She'd grab him in a hug. One time I saw her rub his head in her cleavage while moaning. He'd be there screaming and trying to get away. Of course, he could have escaped anytime if he had gotten really mad and violent, but he wasn't that sort of guy.

One day she was chasing him and he tried to get away by running into another room. There was no escape, as she entered the room and closed the one and only door behind her. For about ten minutes, we could hear him screaming. Finally, the door opened, and out he ran. He ran as far away as he could, as fast as he could.

She had been married before and had a couple of kids, one of which was young. She once told me that "Captain Morgan" was the father of her youngest. Apparently, she liked to drink that spiced rum. She said she got carried away one night and the result was her little son. She started calling my friend the "little one's father," and kept saying she wanted to "do it with him and have another baby." We would tease the guy and accuse him of being that little kid's father. He used to say that there wasn't enough extinguisher powder in the place to make her "white enough" to attract him.

There wasn't much this woman wouldn't say. Well, she had my poor buddy walking on eggshells every time he came to work, worrying about whether or not she'd be there. It was all done in fun, and we all got a good laugh, oddly enough, even my friend laughed.

This went on until the woman was injured on the job and had to leave us. Eventually, she had to leave the job completely. I missed the way she could make the room erupt with laughter, even when she was not tormenting my friend.

My buddy stayed at the academy and endured the harassment from his peers. He was well thought of and was a hard worker. Trouble was that he also had a drinking problem he couldn't lick. It went on for some years, and he eventually lost his job in the fire service and his job at the academy. I haven't seen him for years. I do miss him and wish him well. I still laugh out loud when I remember those days of torment he went through. It was quite a love story: like Beauty and the Beast. I'm not sure which was which.

Bad Directions

Many years ago, I worked with an older guy at station 2. This guy was older than my parents and had kids my age. He was a guy who had come on the job in another era, when they just hired you, gave you a uniform, and put you to work. There was very little training, just on-the-job. He was really a nice guy, but he took some getting used to. He seemed to do everything kind of half-assed, by the seat of his pants.

One weekend day in the summer, we were on duty when a man came into the firehouse looking for directions to the town beach. That was an easy one: it is only up the street. I take a small element of pride in giving directions. I think I do a good job doing that.

However, before I could say a word, my partner started talking. He walked the man out towards the door, pointing towards the street he should take. I saw the man walk to his car and get in. I figured my partner had things under control, so I sat down. My partner came back in and sat down. He turned on something on TV that I didn't care to watch, so I got up and went to stand outside by the open bay doors.

I stood there looking around when I saw a car drive by that I thought I recognized. I looked again and saw that it was the same man who had asked for directions shortly before. He drove past the firehouse and down the street. Somewhere around ten minutes later, that same car drove by the firehouse again, only slower this time. The driver looked over at me and I could see that he wasn't too happy. After he drove by, I decided that I'd better go back inside. I didn't really want to be out there if he passed by again.

I don't know where my partner had told this man to go, but it sure as hell wasn't the town beach. That man didn't look happy at all, and I didn't want to become the victim of a drive-by shooting because my partner couldn't give directions.

A Reception to Remember

I was told that this book wouldn't be complete without a mention of my wedding reception. It was the second marriage for me. There weren't too many relatives of mine, just my mother, sisters, and my three children from my first marriage. I had invited a good many friends, the vast majority of which were firefighters from all over the area. When these people get together to work, they work hard. When they mourn, they mourn hard. And when it's time to play, that's what they do: they play hard.

There was one guy there who had worked the night before. It had been a busy night. Though he was dead tired, you couldn't keep him off the dance floor. He even grabbed a lady bussing tables and pulled her onto the floor to dance. We've got a picture of him and his wife, with a vivid expression of understanding and acceptance on her face.

Another firefighter friend had on a tall stovepipe hat, with painted-on flames going up the sides. Silly? Maybe. But later in the evening, my new mother-in-law was spotted wearing it. Many wore sunglasses...at our *indoor* reception. Why? Who can say? Nobody asked.

One guy took off his tie and tied it around his head. He somewhere found a small sign that read "For Sale" and hung it from the back of his pants. This group of firefighters included one lady, and was the life of the party. They kept people dancing and laughing all afternoon.

My new bride had many relatives there. I had not met a great many of them. Those I had met had had little exposure to how firefighters have fun. My kids had grown up with it, and my mom and sisters knew how I was. Since I was one of the firefighters, they were all used to this. My wife's family and friends looked around at the antics and laughed as hard as anyone. They were having fun and loving those people: those off-duty firefighters.

At one point, the guy with the tie around his head went to the bar to get a beer. The bartender made a comment to him about how these guys were keeping the party really going strong. The firefighter told the bartender, "Yeah, and we don't even know these people."

The bartender asked, "Really?"

The firefighter explained, "We have a business. We hire ourselves out for occasions like this to liven the party." Before he took his beer and left, she asked him for his business card. Of course, he didn't have one. I don't think anyone ever told the bartender the truth, but that's OK.

All those non-firefighters had a great time. I don't know if anyone ever thought about just who these "lives of the party" were, but in another time and place, every one of them would gladly put his or her life on the line to save the lives of others. You can't ask any more from anyone. They're a special class of people: firefighters.

I Guess All Good Things Come to an End

I retired from the fire department on October 13, 2007, after thirty-three years of service. Some people have trouble adjusting to the new way of life. I didn't have any trouble. I still had the fire academy. I still got to see and hang around with firefighters, play with all the toys, and tell stories as well as listen. I had six years as an instructor at that time, and many enjoyable years of part-time employment in support services before that. I got to pass my knowledge to those new recruits whose careers were just beginning.

After a time, I developed my own style of teaching. It seemed to be a good one, as I almost always had a good relationship with recruit classes. One thing I used to really enjoy is being the incident commander at the live burns. I used to play games, little tricks on the students just to see how they would react. These tricks were always instructional in nature.

If a company didn't check their equipment before a burn and found themselves lacking a piece of gear they needed, I'd hold them accountable and tell them to work out the problem, find another way.

If a company forgot to replace the caps on a hydrant, I left them off. Then on the next fire, I'd wait for the engine crew to arrive, expecting to hook up to that hydrant. When they got off the engine, I'd tell them, "Someone left the caps off this hydrant and vandals filled it full of rocks. Now the hydrant is out of service. Get me water."

If they started with something like, "But you said the hydrant is..." I'd come back with, "Get me water!" just like they'd hear at a real fire scene. It's better to learn what to do there at school, than at someone's home at 3 o'clock in the morning.

If the ladder truck was slow getting out of the firehouse, they often couldn't get into proper position on the street because the engines were in the way. I'd then order the aerial ladder to the roof. This usually isn't a problem, unless the truck isn't positioned properly. When they told me that they couldn't get the aerial up, I'd then order them to use ground ladders, a much harder operation, but the roof had to be opened. Even if the truck had been in the right place, if the ladder operator had trouble operating the aerial, then it was ground ladders.

For some evolutions, I'd stand by as an engine company hooked up to a hydrant and put the wrench on it to start the flow. That's when I'd step in and tell them that they just heard the hydrant's shaft snap, making it unusable. Now it was out-of-service. I'd watch as they would work out the problem of finding an alternative water source.

Those burns were fun, but then again, it was always fun teaching the recruits. But things began to slowly change. I found that some days were no longer as rewarding as they used to be, and some things that I once let roll off my back started to bother me. I started to feel kind of like I didn't belong there anymore.

I would go into work with the same people, and perhaps some new ones, and listen to them tell about their shift the night before. I'd listen to them tell about fires they just fought. I always loved the stories. Trouble was that I had no new ones to tell. This started to weigh on me. The longer I was away from the fire service, the more it became just a distant memory.

I didn't belong there anymore. I could feel it. I went in to speak with my boss, the coordinator of recruits, and tried to explain things to him. I said to him that things at the school were changing. The recruit program itself was changing, and was no longer going to be the program I had loved for so many years. My boss let me speak. He listened and understood. In order to avoid doing something I might later regret, he suggested that I take the summer off, and then come back in the fall. I agreed and did as he suggested in the fall. I enjoyed the time off, all the while thinking about the move I was about to make.

After six months, I returned to work. I worked for only three days. In that time, I felt more like an outsider than ever. I even found myself being treated like one by men who knew differently. After those three days, I knew in my heart that nothing had changed: I no longer belonged.

That night, I wrote a letter of resignation to my coordinator. I thanked him for all that I had learned and for being allowed to pass along my knowledge and experience to new firefighters. I said that it was time to say goodbye, take my memories, and go home. The boss said that he was sorry to see me go. An experienced, trained, and knowledgeable instructor is very hard to replace. The academy never likes to lose one, but he understood and accepted my letter of resignation. He wished me well.

In my time at the state firefighting academy, I made lifelong friends. I had experiences others only dream about. I picked up knowledge that was valuable and helped me on my job at the firehouse.

But as they say, "All good things must come to an end." And so, my time at the academy came to an end. With that came the end of my affiliation with the fire service, or so I thought.

A friend told me that it wasn't so, and he was right. I am very much still affiliated with the fire service. This just brought an end to my active participation, but I'll always be affiliated. I guess when you join the brotherhood/sisterhood, you never really leave; you just stop going to work. I have all the friends and memories with me, too, and those are the good things that will never come to an end.

Glossary

10s and 14s *Once a common shift schedule, consisting of 10-hour day shifts and 14-hour night shifts.*

24s *Common shift schedule consisting of 24-hours on duty at a time.*

academy *[See* Massachusetts Firefighting Academy*]*

advanced life support *Paramedics, or an ambulance whose crew consists of paramedics.*

alarms (i.e. two alarms, three alarms) *A request for additional help. Each additional alarm brings a designated amount of additional help to the fire.*

ALS *[See* advanced life support*]*

apparatus floor *Garage area of the firehouse where the vehicles are kept.*

attack line *Hose attached to the engine on one end and a nozzle on the other end, used to fight the fire.*

bag valve mask *Used in place of mouth-to-mouth resuscitation in CPR. Allows for high flow oxygen to be introduced.*

bagging a patient *Assisting a patient's breathing using a bag valve mask.*

bale of straw *Fuel used for live-fire training at the Massachusetts Firefighting Academy.*

basic life support *An ambulance whose crew consists of EMTs.*

big line *A hose with the diameter of 2½". Can also be an attack line.*

BLS *[See* basic life support*]*

board *Spine-immobilizing backboard, or the act of securing a person to a backboard.*

booster hose *Hard, red, rubber hose kept on reels on top of the engine, used for small roadside fires and brush. (Being phased out in favor of other hose.)*

box *One of many predesignated locations in town, assigned a number and used as a reference point when responding to a call.*

box alarm *An alarm for a fire. The location is identified by the number of the closest box.*

breathing apparatus *[See* self-contained breathing apparatus*]*

bunker gear *Protective clothing for firefighting (helmet, hood, coat, pants, boots, gloves).*

burn building *Concrete building at the Massachusetts Firefighting Academy designed for live-burn training. It can withstand multiple lighting of fires over years.*

BVM *[See* bag valve mask*]*

call *A request for assistance, or the response to a request.*

call firefighter *Part-time firefighter who only reports for duty when called in to provide additional help for emergencies. In my town, they do not work regular shifts at the firehouse.*

callback *Recall of off duty firefighters to report to their assigned stations for emergencies.*

callback assignment *The particular firehouse where a firefighter is assigned to go when returning on callback.*

351

Capt. Nickname used to address a captain.

car In my department, car 1 is the vehicle used by the chief of department. Car 2 is the vehicle driven by the duty shift commander.

class B uniform Station work uniform.

coupling Threaded connection used to join a hose to another hose, to the engine, or to a hydrant.

day room Room in the firehouse commonly occupied by firefighters when not engaged in duties or calls.

day shift A scheduled shift, usually 10 hours in length, during daytime hours (i.e. 8 a.m. to 6 p.m.).

dispatcher Person who answers emergency calls from the public and dispatches the proper apparatus per protocol.

duty captain [See shift officer]

duty crew On-duty personnel.

emergency medical technician Person with basic level of medical training, (i.e. CPR, defibrillator, epi-pen).

EMS officer Officer in charge of all aspects of emergency medical services. At the Massachusetts Firefighting Academy, it is the individual assigned to provide emergency medical services for the day.

EMT [See emergency medical technician]

engine Fire department vehicle equipped with a pump and hose, used to supply water to fight a fire.

engine tank A fire engine's holding tank for water. In my town, the tank can hold 500 gallons. Can be used for firefighting until a connection to a hydrant can be made.

epi-kit or ***epi-pen*** *An emergency dose of epinephrine carried by someone with a life-threatening allergy. Also carried in ambulances.*

ER *Emergency Room*

FD *Fire Department*

fire academy *[See* Massachusetts Firefighting Academy*]*

fire ground hydraulics *Formulas and information about water flow as it relates to firefighting.*

first due *Personnel and apparatus expected to arrive first at a call.*

frequent flyer *Fire department jargon for a person who calls the ambulance frequently for problems, real or imagined.*

gauges *Instruments located on the pump operator's panel indicating how much water is flowing through the hoses.*

general recall *[See* callback*]*

gun *Appliance used to supply large amounts of water to a fire. Can be used from its connection at the top of the engine, or removed and fed by a supply hose to make it portable.*

Halligan tool *Forcible entry tool.*

headquarters *In my town, this is station 1.*

IC *[See* incident commander*]*

incident commander *Person responsible for and in charge of all aspects of an incident.*

interior safety instructor *Instructor at a training incident responsible for safety within a structure.*

ladder *Fire department jargon for a ladder truck.*

ladder pipe *Gun affixed to the aerial ladder.*

ladder truck *Vehicle equipped with an aerial device, ground ladders, and forcible entry equipment (used for overhaul).*

LDH *Large diameter hose, usually 4" or 5".*

line *A hose (sometimes made of several lengths of hose joined together to extend the total length).*

live burn training *The use of real fire for training purposes.*

long backboard *A full body backboard for full immobilization of the patient.*

Massachusetts Firefighting Academy *The state facility which provides training for any firefighter in Massachusetts at no cost to the individual. Many towns send their new hires through the recruit program.*

MAST *[See military anti-shock trousers]*

military anti-shock trousers *"Trousers" which wrap around the lower body (legs and abdomen) of a patient and inflated, designed to stave off shock in trauma victims until reaching hospital.*

mechanism of injury *The cause of an injury. Determining the mechanism gives information about what probable injuries could exist.*

mutual aid *The agreement among towns to provide help to one another (manpower and apparatus) when needed.*

MVA *Motor vehicle accident.*

night shift *A scheduled shift, usually 14 hours in length, during nighttime hours (i.e. 6 p.m. to 8 a.m.).*

officer *Someone above the rank of private.*

on air *Breathing the air from an air tank worn on the back.*

oral airway *Tube inserted down throat of victim to keep tongue from obstructing airway.*

overhaul *Searching for hidden fire or hot spots after the fire has been knocked down to assure that it is completely extinguished.*

phase-3 burns *Third of four levels of training burns for recruits at the Massachusetts Firefighting Academy. Each increase in level is an increase in difficulty (size and number of fires).*

pike pole *Pike at the end of a long pole used for opening ceilings and walls during overhaul.*

pipe *Nozzle part of a fire hose.*

private *Entry-level rank for firefighters.*

put out the tone *To have an alert tone sent over the radio to recall off duty firefighters.*

Q-siren *Siren with long, continuous wail.*

quick hitch *Bunker pants folded down over boots for quick donning.*

ranks *Hierarchy in the fire department. The order (from lowest to highest) is private, lieutenant, captain, deputy, and chief. Some departments do not use all these positions and some use additional positions.*

rapid intervention team *Designated team of firefighters that does not engage in the fighting of fire, standing by and kept available for the search and rescue of trapped, lost, or injured firefighters.*

recall *[See* callback*]*

recruit program *Training program at the Massachusetts Firefighting Academy for new firefighters to learn basic skills of firefighting.*

RIT *[See* rapid intervention team*]*

SCBA *[See* self-contained breathing apparatus*]*

Section 12 *Section of the Massachusetts general law detailing requirements for involuntary committal to a hospital for a patient with questionable mental status.*

self-contained breathing apparatus *Air tank, hoses, face piece, and all necessary parts of the breathing system worn on the back of firefighters and used in environments where they cannot or should not breathe the air.*

shift captain *[See* shift officer*]*

shift commander *[See* shift officer*]*

shift lieutenant *[See* shift officer*]*

shift officer *Officer in charge of and responsible for the personnel and equipment during a shift.*

short board *Short backboard used for extricating a seated patient with potential spinal injury from a vehicle. (Being phased out in favor of more modern equipment.)*

smoke pushing *Smoke moving under pressure.*

station coverage *Off duty personnel manning the firehouse while the duty crew is occupied with a call and is unavailable to respond to other calls.*

station 1 *In my town, this is the headquarters station.*

station 2 *In my town, this is the outstation.*

step *Wide, flat platform on the rear of an engine where firefighters stand (and hold onto an upper bar) while responding to a fire.*

strike the box *To have a box number sent through the alarm system, transmitted to the stations in our town and mutual aid towns, indicating that we have a fire at that location.*

subjective report *Written report on an individual student's performance or behavior.*

tap out the box number *To identify a particular box number using a mechanical device (a telegraph) that generates repetitive taps while punching holes into a register tape. The number of taps grouped together corresponds to each digit of the box number. i.e. Box #312: [TAP-TAP-TAP] + [TAP] + [TAP-TAP]*

truck *[See* ladder truck*]*

turnout gear *[See* bunker gear*]*

ventilation *Act of opening a structure (opening windows, cutting the roof) to release smoke and heat to aid the firefighters in battling the fire.*

watch desk *Desk in watch room.*

watch Room *A room, formally used for our dispatcher, now used for greeting the public and routine business.*

well-being check *Going to a person's house to check on their welfare, at the request of family or friends who are concerned because they are unable to reach that person.*

working fire *Fire department jargon for a fire that is free-burning and still growing: pre fire-attack.*

www.ingramcontent.com/pod-product-compliance
Lightning Source LLC
Chambersburg PA
CBHW020731160426
43192CB00006B/183